The
Reference
Shelf

Violence in American Society

Edited by Frank McGuckin

The Reference Shelf
Volume 70 • Number 1

The H. W. Wilson Company
New York • Dublin
1998

The Reference Shelf

The books in this series contain reprints of articles, excerpts from books, addresses on current issues, and studies of social trends in the United States and other countries. There are six separately bound numbers in each volume, all of which are usually published in the same calendar year. Numbers one through five are each devoted to a single subject, providing background information and discussion from various points of view and concluding with a subject index, and comprehensive bibliography that lists books, pamphlets, and abstracts of additional articles on the subject. The final number of each volume is a collection of recent speeches and it contains a cumulative speaker index. Books in the series may be purchased individually or on subscription.

Visit H.W. Wilson's web site: www.hwwilson.com

Library of Congress Cataloging-in-Publication Data

Violence in American society / edited by Frank McGuckin
                p. cm.—(The reference shelf; v. 70, no. 1)
        Includes bibliographical references.
        ISBN 0-8242-0941-9
1. Violence—United States. 2. Violent crimes—United States.
    3. Violence in mass media—United States. I. McGuckin, Frank, 1971– . II. Series
HN90.V5V5484 1998   97–51741
303.6'0973—dc21   CIP

Cover: A woman is cared for by police who responded to her domestic violence call.
Photo: AP/Wide World Photos

Printed in the United States of America

Contents

IV. Stopping the Violence

Bibliography

Preface

The presence of violence in American society and culture extends from the beginnings of European colonization to the present day. Whether we are discussing the 1619 introduction of slavery to British settlements in the Eastern part of the United States, the incredibly high murder rates in "frontier" towns of the mid-19th century, or the 1997 killings of acclaimed fashion designer Gianni Versace, education administrator Betty Shabazz, and Bronx schoolteacher Jonathan Levin, we are discussing violent acts, violent events, and their far-reaching effects. Our knowledge of violence is limited. Theories as to its causes are based in both biology—recall the 1997 discovery of the "aggression gene"—and sociology, which involves a condemnation of those social/environmental factors that seem to breed violent behavior. Other hypotheses embody both camps, suggesting that the human propensity for violent behavior comes from within as well as from without.

Solutions to the problem are no less encompassing. While many believe stricter criminal sentencing and more rigorous law enforcement will eventually deter violent behavior, others believe that not until we have eradicated the social context from which crime is believed to arise will we make any progress. Still others call for psychological and medicinal treatment of those who engage in violent behavior. Whatever the belief, assumption, or conclusion, the quest to better understand and control the presence of violence within our culture has been, and continues to be, a central concern of American society.

A Violent History, the first section in this compilation, reaches back through time and provides theories as to the causes of violence, both in human beings in general and, more specifically, in Americans. This section also demonstrates that our attempt to understand and eradicate that violence is equally prevalent. The first article recalls the staggering violence of the "Wild West," and argues that, historically, violence in America has been propelled largely by young, single men. The actions of these men, particularly during the gold rush years of the mid-19th century, have, according to this author, created the basis for the violent American society many believe exists today. In the following article, Leo D. Lefebure probes the connection between violence and religion as he discusses René Girard's theories on sacrifice and scapegoating. The next two articles examine the quest to understand violence through science. While many scientists assert that our genetic makeup is the basis for violent tendencies, others believe social realities such as poverty and poor education are in fact the cause of violent behavior.

Section II, Violence Manifest, reviews violence as it is felt and witnessed throughout America. Examples of experienced violent acts include robbery, murder, "hate crimes," and spousal abuse. The first article in this section discusses the difference between American crime and crime in similarly industrialized nations. The fact is, American crime, in general, is far more violent and lethal than crime that occurs in comparable societies. The following article, written by the former Newark, NJ director of police, asserts the violence inherent to American crime may be a result of the large number of firearms Americans own.

The remaining articles in this section confront the scope and severity of violence against women. As these articles relay, the problem of violence directed specifically at women is, and has been, a lamentable part of American life. In addition to the emotional and physical trauma spousal abuse inflicts upon its victims, children who witness domestic abuse are profoundly affected. According to several of the authors whose articles are reprinted in Section II, the consensus among child-development specialists is that exposure to spousal abuse can result in poor school performance, discipline problems, trouble getting along with other children, and substance abuse.

Section III, Violent Images, approaches violence as it is continually witnessed on television, in the movies, in newspapers, and advertising. The fact is, violent acts are witnessed by nearly every American on a daily basis. As the authors of articles contained in this section note, while many have vehemently criticized news shows for adhering to an "If It Bleeds, It Leads" credo, others have studied the changes in behavior wrought by continually watching violent actions and events. In short, there is great concern that the media's use of violence as entertainment is creating a profound increase in the amount of violence that exists in real life.

The first article in Section III, by Scott Stossel, relays the efforts of George Gerbner, who is perhaps the most outspoken critic of television's fixation on violent acts. The next two articles follow the debate over the V-chip, which would allow parents to prevent their children from watching television episodes that have been deemed violent. The last article in this section, "A Gore Phobia" from *Esquire*, studies the history of violence in films and the problem of desensitization that writer David Thomson believes to be the consequence of watching movies that contain particularly gruesome imagery.

The last section of this compilation, Stopping the Violence, discusses the range of the efforts, on both the individual and the national levels, devoted to removing violence from the American landscape. According to the articles in this section, across the U.S., citizens, in conjunction with local law enforcement, are patrolling inner-city streets, keeping a close watch on their communities, and monitoring what their children watch on television. Experts argue that to break the cycle of violence, families, churches, and community organizations, as well as local, state, and federal governments, must act together. Articles contained in this section address violence prevention as it exists in three separate areas: home, community, and schools. Michael D'Antonio, from *Redbook*, examines the ways that communities can counter the rise of violence in America, and Marc Kaufman, from *Parents,* describes safety measures that neighborhoods can take to protect their children.

The editor wishes to thank all those who granted permission to reprint the articles contained in this issue of *The Reference Shelf*. Special thanks to Joseph Sora for overseeing this book's compilation, Frank Proto for his numerous resources and endless assistance, and the H.W. Wilson Company.

Frank McGuckin
January 1998

I. A Violent History

Editor's Introduction

Many of the articles contained in this section argue that violence is an inherent aspect of human history. It is, according to these authors, a primordial reality that arises out of the very nature from which human life itself has its genesis. Whether violence is caused by a biological mechanism, such as a particular gene, or is a reaction to the social contexts in which we find ourselves, it is nonetheless a visible, and very real aspect of day-to-day existence. America and American history are by no means immune to this reality. Yet, while violence is and has been a part of existence, it has not been accepted as an unalterable reality. Humanity has consistently, and with great determination, probed into its causes, its manifestations, and its effects upon those who experience it.

According to David T. Courtwright in "Violence in America," single men are far more susceptible to committing acts of violent and disorderly behavior than their married counterparts. Courtwright further argues that insofar as young, single men are any society's most unruly and troublesome citizens, American young men, since the gold-rushes of the mid-19th century, have always had a tendency toward violence and disorder. Courtwright points out that during the gold rushes many young men were forced to function without any sort of family structure, power, or authority. This, according to Courtwright, lay behind the Western United States' staggering murder rates during the gold rush years. It follows that Courtwright believes the major factor in controlling violence initiated by young males lay in the family structure and not necessarily in law, police, or prison.

Leo D. Lefebure, writing in *The Christian Century*, recalls anthropologist René Girard's discovery of the mechanism that links violence and religion. According to Lefebure, Girard has confronted the history of religions, which is "steeped in human and animal sacrifice, and scapegoating," and theorized that humans have used sacrifice as a means of controlling violence. Religious sacrifices are thus the place where religion and violence intersect. Violence today is, paradoxically, a recollection of the early human sacrifices and the need to contain unrestrained bloodshed. While Lefebure believes Girard's theories to be stimulating, he is quick to point out that discussing ancient human history is fraught with difficulty because of the lack of concrete evidence.

The historical attempt to understand violence through science and biology is discussed in the following article from *Discover* by Bettyann H. Kevles and Daniel J. Kevles. While violent tendencies are said to reside in genes—an "aggression gene"—the Kevles are not totally convinced. As the Kevles point out, some, particularly teens, are more prone to violence than others. The Kevles ask how does the so-called "aggression gene" account for the fact that among teens homicides are the second leading cause of death? Do we lose this gene as we age? The authors believe future genetic discoveries may lead to new therapies and further explanations for the biological realities behind violence, but legal and social questions will always remain. As the Kevles point out, poverty, discrimination, and the failure of educational systems are just as likely causes for violence as our genetic makeup.

Tabitha M. Powledge, in "Genetics and the Control of Crime," also provides a history of our attempt to understand the causes for violent behavior. Based on the past insights into violence that the field of genetics has provided, she believes that genetic studies are unlikely to contribute significantly to a discovery of violence's true causes. Powledge asserts that scientists lack the facts necessary to find a relationship between DNA and violent crime. It follows that establishing genetics as a potential solution to violent behavior is difficult. Most behavior, violent or otherwise, seems to result from multiple genes which receive generous input from other genetic information. The complications are enormous, and, according to Powledge, potentially insurmountable. Yet, despite her criticisms she does believe that research within other aspects of human biology may provide more useful information for reducing and preventing violent crime.

Violence in America[1]

Violence is the primal problem of American history, the dark reverse of its coin of freedom and abundance. American society, or a conspicuous part of it, has been tumultuous since the beginnings of European colonization. But while seventeenth-century Virginia was a disorderly place, the Massachusetts Bay Colony was not, and though the South and the frontier and the black ghetto have known especially high levels of violence and disorder, rural New England and Mormon Utah have almost always been tranquil.

Do these differences simply reflect American pluralism? Perhaps New England was less violent because the godly Pilgrims and Puritans settled there. Perhaps Southern and Western communities were more violent because the presence of slaves and Indians aroused fear and encouraged people to carry guns. Such explanations go a long way toward accounting for the regional peculiarities of American violence, but they are not the whole story.

Men, especially young men, are at the heart of American violence. Their behavior is most dangerous in their teens and twenties, the years when they are likeliest to kill, riot, vandalize, steal, and abuse alcohol or other drugs. The surest way to reduce crime, the psychologist David T. Lykken of the University of Minnesota has remarked, would be to put all able-bodied males between the ages of twelve and twenty-eight into cryogenic sleep.

He has a point. Though the median age of arrest is subject to historical variation (it has gone down in the United States in the last century), the arrest bulge has always occurred among citizens in their teens and twenties and declined rapidly thereafter. So far as anthropologists and historians have been able to discern, this has been true of all societies, from Sweden to Samoa. Nations as far apart in time and character as Victorian England and Hefnerian America have shown similar distributions of arrests by age and gender.

Whenever one spots a universal human pattern, the chances are good that it is rooted in biology, in this case hormonal differences. After conception we are sexually undifferentiated until minute genetic differences trigger the development of testes or ovaries. The testes produce testosterone, which organizes the development of male genitals and shapes the central nervous system. Testosterone is why boys are born boys and why they later become men. In the absence of testosterone the fetus will develop into a female.

At the onset of puberty the testes flood the body with testos-

> *"Men, especially young men, are at the heart of American violence."*

---

[1] Article by David T. Courtwright, from *American Heritage* 47:36–40+ S '96. Reprinted by permission of the publisher of *Violent Land* by David T. Courtwright, Cambridge, Mass.: Harvard University Press, Copyright © 1996 by the President and Fellows of Harvard College.

terone, raising levels in the blood to as much as twenty times those in women and prepubertal boys. This surge of testosterone has effects that include increased muscle mass and bone density, hairier bodies, deeper voices, and increased libido, impulsiveness, and aggressiveness. We know that testosterone is causally related to these changes because its presence or absence is easily manipulated. Castrated human males, even castrated criminals, lose interest in sex and fighting. All mammals react in the same way, which is one reason we neuter tomcats and clip the testicles of bulls. When testosterone is artificially replaced in castrated man or beast, its effects soon reappear, proving that the hormone, not the missing gonad, is responsible for the physical and behavioral changes.

Young men awash with testosterone may be a potential source of mischief, but it does not follow that they will get into trouble. Human societies have evolved various institutions to shape, control, and sublimate their energies. The most important of these is the family. Parents are our first governors. They set and enforce limits and guide social behavior. They teach us how to control aggression, defer gratification, work diligently, and care for dependents.

In colonial America such discipline and socialization were shared by surrogate parents—those who supervised apprentices, servants, and young farm workers. In exchange for labor, the master and mistress provided food, shelter, correction, instruction, and sometimes wages to prepare their youthful charges to establish themselves and begin their own families. But the decay of the apprenticeship system in the years from the Revolution to the Civil War and the gradual disappearance of live-in workers eliminated this traditional method of controlling and educating the young. The responsibility reverted to the nuclear family, augmented by schools, churches, and other institutions geared to shaping the characters of young men, such as the YMCA.

Parents do not always behave responsibly, of course. Even so, it is better on average to grow up in an intact two-parent family than in a single-parent family or with no parents at all. Across times and cultures, children who are abandoned or illegitimate or who lack a parent—from death, separation, or divorce—are statistically more prone to delinquency, truancy, dropout, unemployment, illness, injury, drug abuse, theft, and violent crime. The worst effects are most apparent in adolescent boys, who, lacking fatherly control and guidance, are socialized by default in hypermasculine, antisocial families such as gangs.

Children from disrupted families are less likely as adults to become or stay married. This fact has tremendous implications for the social order, because families of procreation, like families of origin, constrain behavior. Married men, as the sociologist Émile Durkheim pointed out, benefit from salutary discipline. Monogamy controls and focuses their sexual energy; children make them mindful of their example; the material needs of their families encourage regular work habits and self-sacrifice.

Married men lack the sense of expendability that plagues bachelor communities, in which the prospective loss of life is often regarded relatively lightly. They are also likelier to be better nourished and healthier than single men. In societies where marriage is the accepted way for adult men to gain the fruits of women's work, the bachelor is at a serious disadvantage. He is, as the anthropologist Claude Lévi-Strauss observed, "really only half a human being." "He that hath not got a Wife," declared Ben Franklin's Poor Richard, "is not yet a Compleat Man."

Here is the prejudice against single men distilled into a single sentence. We usually think of discrimination in American history as centering on race, ethnicity, and gender, but in fact many of the deepest and most unthinking prejudices have involved marital status. Single men have at times been forced to live in segregated neighborhoods and dormitories. Like blacks, they have had their own restaurants and railroad cars. They have consistently earned less and have paid for their singleness through double poll taxes, higher land prices, steeper insurance rates, less generous credit, longer prison terms, and smaller compensation for job-related disabilities. In hard times they have been laid off before married men, and in dangerous ones they have been placed in the front lines. Over time these roles and expectations have become internalized. Social marginality has reinforced single men's senses of superfluity and contributed to the psychology of expendability found in bachelor groups.

What we know about the effects of family on men is consistent with what we know about arrest rates for men in their teens and early twenties. Though physical and hormonal changes are partly responsible, this is also the age range in which men are typically between households. Leaving or having already left their families of origin, they have not yet entered the self-disciplinary regimes of their own families of procreation.

Men who have become stuck in bachelorhood or who have reverted to it are much more susceptible to violent and disorderly behavior. They have more often killed themselves and others, become insane or drug-dependent, or succumbed to illnesses, like tuberculosis, associated with malnutrition and squalor. Consequently their lives have been shorter. In New York State in the early twentieth century unmarried men could expect to live less than forty-four years; those who were married, sixty years. Although life expectancies for both groups have since increased, there is still a significant mortality gap between married and unmarried men.

This gap is caused partly by the selective nature of courtship. Men who start out undisciplined, unattractive, obnoxious, impoverished, inebriated, or otherwise socially or physically impaired find it harder to acquire spouses, and these same traits may result in shorter lives or trouble with the law. But various studies have

"...there is still a significant mortality gap between married and unmarried men."

shown that marriage has a protective effect of its own. Marriage gives men a sense of identity, self-worth, and mastery that translates into greater resistance to mental and physical illnesses. The behavior of married men tends to be more circumspect and healthful, especially if children are present.

Though the first purpose of marriage is the formation of family, one of its chief effects is male social control. The controlling effect works on two generations—both fathers and sons, present and future. Society-wide declines in family bonds have always had long-term consequences. When unmarried men conceive male children out of wedlock, the chances are good that their biological sons will be poor and undersocialized and will have trouble establishing families of their own.

For most of its history America has had a higher proportion of itinerant young single men in its population than the nations from which its immigrants, voluntary or otherwise, came. The proportion of men to women among transported convicts was four to one; among slaves, upward of two to one. The proportion among indentured servants, numerically the most important group of colonial immigrants, was three to one during the seventeenth century and increased to nine to one during the eighteenth. Their nineteenth-century successors, Chinese laborers indebted for their passage, were almost all male. In 1890 America contained twenty-seven Chinese men for every Chinese woman—"more monks than rice porridge," as some of them described the situation.

European immigrants who came without legal or financial fetters were far more likely to arrive in family groups, but even among them there was a surplus of prime-age male workers. Only postfamine Ireland, where economic and marital prospects for young rural women were particularly bleak, furnished more female than male immigrants, and then by just a small margin. Male majorities were the norm, at least prior to the immigration restriction laws of the 1920s.

Our criminal history has thus been played out with a bad hand of cards dealt from a stacked demographic deck. As an immigrant society America had a more or less continuous influx of youthful male workers, helping create a surplus of men for every year prior to 1946. Because these young men outnumbered young women, many of them could not marry. And insofar as young single men are any society's most troublesome and unruly citizens, America had a built-in tendency toward violence and disorder.

To be sure, this demographic leaning could be worsened by cultural predispositions. Southerners and frontiersmen were often contemptuous of other races and touchy about personal honor, which they might sometimes defend by violent means. Some ethnic groups, notably the Irish, drank a great deal of hard liquor. Irish brawling was no myth: New York City coroners' records for

1865 and 1871–73 show that 42 percent of homicide victims were Irish-born, as were only 21 percent of the city's population in 1870. Much of the carnage, Irish or otherwise, occurred in places of commercialized vice, such as gambling halls and saloons. Arguments over table stakes and prostitutes multiplied the opportunities for violent conflict, and the guns and knives men carried increased the likelihood of fatal results. When killings did occur, the police and courts were often unable or indisposed to deal effectively with them. Churches and revivals helped some, but their influence was felt least by lower-class men, who resisted religious conversion and the feminized style of life they often associated with it.

These cultural and social characteristics, together with the abnormal structure of the population, guaranteed that American society would suffer from violence and disorder. But not that it would do so uniformly. The ingredients for trouble—young bachelors, sensitivity about honor, racial hostility, heavy drinking, religious indifference, group indulgence in vice, gun carrying, and inadequate law enforcement—were concentrated on the frontier. An expanding sub-nation of immigrants within a larger nation of immigrants, the frontier was the most youthful and masculine region of the country and consequently the one most susceptible to violence.

"Eighty-nine thousand eager gold seekers from all over the world arrived in California in 1849."

The more remote and unsuited for family farming a frontier region was, the more likely it was to attract a surfeit of boisterous young males. The classic example is California during the gold rush. Eighty-nine thousand eager gold seekers from all over the world arrived in California in 1849. Practically all—95 percent—were men.

Within six months one in every five of them was dead—an astonishing statistic given that almost all had started the journey in good health and in their prime years. So many died that life insurance companies refused to write new policies for Californians, or charged substantial additional premiums for those already covered.

Cholera and scurvy caused much of the mortality. But those who survived illness faced another problem: the ubiquity of bachelor vices. It became apparent early on in California that the sure way to make money was by mining the miners. That could mean providing unexceptionable goods and services like groceries and laundering or more questionable ones, such as tobacco, liquor, gambling, and prostitution. In 1853 San Francisco liquor importers received more bulk or wholesale containers of alcoholic beverages than there were people in the state.

Eyewitnesses were astounded by the amounts of liquor consumed. They saw bottles strewn every few yards along roads and trails, crippled and delirious men dying in shanty bunks while drunkards caroused below. They warned that alcoholic excess weakened men and made them vulnerable to diseases. "The number of deaths is beyond all calculation," wrote a San Franciscan named Jerusha Merrill in October 1849. "Many have no friends to put them under the turf, yet those who take care of themselves and are regular in their habits enjoy good health. I warn all against the gaming house and grog shop."

And against brothels. Like all women, prostitutes were scarce in early California. Miners paid an ounce of gold (sixteen dollars) just to have one sit beside them at a bar or gaming table. San Francisco bar and café owners went further, paying women to serve as topless (and bottomless) waitresses or to pose nude in suggestive positions on elevated platforms. Those who wished to go beyond gawking paid anywhere from two hundred to four hundred dollars for a night of sex. Such prices naturally attracted more prostitutes to San Francisco, which had an estimated two thousand by 1853. Most were infected with venereal diseases.

Professional gamblers outnumbered prostitutes and were just as skilled at siphoning off miners' earnings. "I have seen men come tottering from the mines with broken constitutions," wrote the forty-niner Alfred Doten, "but with plenty of the 'dust,' and sitting down at the gaming table, in ten minutes not be worth a cent." In California men bet on anything, even the prognosis of a shooting victim as he underwent surgery on a pool table.

Much of the gaming and drinking took place in the winter, when men were unable to work, or on Sunday, when they flocked to towns like Coloma to gather news and gossip, lay in supplies, and patronize the saloons and gambling booths. Barkeeps dispensed whiskey for fifty cents or a pinch of gold dust, padding their profits by carefully sweeping up the dust that fell onto their counters.

Sunday was the day for masculine display. Miners tossed gold on the bar and bade their companions to name their drinks; reckless horsemen pulled knives from the ground at full gallop. Itinerant preachers bold enough to mount a stump and declaim against the desecration of the Sabbath were rewarded at collection time—a manifestation, perhaps, of latent guilt—but were ignored on the practical point of reformed behavior.

Devout men who happened to find themselves in this milieu were appalled. One prophesied to an Eastern minister that California "instead of being a blessing will prove a curse to the Union, morally and politically.... You can form no adequate idea of the depths of sin and moral degradation to which most of the people are sunk or rather sink themselves and those too of whom we should not dream such things when they leave the States."

These sentiments were shared by Hinton Helper, who spent three weary and unprofitable years (1851–54) in California and wrote a scathing account of the state's social and economic prospects. Later to achieve fame as a critic of Southern slave society, Helper was an unusual man, simultaneously a racist, an abolitionist, a Puritan, and an amateur sociologist. He argued that California's social disorder stemmed from the Mammonism of its polyglot population and from the want of women, in whose absence "vice only is esteemed and lauded."

Like many other observers, Helper noticed that the moral tone of the mining communities immediately began to change when women arrived. Though worried about the possibility that wives might be seduced away from their husbands by determined bachelors, he nevertheless looked forward to the day when California would experience "an influx of the chaste wives and tender mothers that bless our other seaboard."

If this sounds like Victorianism, it was. But it was also something deeper and more modern. Helper had grasped the fundamental principle of what is now called the interactionist school of sociology: that the self emerges and evolves as people internalize the attitudes that others hold toward them. When the mix of those others changes, so does the sense of self.

The typical California immigrant was neither poor nor vicious. He had been raised in a respectable family in the States, but his home was far away and the hurly-burly of camp life close at hand. His immediate social environment, which consisted of uprooted young men thrown together with opportunists and vice peddlers, shaped his sense of what was permissible and appropriate. His male cornpanions ridiculed conventional virtue as weakness and self-restraint as effeminate. If he avoided the saloons and faro tables, he must stay alone in his tent on Saturday night, bored and lonely. If he refused to smoke or drink, he risked insult and retaliation. A person who would not partake of whiskey or tobacco was "little short of an outlaw," complained a California miner named George McCowen, who took up smoking simply to avoid trouble. People who had never gambled became high-stakes players. In Stockton the proprietor of the leading gambling saloon was a Methodist minister. "Everybody gambled," recalled one San Franciscan. "That was the excuse for everybody else."

The one sure way to change this situation was by family reunification, when disappointed gold seekers returned home or, more rarely, when their spouses journeyed to the camps. "The wives of some of the wildest boys on the creek have come down to join their husbands," observed the forty-niner Alfred Jackson, "and it has sobered them down considerably." It was just this "sobering down" that Helper anticipated would come about when the balance of men and women was restored.

Helper saw something else clearly: that the violence in California was aggravated by the influx of criminals and the habit of carrying deadly weapons, the former encouraging the latter. Miners went about armed with revolvers or bowie knives, which they could buy at local groggeries along with cigars, tobacco, and more than a hundred varieties of alcoholic beverages. The combination of young men, liquor, and deadly weapons produced a steady steam of unpremeditated homicides, most of which arose from personal disputes and occurred in or near drinking establishments. Helper estimated that California had experienced forty-two hundred murders in six years, along with fourteen hundred suicides and seventeen hundred other deaths traceable to disappointment and misfortune.

Helper's murder number seems high (unless he was including killings of Indians, in which case it was almost certainly low), but an abundance of other evidence confirms that gold-rush California was a brutal and unforgiving place. The city of Marysville reportedly had seventeen murders in a single week, prompting the formation of a vigilance committee. Suicide and violent death afflicted every mining region. Witnesses wrote of men suddenly pulling out pistols and shooting themselves, of bodies floating down rivers, of miners stoned to death in gambling disputes. They described men who had become beasts, biting and pulling hair, flogging one another without mercy, cropping boys' ears, laughing at executions.

Miners had their virtues. They were typically open, generous men who valued deeds above words, deplored hypocrisy, and were friendly to strangers, at least when sober and unprovoked. Their language was direct and colorful, their swearing wildly inventive—though abruptly curtailed in the presence of respectable women, whom they treated with courtesy and deference. "I do not recall ever hearing of a respectable woman or girl in any manner insulted or even accosted by the hundreds of dissolute characters that were everywhere," a resident of Bodie, California, recalled. "In part, this was due to the respect that depravity pays to decency; in part, to the knowledge that sudden death would follow any other course."

Historians who have catalogued the murders in frontier mining areas have found extremely high rates of homicide. Nevada County, California, the site of Gun Town, Gomorrah, and other boisterous mining camps, had an average annual homicide rate (using the modern FBI yardstick) of 83 per 100,000 between 1851 and 1856. The mining town of Aurora, Nevada, had a rate of at least 64 during its boom years of 1861 to 1865; however, because its records are incomplete and a grand jury report enumerated other killings, its actual rate may have been as high as 117. That would have been almost identical to the rate in Bodie, California, a nearby mining town that averaged 116 homicides per 100,000 during its boom period of 1878 to 1882.

Non- or postfrontier regions with proportionately fewer men suffered far less homicidal violence. Henderson County, a rural backwater in western Illinois, had an average murder rate of 4.3 per 100,000 during the period from 1856 to 1900—just 19 killings in more than forty years. Two Eastern cities whose records have been analyzed, Boston and Philadelphia, had criminal homicide rates of 5.8 and 3.2 in the two decades after 1860. By comparison the average rates for Boston and Philadelphia in the early

1990s were 19.1 and 28.6, respectively.

The mining frontier was thus several times as violent as today's big American cities, and that's saying a lot. Worse, the historical estimates almost certainly do not include all homicidal killings of Indians. These were particularly common in California, where the distinction between killing Indians in battle and simply shooting them down meant little in practice and where Indian deaths of any sort were of scant concern to law enforcement officials.

The historian Roger McGrath has pointed out that the dark cloud of mining-town violence had a silver lining. He has found that rates of robbery were comparable to, and rates of burglary lower than, those of Eastern cities at the same time. Gun-toting citizens deterred property crime. Would-be robbers and burglars knew they stood a good chance of getting shot, and nothing would happen to anyone who killed them save some highly favorable newspaper publicity. But the same guns that prevented theft made homicide all the more likely. What happened in Aurora and Bodie was a tradeoff: more fatal gunplay for less larcenous crime.

In view of all this it may seem strange that there has been a long-running debate on whether the frontier was violent, pitting those who believe that the reality has been grossly exaggerated against those who hold that it has been at most merely embroidered. This debate has been complicated by the usual skirmishing about the completeness and trustworthiness of records, but the real problem is that the question—how violent was the frontier?—is miscast. There was no such thing as *the* frontier.

Different frontier communities had different social and population characteristics. The Mormon religious colony of Orderville, Utah, and the mining town of Bodie, California, were contemporaneous American frontier settlements, but in terms of gender balance, family life, religious restraint, and vice they might as well have been on different planets. In explaining the historical pattern of Western violence, the key lies in identifying the composition of the local population, not in some intangible variable called frontierness. Mining towns like Bodie, with nine men for every woman, were places where normal marriage and family patterns were disrupted and vice flourished, with all the increased violence that this entailed.

For a nice illustration of this principle, consider the contrast between two American gold rushes of the 1840s and early 1850s—the famous one in California and a largely forgotten one in the Gold Hill region of North Carolina. The latter attracted Cornish miners, many of whom brought their families or married local women, who were much more plentiful than on the distant Pacific coast. Aside from the inevitable deep-shaft mining accidents and sporadic fights, the Cornish immigrant miners experienced little in the way of premature death and violence—nothing to compare with what happened to the young men who flocked to California. One environment was overwhelmingly single and masculine; the other was not. The difference in gender balance translated into a difference in the social order.

The best thing that can be said about California-style frontier violence was that it didn't last long. Most of the surplus men who sought their fortunes along the frontier died, returned home, drifted elsewhere, or eventually were married, usually to young brides who went on to have numerous male and female children, thereby evening out the population and eliminating its tendency to violence and disorder. No frontier region, however notorious, escaped this process. Cowboy watering holes like Dodge City and Fort Griffin, murder-a-day railroad boomtowns like Julesburg and Laramie—all eventually succumbed. When families replaced bachelor laborers and vice parasites, things quickly settled down.

"When families replaced bachelor laborers and vice parasites, things quickly settled down."

Two decades sufficed to normalize most frontier populations, especially those in farming areas where the initial imbalance was less extreme. Washington County, Kansas, a stretch of arable prairie between the Flint Hills and the Nebraska border, had three men for every two women in 1860, but only eleven for every ten in 1880. This was typical. In Midwestern farming areas the demand for farm hands ensured that the number of women almost never exceeded that of men, but the additional male workers were usually attached to families.

Immigrant groups that initially had more men than women also adjusted. The passage of time balanced the sexes both regionally and ethnically, except when, as in the special case of the Chinese, the government enacted prejudicial laws that made family formation or reunification difficult. Chinatowns were home to vice dens and hatchet men in the later half of the nineteenth century for the simple reason that by dint of the exclusion policy, they were home to male workers without families.

By the mid-twentieth century America's overall male surplus was disappearing, as a result of shifts in immigration patterns and the fact that women's life expectancy was improving faster than men's. With a balanced population and a prosperous industrial economy, postwar America enjoyed a sustained marriage boom. The two popular images of the 1950s—as the decade when Americans settled down to raise their children in safety and plenty and as the decade of conformity—both arose from this marital efflorescence. Men worked hard, paid off their mortgages, and sacrificed for their children. Church attendance rose, violent crime fell. It looked as if America's built-in propensity for violence and disorder—the excesses of excess men—had finally run its troubled course.

Then came the 1960s and 1970s, the coming of age of the baby boomers, the sexual revolution, and a sustained rise in violent crime and drug abuse. It was not simply that there were more young and therefore trouble-prone men in the population, though that was true enough. It was that more of these men were avoiding, delaying, or terminating marriages. Overall, the number of American men living alone roughly doubled between 1960 and 1983, an unprecedented change for prosperous times. In 1960 Americans spent an average of 62 percent of their adult lives with spouses and children, an all-time high; in 1980 they spent 43 percent, an all-time low. "This trend alone," remarks the sociologist David Popenoe, "may help to account for the high and rising crime rates." Violent crimes were largely committed by unattached males. When their numbers rose, so did crime.

Though marriage and conventional family life grew less common among young men after 1960, sexual intercourse did not. The result, despite widespread contraception and abortion and a decline in fertility, was a huge increase in the percentage of children who were illegitimate and raised in fatherless families. The much higher frequency of divorce also increased the number of poorly supervised, poorly socialized, and just plain poor children.

These problems were national in scope, but they were most severe in black America, particularly in urban ghettos. By the early 1990s there were some black neighborhoods in which two-thirds or more of all families were headed by single mothers and three-quarters of all births were illegitimate. Conservatives attributed this trend to welfare: Programs like Aid to Families with Dependent Children had backfired by permitting black women to "marry the state," secure in the knowledge that others would pay for their children. Liberals countered that welfare benefits were in no sense overly generous and that family formation and stability required good jobs that deindustrialization, government cutbacks, union decline, automation, retrenchment, and global competition had made increasingly hard to find. In 1990 the City of New York announced an examination for prospective sanitation workers, starting salary twenty-three thousand dollars, no high school diploma required. More than a hundred thousand people signed up to compete for two thousand positions.

Regardless of who or what is to blame for family decline, it is clear enough that the endemic violence of inner cities is closely related to their numbers of illegitimate children and single-parent households. Young black men growing up without fathers and into adult lives without families are in a sense twice single and a good deal more than twice as likely to become involved in shootouts or run afoul of the law.

All of this has been compounded by the everyday realities of ghetto life: social isolation, abnormal demography, and the omnipresence of guns, alcohol, drugs, and vice. These problems helped make the white frontier boomtowns of the nineteenth century into violent hot spots, and they have done the same for black ghettos. In fact, except for the apparent paradox that the ratio of men to women is low in the inner city whereas it was high on the frontier, in an important sense ghettos are the raw frontiers of modern American life, the primary arenas in which the recurrent problem of youthful male violence continues to be played out.

Calling ghettos in the decaying hearts of big cities *frontiers* may seem odd, but it is not anachronistic. When the Secretary of Housing and Urban Development, Henry Cisneros, toured Chicago's Ida B. Wells public housing project in 1993 (accompanied by a security patrol), he found what he saw to be "almost like a western frontier." Local residents began calling North Kenwood, also in Chicago, "the Wild West." The founders of Jamaican drug gangs took their generic name, posses, from Western films. And one youthful New York City drug dealer evoked the analogy when he went upstate in search of sweeter profits and softer markets. "There's more opportunity in Buffalo," he explained. "You know back in the days when you went West to claim gold? Buffalo's like that."

> *"No trend increases forever, and baby boomers will continue to commit less crime as they age."*

A good analogy, like a good argument, should not be pushed too hard. There are also important differences between the frontier and the ghetto. Far more ghetto youth are illegitimate, hence undersocialized, and unemployed, hence unproductive in the legitimate economy, than were settlers along the nonagricultural frontier. If the dominant pattern of frontier vice was work and spree, that of ghetto vice is often hustle and spree, which adds another dimension of crime and degradation to the violence surrounding the vice industry. The dollars miners and cowboys spent on liquor and prostitutes were at least come by honestly.

Historical sources (as opposed to, say, the novels of Larry McMurtry) make it clear that there was less sociopathic violence on the frontier. The reasons people did have for killing—nobody calls me that, goddamn skulking savages, coolies take our wages—may seem lamentable to modern eyes, but at least they were reasons. Settlers were not much worried that a kid with a gun and no regard for human life would mow them down while rampaging after someone else. People were not, in fact, much worried about kids at all.

They are now. One of the most disturbing and politically explosive aspects of inner-city violence, terrifying to blacks and whites alike, has been the rapid increase of felonious crime and gunplay among unsupervised inner-city youths, not excluding children. Miami's Chief of Police, Donald Warshaw, has encountered ten-, eleven-, and twelve-year-olds "running around with guns and drugs, and when we track down their parents, we find they are on drugs too. It's out of control."

Crime and homicide rates will fluctuate in coming years. No trend increases forever, and baby boomers will continue to commit less crime as they age. But the problem of youthful ghetto violence will persist. Despite a decline in the overall murder rate in recent years, many experts predict that it will soon rise again, both because there will be more teenagers and because more of those teenagers will be illegitimate.

What has happened in the inner city may be a harbinger of worsening social-order problems everywhere. Changing labor-market realities and the eroticization of the media-based consumer culture have undermined family stability throughout the United States. Indeed, measures of white family disruption and illegitimacy three decades into the sexual revolution almost exactly match those for black Americans when Daniel Patrick Moynihan pulled his famous fire alarm back in 1965.

Seen in perspective, these events are a continuation, possibly the culmination, of a momentous historical trend, the decline of the family as the basic social unit and the appropriation of its functions by the state, professions, and corporations. Two centuries ago America's families were its society, or at any rate its centers of desire, conception, labor, production, consumption, authority, discipline, training, credit, and care for the sick, aged, and dying. But during the nineteenth century, families began losing power and authority. The usual suspects are the commercial and industrial revolutions; urbanization; the rise of public schools, factories, asylums, prisons, and hospitals; and the creeping intrusions of bureaucracies and professions into the domain of the home. Over the course of the twentieth century (with a pause for the temporary and, some say, anomalous marriage boom of the 1940s and 1950s), the nuclear family itself began to break up. More and more of the family's socializing and punishing functions devolved upon the professions, private enterprise, and the state, the parent of last resort.

State parenting is neither cheap nor satisfactory for maintaining social order. The voice of family-instilled conscience is always more cost-effective than that of a police officer, especially if the officer is part of a criminal justice system that has become irrelevant to all but serious offenses and then not guaranteed to produce results. Voters obviously have become frustrated over this failure, which has contributed heavily to the conservative gains in state and national politics.

Some of this anger might be better directed into a mirror. While politicians have made inroads against violence, they have usually done so at the margins. Lives gained or lost at the margins are still lives gained or lost, and laws and law enforcement do matter. But the key to controlling youthful male violence lies not in legislation or police or prisons but in society's basic familial arrangements. And that means it lies in all of us.

Victims, Violence and the Sacred: The Thought of René Girard[2]

Religious traditions promise to heal the wounds of human existence by uniting humans to ultimate reality. Yet the history of religions is steeped in blood, sacrifice and scapegoating. The brutal facts of the history of religions pose stark questions about the intertwining of religion and violence. How does violence cast its spell over religion and culture, repeatedly luring countless "decent" people—whether unlettered peasants or learned professors—into its destructive dance? Is there an underlying pattern we can discern?

The French literary critic and anthropologist René Girard has provided a compelling set of answers to these questions. He claims to have discovered the mechanism that links violence and religion. The extent of his claim is even more audacious: he believes that in the mechanism linking violence and religion lie the origins of culture.

A growing number of biblical scholars, theologians, psychologists and economists have turned to Girard's wide-ranging theory to understand their respective fields. His works have been widely read in his native France, and international conferences have explored the implications of his theory for different fields. Robert Hamerton-Kelly and James G. Williams have interpreted the Bible in light of Girard's theory. Catholic theologian Raymund Schwager has used Girard's proposal extensively in his theological reflections. Working closely with Girard, French psychiatrists Jean-Michel Oughourlian and Guy Lefort have proposed an "interdividual" psychology which stresses the radically social nature of the self and interprets phenomena such as desire, possession, hysteria, trance and hypnosis in Girardian terms. French economists Paul Dumouchel, Jean-Pierre Dupuy and André Orléan have interpreted such economic problems as the market, competition, scarcity, wealth and monetary value in light of Girardian theory. The Colloquium on Religion and Violence meets regularly to explore the application of Girard's ideas to a wide range of areas, and the colloquium's journal, *Contagion: Journal of Violence, Mimesis, and Culture*, publishes research on Girardian theory. A recent book by Gil Bailie, *Violence Unveiled: Humanity at the Crossroads*, has brought Girard's ideas to a larger audience in the U.S.

According to Girard, human culture has been founded on two

---

[2] Article by Leo D. Lefebure, professor at University of St. Mary of the Lake, Mundelein, IL, from *The Christian Century* D 11 '96. Copyright © 1996 *Christian Century Foundation*. Reprinted with permission.

principles, which he calls "mimetic rivalry" and the "surrogate victim mechanism." Mimesis refers to the propensity of humans to imitate other people both consciously and unconsciously. Girard developed a mimetic theory of the self in his early work as a literary critic (*Deceit, Desire, and the Novel: Self and Other in Literary Structure* [French, 1961; English, 1965]). Such novelists as Cervantes, Stendhal, Dostoevsky and Proust taught him that humans learn what to desire by taking other people as models to imitate. Aware of a lack within ourselves, we look to others to teach us what to value and who to be.

Girard observes that the desire to appropriate another person's possessions, loves and very being may seem innocent at first, but it poses a fundamental threat to community life. In imitating our models, we may come to approach their power and threaten their own position—in which case they quickly become rivals who tell us not to imitate them. When we imitate the model's thoughts, there is harmony; when we imitate the model's desires, the model becomes our obstacle and rival.

Mimesis thus inexorably leads to rivalry, and rivalry leads sooner or later to violence. From his study of mimetic desire in the modern novel, Girard turned to the relation of violence and the sacred in early cultures, especially in primal religions and Greek tragedy. In 1972 he published *La Violence et le Sacré* (English: *Violence and the Sacred*, 1977), a work that ranged widely through the fields of ethnology and anthropology. In Girard's judgment, the conflicts that result from mimesis repeatedly threaten to engulf all human life. Escalating violence renders humans more and more like each other, leveling distinctions and sweeping people up into ever greater paroxysms of violence. Mimesis leading to violence is the central energy of the social system.

"Escalating violence renders humans more and more like each other..."

During the course of evolution, Girard believes, a long series of primal murders, repeated endlessly over possibly a million years, taught early humans that the death of one or more members of the group would bring a mysterious peace and discharge of tension. This pattern is the foundation of what Girard calls the surrogate victim mechanism. Often the dead person was hailed as a bearer of peace, a sacred figure, even a god. Fearful that unrestrained violence would return, early humans sought ritual ways to re-enact and resolve the sacrificial crisis of distinctions in order to channel and contain violence. "Good violence" was invoked to drive out "bad violence." This is why rituals from around the world call for the sacrifice of humans and animals. For Girard, the sacred first appears as violence directed at a sacrificial victim, a scapegoat. Every culture achieves stability by discharging the tensions of mimetic rivalry and violence onto scapegoats. Scapegoating channels and expels violence so that communal life can continue. As mimetic tensions recur, a new crisis threatens, and sacred violence is once again necessary.

In Girard's view, myths from around the world recount the primordial crisis and its resolution in ways that systematically disguise the origins of culture. Later cultures use judiciary systems to contain violence. But even when cultures no longer practice sacrifice directly, they still continue to target certain individuals or groups as scapegoats so that violence will not overflow its banks and threaten others. The lynch mob is at the foundation of social order.

According to Girard, every culture arises from the incessantly repeated patterns of mimetic rivalry and scapegoating. Some authors, like the Greek tragedians, caught a glimpse of the underlying dynamics of the cycle and the arbitrariness of the choice of victim. But only the Bible, Girard contends, offers a full unveiling of the pattern of violence and a rejection of it.

Girard began his career as a secular thinker unaffiliated with any religious tradition. The course of his research and reflection led him to conclude that the Christian revelation unveils the patterns of violence and provides the divine response. Having become convinced that the gospel alone reveals the truth of the human condition, Girard entered the Catholic Church. Girard expressed his Christian perspective in *Things Hidden Since the Foundation of the World* (French, 1978; English, 1987) a book composed in dialogical form with Oughourlian and Lefort as interlocutors. His later work, *The Scapegoat* (French, 1982; English, 1986), continues his exploration of biblical themes and offers a good introduction to his thought.

According to Girard's interpretation of the Bible, the people of Israel were, like all other people, steeped in the surrogate victim mechanism. But the biblical authors, especially the psalmist, the prophets, and the sages of Israel, recognized the primordial pattern and denounced it. Many psalms express the perspective of the victims, and the author of the Book of Job sides with the maligned Job rather than his friends. The Suffering Servant poems present the age-old mythological drama: a crowd surrounds an innocent victim and heaps abuse upon him. The point of view, however, has changed. The biblical author does not accept the charges; the victim is innocent and is vindicated by God.

Such is also the message of the New Testament. In Jesus, God appears in history as the innocent victim, who goes to his death as the scapegoat. Far from demanding victims, God identifies with the victims and thus exposes the surrogate victim mechanism as a fraud and deception. God responds to our violence with nonviolent love. Paul's conversion turns on the realization that he is persecuting God. The realization that God is on the side of the victims is, for Girard, the center of biblical revelation.

Girard laments that throughout its history the church has largely ignored this message. It has misinterpreted the death of a Christ as a sacrificial offering to a God who demands victims. For centuries the true meaning of the gospel was lost, and Christians continued the cycle of scapegoating others, especially Jews. The anti-Jewish texts of the late Middle Ages offer Girard some of the clearest examples of the scapegoating mechanism at work.

At last, however, the message has begun to register. According to Girard, modern movements on behalf of oppressed peoples, even though often outside or opposed to established Christianity, are the heirs of the Hebrew prophets and the New Testament. As Friedrich Nietzsche noted, Christianity sides with victims, not conquerors.

Prior to biblical revelation, Girard claims, cultures achieved relative levels of social stability through scapegoating certain individuals. Over the centuries the impact of the gospel on culture has largely destroyed the power of the surrogate victim mechanism. Conventional culture is now in a painful process of disintegration. History as we have known it for millennia is coming to an end, and we face a dramatic, even apocalyptic, choice: total destruction or total renunciation of violence.

"Conventional culture is now in a painful process of disintegration."

What is striking about Girard's proposal is the wide range of data that do bear the hallmarks of mimetic rivalry and the surrogate victim mechanism. The insights of great novelists and dramatists into the volatility of mimetic desire, as interpreted by Girard, are profound and persuasive on an intuitive level. Similarly, the analysis of the surrogate victim mechanism can find much evidence in a wide range of cultures. It is frightening to note how often social bonding has taken place through the exclusion of certain groups and through periodic violence directed at unfortunate individuals. Lynch mobs and pogroms punctuate human history.

When mimetic theory is extrapolated into the explanation of all institutions of all human cultures, however, doubts arise about the status of the evidence and the assumptions of the argument. Too often discussions of Girard tend toward an all-or-nothing choice: either uncritical enthusiasm or skeptical dismissal. It is helpful to distinguish between the intuitive power of Girard's proposal, which can be quite compelling, and the logical status of many of the claims advanced, which remains problematic. Girard has proposed a hypothesis which is most intriguing, but it has by no means reached the stage of empirical verification, and in many cases it is difficult to see how verification could be achieved.

The theory of the primal murders and the primordial origin of religion and all human culture in the surrogate victim mechanism is highly speculative because we lack adequate data from the period that Girard takes as foundational for all human culture. Girard seeks to reconstruct a form of mimesis prior to symbols, a mimesis which would take place as the origin of human consciousness and of culture and religious symbolism. However, there remains a gap between what we can reconstruct of the primitive drives of hominids and the emergence of higher cognitive and symbolic capacities. Girard claims to have found the missing link, but one wonders whether the power of mimesis and the effect of the primal murders can really account for the entire range of development of early humans. Was the surrogate victim mechanism really the motor driving the development of the human brain in interaction with cultural factors, as Girard claims? How can we possibly know?

In addition, the link between the putative crisis of distinctions and the first manifestation of the sacred remains tenuous. For Girard, "the sole purpose of religion is to prevent the recurrence of reciprocal violence" (*Violence and the Sacred*). Girard also claims that "humanity's very existence is due primarily to the operation of the surrogate victim." Furthermore, he argues that "the origin of symbolic thought lies in the mechanism of the surrogate victim," and that this mechanism also "gives birth to language and imposes itself as the first object of language." "It is the surrogate victim who provides men with the will to conquer reality and the weapons for victorious intellectual campaigns." All this seems overstated, and it is hard to see what would count as verification from the earliest periods of human existence.

Moreover, the evidence of later ages is itself ambiguous. There are many texts and practices that fit Girard's theory rather well, but others are less clear. Joseph Henninger has pointed out that many cultures have offered bloodless sacrifices, such as fruits, grains, foods from plants, milk and milk products, and alcoholic libations. These are presented to supernatural beings who often do not need them, and the primary motives are thanksgiving and homage. Henninger argues that the offering of first fruits in many cultures involves intellectual assumptions and emotions that are far removed from the scapegoating patterns that Girard identifies. Moreover, there is no evidence that the sacrifice of humans and animals is more ancient than the offering of first fruits.

Girard's theory risks being a tour de force which explains too much by explaining everything. Girard claims that most of historical culture is involved in a conspiracy to cover over its origins, and this sets up a logical difficulty in assessing the evidence. If the surrogate victim mechanism appears only in fragmented form, supporters of the theory can claim that this reflects the attempt to cover over the guilty, violent origins of culture. The problem with such a hidden mechanism is that the claim cannot be refuted.

Questions also arise concerning Girard's interpretation of modern history (a perspective that Baillie has made the center of his own work, *Violence Unveiled*). Girard gives the biblical tradition credit for awakening concern about the plight of victims and for being the driving force in the development of modern science and the quest for social justice. Amid the manifold forces at play in recent centuries, one factor is named over and over again—the biblical tradition—while the role of other factors is marginalized or dismissed. Certainly, Christianity had a massive influence on the sociopolitical and intellectual history of Europe, but it seems simplistic to posit the subterranean influence of the gospel alone as the driving force of modern cultural history, especially when so much of modern history understood itself as a reaction against Christianity.

According to Girard, the mass murders of the 20th century have occurred because the gospel has undermined the traditional sacrificial system that previously protected societies from outbreaks of unrestrained violence. Now that the sacrificial system is collapsing, the old mechanisms try more and more desperately to function and so demand more victims. Whether this adequately explains the mass murders of this century is doubtful. Earlier ages knew mass slaughter, but they did not have the technology to kill on the same scale. If earlier centuries had been able to perform actions like the fire-bombing of Dresden or the nuclear bombing for Hiroshima, they probably would have done so. Whether the scale of the purges of Stalin or Mao and other mass murders can be explained as due primarily to the gospel's unmasking of the scapegoat mechanism is unlikely.

Girard concludes his reflections with an appeal about the future. "For the first time," he says, humanity faces "a perfectly straightforward and even scientifically calculable choice between total destruction and the total renunciation of violence." In this apocalyptic context, Girard presents a stirring call to wake up, to acknowledge the dynamics of history, to renounce the patterns of violence and scapegoating, and to allow the nonviolent appeal for the gospel to transform the earth. It is a powerful and moving appeal.

However, it is difficult to see how such an all-or-nothing choice for the future could be "scientifically calculable." It seems more likely that neither alternative will take place, at least in the foreseeable future. Rather than either a total destruction of human life or a total renunciation of violence, we are more likely to muddle through with limited conflicts repeatedly breaking out but not escalating to total destruction, whether nuclear or ecological.

One problem in assessing the appeal for nonviolence is that Girard does not define exactly what behavior counts as violence. If violence is something broader than causing physical injury to another person, then different cultures have very different perspectives on what constitutes violent behavior. The failure to define the meaning of violence leaves the call for a renunciation of violence vague. The dramatic rhetoric of either total destruction or total renunciation of violence leaves us in a situation in which the very meaning of effective action is unclear. Is an economic boycott that seeks to end injustice an act of violence? At what point do economic sanctions that result in the deaths of children become an act of war? Buddhists pondering the First Precept note that if you boil water, you commit an act of violence against the microorganisms in it. Girard insists on surrendering the distinction between "good" and "bad" violence, but the lack of a working definition of violence leaves the concrete means of influencing the course of events unclear.

Alfred North Whitehead asserted with his characteristic playfulness: "It is more important for a proposition to be interesting than that it be true." Propositions for Whitehead are "tales that might be told," visions of possibilities relevant to a particular situation. Even if it turns out that the universalizing claims of Girard's theory are not sustainable, his work nonetheless calls attention to widespread dynamics of cultural and religious life that have too often been neglected by theologians. For this, we owe him a debt of gratitude.

Scapegoat Biology[3]

Biological explanations of violence are much in vogue. Part of the reason is that scientists studying the seat of behavior, the brain, and its genetic underpinnings, have learned a lot in recent years. Tendencies toward violence, they tell us, may reside in our genes or be hard-wired into our brains. Some neuroscientists have mapped brain abnormalities in laboratory animals and human murderers that seem to correlate with aggressive behavior. Others have teased out apparent connections between violent behavior and brain chemistry.

Being scientists, these researchers often try to tone down and qualify the connection between violence and biology. But even a faint message seems to fall on extraordinarily receptive ears. The findings of a team of Dutch and American scientists, for example, were recently exaggerated not only by the lay media but by the technical press as well. The researchers had come across a Dutch family in which, for five generations, the men had been unusually prone to outbursts, rape, and arson. These men were also found to have a genetic defect that made them deficient in an enzyme that regulates levels of the neurotransmitter serotonin. Han Brunner, a geneticist at University Hospital in Nijmegen, the Netherlands, and a member of the team, cautioned that the results concerned only one family and could not be generalized to the population at large, but the caveat was ignored. Stories everywhere, in both the scientific journals and the general media, spoke of his finding an "aggression gene."

There are other examples. In a 464-page assessment of the state of violence research in 1992, the National Research Council devoted only 14 pages to biological explanations. Of those 14, genetics occupied less than two pages. All the same, the *New York Times* covered the report with the headline STUDY CITES ROLE OF BIOLOGICAL AND GENETIC FACTORS IN VIOLENCE. Indeed, the proliferation of genetic explanations for violence prompted a *Time* writer to note wryly: "Crime thus joins homosexuality, smoking, divorce, schizophrenia, alcoholism, shyness, political liberalism, intelligence, religiosity, cancer, and blue eyes among the many aspects of human life for which it is claimed that biology is destiny."

Editors, of course, usually know what's on the minds of their audience: from rapes and murders in Rwanda or Bosnia to wrong-turn drivers cut down in a Los Angeles cul-de-sac, senseless violence has seemingly become the norm. Theater and movie audiences in the 1950s were shocked by *The Bad Seed*, the tale of a prepubescent pigtailed blond girl who was revealed to

---

[3]Article by Bettyann H. Kevles and Daniel J. Kevles, from *Discover* 18/10:58–62 O '97. Copyright © 1997 Disney Magazine Publishing Group. Reprinted with permission.

be a multiple killer. Today Americans are numb to nightly news reports of assaults in once-protected middle-class neighborhoods, child and spousal abuse in outwardly respectable homes, and clean-cut teenagers or even young children killing each other. The American Academy of Pediatrics made violence the theme of its meetings in October 1996, and the American Medical Association has alerted us to the "epidemic of violence."

This morbid fascination is to some extent justified: violence is pervasive. Homicide is the second leading cause of death among teenagers and young adults and the leading cause among African American women and men between the ages of 15 and 34. In the past few decades, the demographics of violence in the United States have taken a turn for the worse. Almost 80 percent of murders used to involve people who knew each other. That figure has fallen to less than 50 percent. These statistics suggest that your chances of being wiped out by someone you've never met, and probably for no reason at all, have risen.

"The escalation in random violence, especially among adolescents, has generated a hunger for explanations."

The escalation in random violence, especially among adolescents, has generated a hunger for explanations. Biological accounts of murderous behavior do as well as any, and better than most. They are easy to grasp in principle, and they are socially convenient, locating criminal tendencies in our natures, about which we can currently do little beyond incarcerating the wrongdoers, rather than in nurture, which we might be able to remedy if we chose to invest the time and money.

The long, embarrassing history of biological theories of violence suggests caution. In the mid-nineteenth century, phrenologists—who diagnosed personality traits by the location of bumps on the head—worked out a behavioral map of the human skull, determining that area number 6 (out of 35) was the seat of destructiveness. In the early twentieth century some biologists and psychologists sought to extend the newly minted science of genetics to explanations of pernicious behavioral traits. Like today's scientists, they worked in a context of mounting social problems, including the disruptions of industrial capitalism and the flooding of immigrants into the nation's cities. They convinced themselves that poverty, alcoholism, prostitution, and criminality leading to violence all arose, in the main, from a trait called feeblemindedness, an inherited condition that they claimed was transmitted from one generation to the next as regularly and surely as the color of hair or eyes. Henry Goddard, the leading authority on the subject in the United States, taught that the feebleminded were a form of undeveloped humanity, "a vigorous animal organism of low intellect but strong physique—the wild man of today."

Perhaps not surprisingly, Goddard's theories were suffused with the bigotry of his era. Feeblemindedness was held to occur with disproportionately high frequency among lower-income and minority groups—notably recent immigrants from eastern and southern Europe. The biologist Charles Davenport, director of the Carnegie Institution Station for Experimental Evolution in Cold Spring Harbor, New York, and one of the country's prominent eugenicists, predicted that the "great influx of blood from Southeastern Europe" would rapidly make the American population "darker in pigmentation, smaller in stature, more mercurial...more given to crimes of larceny, kidnapping, assault, murder, rape, and sex-immorality."

Such explanations of violence were commonplace in their day, but of course they proved to be hogwash, of no greater merit than the phrenological theories that had preceded them. The scientists responsible for them generally ignored the role of environment in shaping human behavior. They neglected to consider that the genetic contribution to aggression might well be very limited and, to the degree it might exist, very complex, the product of multiple genes acting in concert.

All the same, blaming violence on biology never lost its appeal to the media, the public, and even some scientists. In the mid-1960s a team of British researchers reported that a disproportionate number of male inmates in a Scottish hospital for patients with "dangerous, violent, or criminal propensities" had an extra Y chromosome accompanying the normal male complement of one X and one Y. Eventually, further research showed the double Y to be irrelevant to violent behavior, but not before lawyers representing the notorious Chicago multiple murderer Richard Speck announced that they planned to appeal his case on the grounds that he was XYY and therefore not responsible for his criminal acts. As it turned out, Speck didn't have the double Y chromosome after all, but the publicity helped inspire others to take up the banner. *Time* and *Newsweek* spotlighted the alleged relationship between chromosomes and crime, and a series of novels such as *The XYY Man* and *The Mosley Receipt* by Kenneth Royce featured an XYY character who struggled against his compulsion to cause havoc.

Today's biological theories of violence are far more sophisticated than their forebears. Unlike the earlier theories, they are concerned with behavior in individuals rather than groups, and they tend to be sensitive to the role of environment. They are also the product of some of the most powerful tools of modern science, including the ability to identify and isolate individual genes and to obtain pictures of the living brain. Unlike the phrenologists, neurobiologists can see—and show us—what may be wrong in a criminal's head.

Brain scans in particular seem to give a dramatic view into the biological dynamics of violence. Early PET-scan studies in the 1980s revealed that the brains of convicted criminals who had been victims of child abuse had areas of inactivity relative to the brains of control subjects (probably the result of getting banged on the head while they were babies). By early 1997, a psychologist at the University of Texas Medical Branch in Galveston could conjure up red-and-blue reconstructions of the brains of violent offenders and use them to support his view that their hair-trigger tempers were the result of an impairment of the frontal and parietal lobes of their brains.

Neuroscientists have isolated and begun to study the roles of several neurotransmitters in suicidal patients, depressives, and people prone to impulsive violence. They have connected both excesses and insufficiencies of serotonin and dopamine with impulsive violent behavior and with diseases of the brain such as Parkinson's. At the same time, the mapping of the human genome is providing pictorial representations of where our genes reside in relation to one another. We can now see our genes as strings of beads, and it seems only a matter of time before the bad bead on the string will be correlated with the suspect area in the brain scan.

"Other studies have focused on the role of serotonin in aggression."

Among the most interesting studies in progress is a project at Brookhaven National Laboratory on Long Island linking dopamine, cocaine addiction, the rise of euphoria, and subsequent violent behavior. The research seems to indicate that people who do not produce enough dopamine—whether through a genetically encoded trait or from some environmental cause—might seek out addictive drugs to avoid feeling depressed. Whatever the cause, brain scans of recovering addicts show damage in parts of the brain that neurologists have identified as controlling acceptable interpersonal behavior. Other studies have focused on the role of serotonin in aggression. Researchers at UCLA observed a colony of vervet monkeys whose social structure they could manipulate by controlling serotonin levels in individual animals. High levels raised the status of male monkeys in the hierarchy of the colony, and high status goes with dominant behavior.

Both scientists and popularizers have predicted that the new behavioral genetics will lead to the kinds of therapies and cures that medical genetics hopes to achieve for physical disease. Yet for all its sophistication and, in some cases, caution and care, the new biology of violence is at risk for many of the difficulties that have afflicted the entire field of human behavioral biology since the early decades of this century. Researchers continue to find it difficult to eliminate or compensate for environmental influences in their studies. For instance, putting together a control group of families that have the same complicated situations as a subject group is an inexact process, to say the least. Controlling for the existence of, say, poverty is relatively straightforward, but controlling for a family's attitude toward its own poverty—and attitude will have a big impact on how well family members cope with it—is practically impossible.

Many theories also suffer from imprecise definitions of the traits they purport to explain, or they lump disparate behaviors together—such as putting all manifestations of violence under the catchall category of "aggressiveness." These call to mind

Charles Davenport's efforts to find genetic explanations for "nomadism," "shiftlessness," and "thalassophilia"—a love of the sea that he discerned in (male) naval officers and concluded must be a sex-linked recessive trait. Contemporary scientists have attributed to genes the propensity to crave thrills, to have leadership qualities, to be unhappy, to divorce, and to wear a lot of rings (or "beringedness," as one psychiatrist calls it). Researchers from City of Hope, the Duarte, California, research hospital, declared that the D^2 dopamine receptor gene was associated with an entire constellation of destructive behaviors, including autism, drug abuse, attention-deficit hyperactivity, post-traumatic stress disorder, pathological gambling, Tourette's syndrome, and alcoholism.

The new biology of violence has often drawn excellent correlations from studies with animals, particularly mice and monkeys. But what animals have to tell us about human behavior is severely limited. It is difficult to see how the sex lives of adolescent mice, for instance, has [sic] much at all to do with our sons and daughters. When a male rodent mounts a female, and the female assumes an accepting position, they are not doing so as a result of social pressures: both animals are acting according to biological signals alone. It doesn't take a Ph.D. to know that such is not the case with boys and girls. Monkeys, on the other hand, are certainly behaviorally closer to humans. After all, they undergo many of the same developmental stages, and anyone who has watched adolescent vervets knows that they sometimes act a lot like college students the week after exams. But monkeys are not people by any measure.

Despite all that neuroscientists have learned about brain chemistry and structure, they in fact still know very little about how the brain works, let alone how it governs action. Much confusion over research on the biology of violence occurs because the public does not always appreciate the largely correlational aspect of the research. Scientists in general cannot yet say that a specific abnormality in the brain *causes* a person to exhibit a particular violent behavior; they can say only that the two tend to occur in the same individual. Although in some cases an abnormality may indeed be said to cause a behavior, it is sometimes equally plausible that a behavior causes an abnormality. Further muddying the waters is the obvious and unenlightening fact that all behavior—even learned behavior—is in some sense biological. We initiate a biological process every time we use a finger to press a button or pull a trigger. The biological activity that scientists observe can often be the result of our experience in life or even "pre-life" in the uterine environment. Researchers are still a long way from predicting, much less preventing, most outbursts of violence.

Meanwhile, even the hope of using biology to foretell an individual's tendency to violence poses grave difficulties for a democratic society. The prospect strikes directly at conventional notions of human dignity and freedom. If we could tell that someone has a 65 percent chance of behaving violently if he consumes alcohol, how should that information be used? Should it be made public, thus stigmatizing the person? Should legislation be passed making it illegal for such people to drink? Since the advent of the xyy research, many have worried that screening children for biological propensities to violence could lead to a self-fulfilling prophecy. Telling children that they are prone to violence might just encourage them to meet those expectations.

Another difficulty arises from the not unreasonable notion that if biology is destiny, then responsibility becomes moot—a point not lost on defense lawyers. In 1982, John Hinckley, who shot Ronald Reagan and James Brady, was sent to a mental hospital instead of prison in part because a jury accepted ct scan evidence that he was suffering from "shrunken brain" and had therefore not been responsible for his actions. While brain scans have not been used successfully to exculpate murderers, they have been employed to avoid the death penalty, and in the last several years criminal defense lawyers have proposed that a deficiency in the enzyme that regulates serotonin might make a good legal defense.

"We need better education, nutrition, and intervention in dysfunctional homes and in the lives of abused children..."

We would probably all like to cure society of violent behavior with something akin to a vaccine to prevent its spread and an antibiotic to cure what we already face. But the medical analogy gives undue weight to the biological basis of the behavior. "We know what causes violence in our society: poverty, discrimination, the failure of our educational system," says Paul Billings, a clinical geneticist at Stanford. "It's not the genes that cause violence in our society. It's our social system." We need better education, nutrition, and intervention in dysfunctional homes and in the lives of abused children, perhaps to the point of removing them from the control of their incompetent parents. But such responses would be expensive and socially controversial. That are searching, instead, for easy answers in the laboratory is a sign of the times.

Genetics and the Control of Crime[4]

If any of those who attended the now-notorious recent conference on genetics and criminal behavior had hoped to learn how genetic research can solve our crime problems, they must have gone away sorely disappointed. Originally scheduled for 1992 at the University of Maryland, the meeting was canceled after being roundly denounced as racist, then was resurrected last September at a smaller and more remote venue on Maryland's Eastern Shore. Even reconfigured and relocated, however, the conference still commanded a flood of public attention.

The media mostly ignored the participants' debates about what the term *heritability* means and the worth of genetic association studies. Coverage focused instead on the far more telegenic brief demonstration organized by the Progressive Labor Movement and a group of people describing themselves as psychiatric survivors. ("Jobs not Prozac," read one placard, and "This Conference Predisposes Me to Disruptive Behavior Disorder.")

Given all the hullabaloo over the meeting, one would have thought the participants were about to announce a devastatingly persuasive array of research findings for immediate application by crime fighters. The take-home message for those who actually listened to the meeting's content, however, was that the field of genetics is unlikely to contribute significantly to reducing or preventing crime. In short, crime is never going to be very big in the genetics business, and genetics is never going to be very big in the crime business, forecast Franklin E. Zimring, of the University of California School of Law in Berkeley.

It is not simply that scientists lack facts about the relation of DNA to crime (with, to be sure, one noteworthy exception: more than 80% of those arrested for any crime, and more than 90% of those arrested for violent crime, possess a Y chromosome). Nor is it just that ignorance renders it premature to incorporate genetics into crime policy.

The difficulty is considerably more basic. The more that is learned, the clearer it becomes that the knowledge gained is unlikely to generate practical strategies for dealing with that motley mass of disparate actions—ranging from stock fraud to serial homicide—we lump under the catchall rubric *crime.*

Genes and Crime

Take, for example, the much-mentioned 1993 study that described an X-linked mutation associated with mild retardation

---

[4]Article by Tabitha M. Powledge, from *BioScience* 46:7–10 Ja '96. Copyright © 1996 Tabitha M. Powledge. Reprinted with permission.

and aggressive, sometimes criminal, behavior in one large Dutch family. The mutation causes complete deficiency of the enzyme monoamine oxidase A (MAOA), which metabolizes the neurotransmitters serotonin, dopamine, and noradrenaline. Much excitement about its possible social implications attended this publication *(Science* 262: 578–580), and geneticists around the world rushed to scour their own populations for a similar MAO defect. So far, they have been utterly unable to find it.

No one disputes that the Dutch team identified a real single-gene defect that results in antisocial behavior. But it now looks as if the abnormal gene is what geneticists call a "private" mutation, likely to be found at most in a handful of other families, with approximately zero relevance to crime control.

"The type of data that genetics research provides is actually not the sort that crime fighters need..."

Even if the mutation were far more common than it appears to be, it is not clear what crime fighters could or would do about it. The Dutch men who possess this abnormal gene may typically engage in impulsive aggression, but the time, place, type, and seriousness of their crimes (which include exhibitionism, attempted rape, and arson) have been diverse and unpredictable, as David Goldman, a geneticist at the National Institute of Alcoholism and Alcohol Abuse, pointed out.

Although this onetime genetics bombshell has dwindled into something of a dud, not everyone has been deterred from trying to make policy with it. Contrary to frequently expressed fears that genetic research will be wielded by a malicious state against poor and powerless minorities, however, it is actually creative (or desperate) defense attorneys who have dragged the MAOA mutation into the public arena. They claim that in 1991, the gene drove their client to shoot a Domino's pizza manager in the face. According to Goldman, several genetics labs have been asked to test the man for the MAOA mutation, but all have declined.

The type of data that genetics research provides is actually not the sort that crime fighters need, because genes are not a proximate cause of crime, Zimring argued. Those professionally concerned about reducing crime, he said, seek short-term solutions with an impact on known offenders.

Also, genes relevant to criminal behavior—those that affect aggression, for instance—are likely necessary to normal functioning. According to Dorothy Nelkin, a sociologist and historian of science at New York University, one of the arguments in favor of the Dutch mutation being present in the family of the convicted man was that a lot of his relatives were successful businessmen.

Genetic information is also not predictive enough. Finding a single-gene defect like the MAOA mutation is an exceedingly rare event in behavioral genetics. Like other complex traits, most behaviors appear to result from the actions of multiple genes, with generous input from outside the DNA as well. One of the meeting's favorite metaphors was lemonade—compounded from distinct ingredients like lemon juice and sugar, but melded irrevocably, and ultimately inseparable. For one thing, what matters is not whether someone possesses a gene, but whether that gene is expressed, as Margaret McCarthy, of the University of Maryland School of Medicine, showed.

In a stunning five-minute exegesis, McCarthy reviewed several studies of the role of testosterone in aggressive behavior among experimental animals. Testosterone, it turns out, unlike cocaine or heroin, does not act directly on the brain to trigger behavior. Like other steroid hormones, testosterone instead regulates gene expression, acting on many different sites in a cell's DNA. "We have very little clue as to what these sites are, but they are multiple in the brain," she said. "That turns on the gene products, and it is these gene products that then alter the behavior."

Everyone who reads newspapers, McCarthy pointed out, thinks that there is a direct relationship between testosterone levels and aggression. The real story is considerably more complicated. When two male experimental animals with similar genes and similar testosterone levels fight, the winner's testosterone rises and the loser's falls, resulting in different levels of gene expression. The fight also stimulates production of other steroids, the glucocorticoids, the so-called stress hormones, which turn on another set of genes, and initiate another set of gene products.

The two animals, whose genetic endowment is similar, are now in quite different states. If the aggression does not recur, a stable social hierarchy will be established and the testosterone levels of the two animals will return to approximately their original similarity. If this social hierarchy is disrupted, however—by repeatedly introducing strange males, or by limiting resources, for example—testosterone will end up having a large effect on gene expression, as will the glucocorticoids.

"Given enough of these encounters, you can exert more-or-less permanent effects on gene expression in these animals," McCarthy said. The result: animals that are genetically similar respond to the same stimulus quite differently.

"We keep talking about genes, and genetic variability, but genes are not static," McCarthy noted. "It doesn't matter a whit if you have a gene if it doesn't get turned on. It has to be regulated. What genes we inherit are only relevant in terms of their expression."

It is possible that genetic research may eventually contribute something to our knowledge of crime, and perhaps even to its control. But the contribution will be indirect. Research on genetic aspects of behavior such as mental disorders, or alcoholism and other addictions, could ultimately have some impact on the social consequences of those conditions, which can include breaking the law. Diana Fishbein, of the U.S. Department of Justice, one of the few criminologists who is a biology enthusiast, called for more research into conduct disorder, attention-deficit disorder, and certain other temperamental traits like impulsivity.

Crime and Biology

Although genetics per se is unlikely to tell us much of practical value about crime, other aspects of human biology may be more useful. Adrian Raine, of the University of Southern California at Los Angeles, showed PET scans comparing brain activity in 42 murderers with that in an equal number of normal controls. The murderers tended to have less prefrontal activity, consistent with Raine's hypothesis that a damaged prefrontal cortex can lead to impulsive aggressive behavior.

Because murderers, like the rest of us, are a heterogeneous group of people, Raine cautioned strongly against regarding such scans as diagnostic. "You cannot do brain imaging on people and predict who is normal and who's a murderer," he said. "We cannot use any single measure to predict who's going to become violent, who's going to be a criminal." In short, applying research of this kind to crime control often raises exactly the same ethical and policy issues whether the study focuses on genes or on other aspects of human biology.

Raine acknowledged that prefrontal dysfunction might be genetic, but he believes it is much more likely to be produced by nongenetic events such as accidents, head injuries, and child abuse. Vigorously shaking a young child can lacerate the delicate nerve fibers that link the prefrontal cortex to the limbic system, he noted, and so perhaps generate aggressive violent behavior.

Birth itself may play a role. A 1993 report from the National Academy of Sciences found indications that birth complications predisposed to violence. In a follow-up, Raine and his colleagues studied more than 4200 Danish men born between September 1959 and December 1961. They found highly significant interacting effects among men whose birth had been difficult and who had also experienced maternal rejection in infancy (using measures such as whether the pregnancy was unwanted and whether the infant was institutionalized for at least four months). Members of this group were much more likely than others in the cohort (including those with birth complications alone or maternal rejection alone) to have engaged in violent crime by the age of 18. They accounted for only 4.5% of the sample, but committed 18% of the violent crimes.

The researchers speculate that violence may erupt from brain dysfunction brought on by birth trauma when it is combined with disruption of the mother-infant bond. Although in 1994 (*Archives of General Psychiatry* 51:984–988) they cautioned that they do not yet know whether the findings might apply across cultures. When Raine reported on this study, he urged greater public attention to reducing birth complications—and on teaching parenting skills—as a way of reducing violence.

Metals known to have a toxic effect on the brain and cognitive processes may also cause violence, according to an unpublished study by Roger D. Masters and his colleagues at Dartmouth that was circulated at the meeting. Intrigued by the variability in the homicide rate between similar-seeming U.S. cities—the murder rate of 19/100,000 population in Jersey City is twice that of Newark, with comparable differences between St. Louis and Kansas City, or Atlanta and New Orleans—the researchers used data from the Environmental Protection Agency's Toxic Release Inventory to look at geographical variations in lead and manganese. (Other researchers have reported these two neurotoxins in the hair of violent criminals, although not consistently.)

Masters and his colleagues found high correlations between violent crime and releases of the two toxic elements and their compounds in a sample of 573 counties with a total population of 80 million from eight states. Counties with only one of the metals had violent crime rates of between 340 and 380 per 100,000, not significantly higher than average. The higher rates were found principally in the 23 counties with moderate rates of manganese and high rates of lead (on average, 520 violent crimes per 100,000), and especially in the 18 counties with high rates of both (700 per 100,000).

"...rather than the criminal's genes, easy access to a handgun led to the murder of the manager at Domino's."

The researchers speculate that any effects of the neurotoxins may be increased due to an interaction between the metals and poor diet, especially during childhood. In particular, they say, vitamin and mineral (especially calcium) deficiencies play a central role in manganese uptake.

A few other factors were associated with violence in this study, among them alcohol-related deaths, population density, and poverty among African Americans. No significant effects were found for some variables widely believed to be associated with crime, such as number of African Americans, per capita income of Hispanics or African Americans, and unemployment rates. The study also tossed a small bouquet to the much-denigrated Welfare State: higher monthly expenditures for Aid to Families with Dependent Children were associated with lower rates of violent crime.

Policy Implications, If Any

Given the meeting's intended focus on genes, there was a surprising degree of agreement among biologists and nonbiologists alike that society already knows much about how to reduce and prevent violent crime, and most of it has nothing to do with biology or genetics. Gun control topped the list. (In fact, it can be asserted that, rather than the criminal's genes, easy access to a handgun led to the murder of the manager at Domino's.)

Several meeting participants called for renewed attention to social programs. Said Fishbein, "I think bleeding hearts are very underrated in this society."

The meeting did not settle the controversy, simmering since 1992, about whether such a conference should have been held at all. The demonstrators claimed that even the thought of genetic research on crime is irredeemably racist and genocidal. As they penetrated the meeting room, they chanted, "Maryland conference, you can't hide. We know you're pushing genocide," and later, "Jobs yes, racism no."

Several participants, including Paul R. Billings of the Palo Alto Veteran's Affairs Medical Center, argued that any discussion of these issues may make them seem important enough for society to take seriously. Others were appalled at the idea that some subjects should be off limits for debate and research. Adrienne Asch, of Wellesley College, told the demonstrators, "You're not going to solve the problem by closing down ideas."

There is of course no guarantee that, just because they are foolish and useless, there will be no attempts to base crime policy on genes. "We're not conducting our academic research in a vacuum. It will have very real political implications," warned Katheryn Russell, a criminologist at the University of Maryland. Jerome G. Miller, of the National Center on Institutions and Alternatives, agreed, arguing that the making of social policy has nothing to do with scientific facts, but that policy makers muster any facts that can bolster an ideological position.

Participants gave considerable attention to cautionary tales of the eugenics movements here and abroad earlier in this century, which resulted in discrimination, forced sterilization, and genocide. Russell pointed out that a lot of well-meaning people espoused eugenics, and a lot of defenseless people were hurt as a result.

"How do we know that the bad old days are over?" asked Billings. The perspective of many scientists is narrow, he said, and there is no evidence that today they are any more aware of the side effects and malevolent uses of their work than were scientists in the past. Moreover, society's old beliefs about this subject have not been corrected either by public education or the media, he noted.

But several participants argued that today in the United States, people face little danger of a government-imposed eugenics program. The greatest potential for bigotry and injustice lies elsewhere. Reproductive consumerism is one potent force. Important social questions about genetics, predicted Diane Paul, a political scientist at the University of Massachusetts, will arise from the desires and demands of individual families.

Genetic discrimination is also likely to emerge from economic pressures. Insurance companies are likely to seek to exclude persons they deem genetically vulnerable in order to keep down their costs. Said Nelkin, "Genetic explanations are very convenient at the moment of the dismantling of the Welfare State."

Toward the meeting's end, Asch called on participants to draw up a "to-do list" of useful genetic research that would help deal with crime. One participant suggested calcium supplements and advice on breast-feeding and child rearing for pregnant teenagers. Not genetic, Asch pointed out.

Another declared something should be done about violence on TV and in the movies. That is not genetic either, Asch replied. She waited expectantly for a long moment. Only silence filled the air.

II. Violence Manifest

As Section I contains articles that discuss the causes and bases for violence and violent actions, Section II discusses the nature of violence as it is actually experienced by many Americans. It follows that the articles in Section II describe a wide range of manifestations of violence, including racism, spousal abuse, and violent crime. Again, as the articles in this section demonstrate, while violence embodies a variety of destructive actions, the quest to understand it and prevent it is similarly multifaceted.

In a book review of Franklin E. Zimring's and Gordon Hawkins's *Crime Is Not the Problem: Lethal Violence in America*, James Q. Wilson discusses the difference between American crime rates and those of comparably industrialized nations. According to Wilson's review, the central difference lies in the United States' far higher rate of violent crime. Simply put, Americans "kill each other" far more frequently than do citizens of other nations. Zimring and Hawkins believe this to be a direct result of the great extent to which Americans possess firearms.

Wilson's review of Zimring's and Hawkins's book asserts that one of the most direct causes for the prevalence of violence in America is the sheer number of weapons that Americans own. A number of organizations—including the Children's Defense Fund, the HELP Network, and Handgun Control, Inc.—are exploring new approaches to gun violence that go beyond the crime issue. One method such groups advocate is to treat violence resulting from firearms as a public health crisis and educate the public as to the risks of keeping guns in the home. Another tactic is to treat guns as a consumer product that is subject to restrictions and safety standards.

"End the Domestic Arms Race," by Hubert Williams, the former police director of Newark, New Jersey, discusses the staggering number of guns in America. According to Williams, there are over 200 million guns in the private sector. Williams believes this to be the largest factor behind the almost "40,000 Americans [who] died from gunshot wounds" in 1994. In his article, Williams recalls suggestions that have been made to Congress on how to reduce the violence that is thought to be a result of firearms. Such suggestions include heavily taxing handguns and ammunition, and banning handgun ownership for anyone under 18 years of age.

Racism often acts as a catalyst for violent behavior. According to Stephan Talty, writing for the *New York Times*, while "the majority of skinheads are nonracist and nonviolent," their white supremacist "racist counterparts" are in fact exceedingly violent. In "The Method of a Neo-Nazi Mogul," Talty profiles a white supremacist and describes his use of the Internet as a means of reaching a surprisingly large audience.

In 1997, *Essence* magazine reported that two million women in the United States were victims of domestic violence. A study conducted by New Haven, Connecticut's Domestic Violence Training Project found that women suffer more injuries as a result of domestic violence than from car accidents, rapes, and muggings combined. In 1994, for the first time ever, the Clinton administration and Congress allocated funds to the Centers for Disease Control and Prevention (CDC) with the aim of investigating and reducing violence against women. Jeannine Amber, author of "Young and Abused," discusses the possible causes of abuse, the characteristics of abusive men, the difficulty women have in ending abusive relationships, and various methods of dealing with abuse.

Sarah Buel, assistant district attorney of Norfolk County, Massachusetts, is one of America's most active weapons against domestic violence. Having been a victim of domestic violence, Buel is well aware of the problems faced by battered women. In

"Why They Stay: A Saga of Spouse Abuse," Hara Estroff Marano profiles Sarah Buel, describing how she travels the country training judges to deal with abuse cases and addressing seminars and conferences on the nature of domestic violence. According to Marano, Buel believes that handling the problem effectively requires a coordinated community effort and not simply the isolated, case-by-case efforts of attorneys and judges.

Hostility in America[1]

One of the more frustrating difficulties facing students of crime is our inability to compare crime rates across countries. Interpol gathers crime data from national police agencies, but it does so in a way that makes its reports next to worthless.

The agency fails to assess the quality of the accounts that it receives, and it presents them in a way bound to cause confusion. Thus, not long ago, someone published an op-ed essay in which the author claimed that the Netherlands had a higher murder rate than did the United States. That is, to put it mildly, an implausible idea. In his defense, however, he displayed the Interpol report. At first glance, the document seemed to confirm his view, until one noticed that every homicide reported for the United States was completed—that is, there was a dead body—but the homicides reported for the Netherlands included both completed and attempted (no dead body) homicides. The attempts, of course, far outnumbered the actual murders, and there was no explanation of how the Netherlands decided which actions were attempted murders and which were just everyday assaults. We do not know very much, in short, about how the characteristics of nations or their various criminal justice policies affect crime rates.

Franklin Zimring and Gordon Hawkins, two members of the Earl Warren Legal Institute at the University of California at Berkeley, have plunged into this thicket, fully aware of the snags that it contains, to sort out how American crime rates differ from those of comparably industrialized nations. No one will be surprised to learn that the United States has a far higher rate of violent crime, especially homicide, than Western Europe or Australia. But some may be astonished to learn that the rate of property crime here is similar to the rate of property crime elsewhere, and in many cases it is much lower. Zimring and Hawkins conclude that what is often described as the American "crime problem" is in reality a lethal violence problem, and that the main goal of public policy ought to be to reduce violence.

To do that, we must first understand why our rate of violence is so much higher than in England, Australia, France or Germany. The answer given by Zimring and Hawkins is that we kill each other more often (and engage in property crimes, such as robbery, that often have fatal outcomes) in large part because Americans are more heavily armed than are other societies. Opponents of gun control will reflexively object to this conclusion, but, if they are to prevail, they will have tough going against the arguments made here. Using data from the World Health Organization, a group that counts dead bodies instead of

---

[1]Article by James Q. Wilson, from *The New Republic* 217:38–41 Ag 25 '97. Copyright © 1997 *The New Republic*. Reprinted with permission.

merely repeating police reports, and gathering facts from big-city police departments abroad, Zimring and Hawkins show that American cities are not very different from foreign ones of similar size with respect to theft or burglary, but they are vastly higher with respect to robbery and homicide. New York City has less theft and burglary than London but vastly more robberies and homicides. The same difference exists between Sydney, Australia, and Los Angeles.

Robbery involves the threat of violence; burglary need not involve violence, though violence may occur if the dwelling is occupied when the burglar enters. In neither crime is death likely. But thefts in American cities are more likely to lead to death than are thefts in other nations. In 1992, there were seven deaths in London resulting from a burglary or robbery; in New York City, there were 378, even though New York has fewer such crimes than does London. American property crimes are much more deadly than English ones, in large measure because our thieves are armed. And much the same story can be told about assault. When one Londoner attacks another, death occurs in less than one-half of 1 percent of the cases, but when one New Yorker attacks another, death is the result in over 3 percent of the cases. The reason in part is that firearms are used in 26 percent of all New York assaults but in only 1 percent of assaults in London.

"...the death rate in New York City is...three times as high as it is in London."

Still, the use of guns is not the whole story. If one looks only at robberies in which no gun was involved, the death rate in New York City is still three times as high as it is in London. Even in murder cases, guns are not essential: 30 percent of all American homicides did not involve a gun. This means that New Yorkers without a gun kill one another more often than do Londoners however armed. Obviously something more than weaponry makes New York a more lethal environment than London.

Since guns are not the whole story, we have extraordinary differences among our states in how frequently people are killed. Maine and North Dakota have the lowest homicide rates in the country, less than one-tenth of the rates in Louisiana and Mississippi, but the reason cannot be that no one in Maine or North Dakota owns a gun. Rural states are probably armed to the teeth, as anyone knows who has visited them during deer hunting season. The answer must be that personal encounters in rural states are more law-abiding and less productive of personal violence. North Dakota not only has the second-lowest murder rate, it has the second-lowest property crime rate.

Zimring and Hawkins suggest that many American communities are more dangerous not only because guns are more available, but also because personal conflicts are more frequent and more violent. In their words, firearms are "neither a necessary nor a sufficient cause of violent death," but they are a contributing factor. If two men meet in a bar or on a street corner and have an argument, the result of that quarrel will depend heavily on what weapons might be available with which to manage any escalating violence. If there are only fists, only a fist fight can ensue; if there are guns, there may be a fatal shootout. Many years ago Zimring published articles suggesting that murder was often the consequence of an ambiguously motivated assault: at the outset, nobody intended the death of the other, but, as the fight progressed and a gun was at hand, death was the result. To reduce deaths one must either reduce the likelihood of fights or disarm the fighters.

In their new book, Zimring and Hawkins largely reject other popular explanations for violence. They have little use for studies of the impact of the media, and I think that their rebuttals are essentially correct. Violence in the media is everywhere, in London as much as in New York, in Sydney as much as in Los Angeles, and yet those places differ dramatically in lethal behavior. When all cities are exposed to the same media, it is hard to see how the media can explain differences in violence. No doubt there are copy-cat killers, but their numbers are too small to explain why people in Tokyo almost never kill and those in Atlanta often do.

Violence also accompanies drug dealing, but the proportion of murders that are connected to the drug trade is too small to make much of a difference. The best estimates are that no more than 10 percent of all killings are connected to the drug trade, though from time to time the percentage is much higher in a few cities. Moreover, the laws on drug-dealing are about as tough in Australia as they are here, but drug-connected deaths are about sixty times more common in Los Angeles than in Sydney. In the United States, drug dealing on a large scale has probably created an array of armed gangs that make violent encounters, and thus lethal ones, more likely. But why? That is like asking why the vast majority of drug users are in this country even though almost every country has similar laws.

There is another contributing factor that the authors confront, but not, I think, quite adequately. They ask whether the very high rate of violence among African Americans explains the American homicide rate. There is no denying the core facts. Blacks are five times as likely to kill as are whites; black males are six times as likely to kill as are white males. Homicide is the leading cause of death among young black males, but it is the tenth cause for Americans as a whole. Zimring and Hawkins do not have much to say about why this is true, except to argue that it is probably because African Americans live disproportionately in urban "slum neighborhoods" and because less violent middle-class blacks live in "racial zones" that put them in close proximity to poor blacks.

This is not much of an explanation. Just limiting ourselves to big-city residents reduces the black-white difference in homicide from eight times nationally to only (only!) four times at the big-city level. Moreover, other equally poor and geographically isolated urban groups have much lower crime rates. Koreans, Vietnamese and Chinese are often poor, and recent arrivals, and many of them live in similar "racial zones," but they kill at a far lower rate than do African Americans.

Now, explaining these differences is not easy. I am not certain what it is, but I expect that it has much to do with the legacy of slavery, lynching and past failure to enforce the law when blacks harmed other blacks. Oddly, Zimring and Hawkins write as if the explanation is either unimportant or obvious. It is, in fact, neither. If African American murder rates were the same as white murder rates, the national murder rate would drop substantially. The effect of lowering the black murder rate to equal the white one would not make America as safe as other industrialized nations, but it probably would have at least as big an effect as banning the existence of all handguns. Non-gun homicides in New York City are three times as common as all homicides in London, a number that is only a bit smaller than the difference in white-only homicide rates between the two countries.

"Young people, white and black, were becoming much more lethal in the late 1980s, probably owing to the spread of gangs..."

In fact, Arnold Barnett of MIT has made some calculations that suggest that the homicide rate of adult black males has in fact been coming down much faster than the white homicide rate. No one is quite certain why this has occurred, though certain possible explanations—social progress, residential relocation—are obvious enough. We tend to forget these trends and to dwell instead on the great increase in juvenile homicide rates that took place between 1985 and 1992. Young people, white and black, were becoming much more lethal in the late 1980s, probably owing to the spread of gangs, their involvement in drug trafficking, and easier access to guns. The increase was greater for blacks. In the last few years, that rate has declined a bit, and this probably helps to explain why the homicide rate generally in the country has experienced so sharp a dip.

But this dip may prove to be short-lived. Census figures show that there will be an increase in the proportion of young people on the streets in the next few years, and there is no reason yet to suppose that those who now lead a life of no fathers, gangs for friends and easy dollars in the drug trade have decided to abandon that life. Rescuing young people from those conditions, a frightfully difficult and expensive proposition, may be as effective as figuring out a way (none now exists) to deny them access to the knives and guns with which they can kill others.

Zimring and Hawkins neglect almost all of these issues in their desire to reassure us that there is no "black problem" in crime. I'm sorry, but there is. It is certainly not the whole problem, and solving it would certainly not solve America's violence problem; Zimring and Hawkins are right to point out that equalizing racial differences in murder, desirable as that may be, would still leave America's homicide rate at least twice as high as the rate in other major industrialized nations. An all-white America would be much more lethal than Italy, Canada, France, Germany and England, and vastly more lethal than Japan.

But that is not the end of the story. It is impossible to deny that very high rates of violence among African Americans (rates that may have been coming down of late among black adults) not only contribute mightily to the problem of life in our cities, they also disfigure and polarize any effort to deal with our most serious domestic problem. The authors at least acknowledge this effect. As long as black violence is at so high a level, they observe, it will reinforce "white fear in ways that palpably contribute to the exclusion of blacks from the social mainstream."

By this point the reader expects that Zimring and Hawkins will offer some remedies for murder. Given their analysis, there are only two such remedies: reduce the availability of guns or lower the frequency of hostile encounters. But they suggest neither. Though they devote two long chapters to "Prevention," reading them reminds me of watching Mike Hargrove getting ready to bat. He comes to the plate. He stretches his shirt, tugs at his glove, pulls at his pants, shifts his cap, adjusts his grip. He gets in place. Then he backs out and does this all over again. To watch Hargrove at bat was like killing time during a rain delay. Will this ever end?

In this book, Zimring and Hawkins write that a "book of this kind would be a terrible place to posit a detailed and comprehensive program of loss prevention from violence...." A terrible place? Franklin Zimring has devoted much of the last thirty years of his professional career to studying the impact of guns on violence, and he still has nothing to say about what we should do? If not now, when?

Of course, he does have a few things to say, but mostly by way of criticizing other people's ideas. Zimring and Hawkins dislike many of our prison policies because they think that, under the impact of those policies, we send too many nonviolent offenders to prison. They argue that, in California, the "three strikes" law has had no connection to the recent reduction in the rate of violent crime, but they leave the explanation of this controversial judgment to a document that they do not bother to summarize. (You will have to look it up. But I warn you, it will be a waste of your time.) They attack people who support various popular anti-crime programs for making absurd predictions and failing to evaluate the results.

They are probably right about this. But what programs do they favor, and how should we evaluate them? They speculate about regulating handguns, but they offer no idea as to how it might be done better. They ruminate about violent encounters, but they suggest no way to reduce their frequency except to suggest that victims be "as cooperative as possible" if they are threatened by a robber. They note that some people are trying to teach violence avoidance in the schools, but they conclude that there are "insufficient data to form a judgment" as to whether these plans work.

Perhaps Zimring and Hawkins are vague because they do not have any good ideas. That is not an embarrassing predicament. Very few people have good ideas about this subject, and for good reason. Eric Monkkonen, after years of careful digging in historical records, has been able to show that the homicide rate in New York City has exceeded that of London by a factor of at least five *for the last two hundred years*. Similarly, Roger Lane has shown that in the early nineteenth-century Philadelphia had a high homicide rate. Big-city Americans were killing each other at a far higher rate than were Londoners long before the invention of radio and television, and long before the introduction of semi-automatic weapons (and automatic ones) or the sale of any drugs (other than alcohol). It is very hard, I think, to devise an easy way to reduce a homicide rate that has been so high for so long. The hostility of American encounters is at least as important as the presence of American guns. If New York City can have a *non*-gun homicide rate that is three times larger than the total homicide rate in London, then removing all guns from the United States (which is impossible) would still leave us in a troubling condition.

"There are no point-of-sale restrictions that will reduce this huge stock by very much."

Suppose we take Zimring's and Hawkins's analysis of the problem as correct, and then try to imagine what might be done. We must begin with the fact that the private ownership of guns cannot be substantially reduced. There are no point-of-sale restrictions that will reduce this huge stock by very much. Moreover, point-of-sale restrictions overlook the fact that most guns used in crimes are stolen or borrowed. And no government can do very much when people believe, with some empirical support, that having a gun makes you safer.

Using the data compiled by the National Crime Victimization Survey (NCVS) of 56,000 families, scholars have estimated that there are, at a minimum, between 65,000 and 80,000 defensive gun uses per year. Some estimates based on private polls suggest much higher defensive uses, ranging up to 1.5 or even 2.5 million. The data supplied by private polls are controversial, since so much depends on inferring society-wide effects from the answers of a tiny number of respondents. (If, to take a recent study, only 54 people out of 2,500 surveyed said they used a gun to defend themselves, then each of the 54 represents 68,000 Americans. Reporting errors—lies, exaggerations, poor memory—on the part of just a few people can have huge effects on the total number of defensive gun uses.) So consider instead the much larger and more reliable NCVS, conducted by the Census Bureau, according to which defensive gun uses in America are not trivial: 65,000 to 80,000 uses each year. No democratic government can afford to say that, while it is having its own trouble protecting people against crime, it wants to deprive these 65,000 people of the means to protect themselves. Under such conditions, you don't need the National Rifle Association to defeat a government effort to disarm Americans.

There are more desirable and less controversial forms of gun control. The most important is to reduce the chances that a person will carry concealed on his person an unlicensed weapon while he walks about town. With a bit of new technology that is now being developed, it may become much easier for the police to spot and to question such gun carriers. Doing this may reduce the rate at which guns will cause angry encounters to escalate into lethal violence.

We also might wonder a bit about the magnitude of our penalties for homicide. They are about the same here as in Europe— that is to say, they are short in both places. Nationally, the median homicide inmate is released from prison after only about six years, while in California the release comes after about three-and-a-half years. Even many offenders sentenced to prison "for life" spend much less time there. Some inmates, of course, spend a lot of time in prison. But the small number of years the median (and the average) offender serves suggests the low price that we generally place on the average victim's life. These sentences should be made longer.

And much remains to be done, finally, to lead children away from a life on the street. We are still trying to learn how best to do this, but a growing body of evidence suggests that early intervention in the lives of very young, at-risk children and their mothers (often there is no father) can make a lasting difference. It will take another generation to learn whether these plausible guesses will bear lasting results for a large number of children, but the nation's perpetually high homicide rate suggests that it might be time well spent.

Above all, we will have to learn to think about our crime problem historically. It took England several centuries of tough rule, brutal punishment and the inculcation of class-based values to achieve a low homicide rate. America has spent less time at the task, and it has sought to inculcate different values. As someone once said, the low murder rate in England is produced the same way you produce good lawns: plant good seed and then roll it for three hundred years. Zimring and Hawkins offer some sensible data on violent crime rates, but they plant no seeds and they roll no lawns.

End the Domestic Arms Race[2]

The reality of policing in America includes dealing with citizens who possess firearms: About 200 million guns are in private hands. So huge is the domestic arsenal that American police must be aware that a firearm may be at hand in any situation they encounter. Tragically, in thousands of situations each year, the potential for injury or death by firearms is realized.

Since November 1994, seven police officers and federal agents in the Washington area have been killed in ambush attacks. In the past few weeks, two young Washington police officers were murdered in cold blood. One, a highly commended officer, was shot as he sat in his patrol car at a stoplight by a man who walked up to him and, without provocation, fired three bullets into his head; the other officer—the victim of a robbery as he parked his car in front of his home where his wife and young son were asleep inside—was murdered by his attackers because he was a police officer. On Feb. 28, two men in full-body armor, armed with a deadly cache of assault weapons loaded with armor-piercing ammunition—known as "cop killer" bullets— engaged the Los Angeles Police Department in an hours-long, rolling gun battle in broad daylight on a busy commercial street. When it was over, the two gunmen lay dead, and 11 police officers and six citizens had been shot or injured.

"In 1994 almost 40,000 Americans died from gunshot wounds."

At 5 PM on Feb. 23, a transient foreign national entered the observation deck of the Empire State Building and, armed with a 14-round semiautomatic pistol he was able to legally purchase in Florida, unleased a barrage of bullets, killing one young man and wounding six others. The assailant bought his gun at the same gun shop where mass killer William Cruse legally purchased the weapon he used to kill six people at a Florida shopping center in 1987.

In 1994 almost 40,000 Americans died from gunshot wounds. By the year 2003, according to the Centers for Disease Control, the leading cause of death by injury in the United States will be from gunshots. America also has the distinction of having the highest rate of firearms-related deaths of children among the world's 26 richest nations.

In 1992 handguns were used to murder 13 people in Australia; 33 people in Great Britain; 60 people in Japan; 128 in Canada; and more than 13,000 in the United States. More Americans die from firearms injuries every two years than died during the entire Vietnam War.

The statistics are numbing. America has an epidemic of gun violence. Yet we regulate guns less than we do automobiles, chil-

[2]Article by Hubert Williams, writer, police director of Newark, NJ from 1974 to 1985, and president of the Police Foundation, from *The Washington Post* Mr 26 '97. Copyright © *The Washington Post*. Reprinted with permission.

dren's pajamas and teddy bears.

The legacy of disability and death that guns (especially handguns) have wrought on American society is of concern to law enforcement personnel, health officials, educators, policy makers, families and communities all across America. The impact that guns have on our lives continues to generate passionate debate. Americans are ambivalent about guns: They fear them, and at the same time they feel safer possessing them, as reflected by the growing number of states that have or are considering concealed weapons laws, often called "right-to-carry" laws.

For the nation's police, the nexus of drugs and guns creates daily and deadly challenges to their ability to control crime and ensure public safety. It used to be anathema to kill cops, but that line has been crossed, if not crossed out altogether. The nation's police have become the targets, outgunned by gang bangers, drug thugs and fanatical gun freaks who believe they're on a righteous mission.

Law enforcement's inevitable and understandable response to the escalating violence is to augment its capacity to respond with high-powered munitions of its own. The stakes have been raised, but the price of public safety must be measured in more than dollars. Democracy requires a delicate balance of interests; in this case the police must provide for public safety without sacrificing the freedoms that Americans treasure. Will more and bigger guns make us safer from the violence that has us gripped in fear?

In the short term, of course, the police must be given the firepower that's required to combat the firepower they now face. In the long run, however, we need fewer guns. Semiautomatic weapons and other weapons of war have no legitimate place in civil society and ought to be banned outright, right now. Unless we muster the national resolve to do so, the body count will continue to rise and democracy remains the ante in this deadly, high-stakes race to arm ourselves against each other.

The Method of
a Neo-Nazi Mogul[3]

Most white supremacists are, by nature, nostalgic and would rather be living deep in the Aryan past. Not George Burdi. He is a racist from the future, and he is impatient for it to arrive.

At 25, Burdi is an archetype of the forward-looking neo-Nazi: he is taking an old idea (hard-core white supremacy), revitalizing it through a young art (rock-and-roll) and bringing it to mainstream America through a newly powerful network (the Internet). His tiny empire, Resistance Records Inc., includes a record label, a magazine, an Internet home page and a weekly electronic newsletter. Burdi, a k a George Eric Hawthorne, is also the lead singer in a rock-and-roll band called Rahowa, short for Racial Holy War.

Remie666 is the on-line name of a 16-year-old Panorama City, CA, fan of Burdi and Resistance Records. In an E-mail note, he describes himself as "straightay"—Aryan Youth—and in a phone interview he says he uses the Internet to read Burdi's writings, to hear music samples and order CD's of white-power bands, to learn about new white-power novels and to E-mail other racist skinheads. "The Internet has quadrupled the number of white-power skins I'm in touch with," he says.

Another white-power devotee, a 27-year-old computer engineer in Dallas whose on-line name is Bootboy, has also seen the surge. "I have operated a P.O. box and a voice-mail system for four years now," he says. "And I have received more contacts, good ones, over the Internet in four months than I have in all four years. I get E-mail from other white-power skins from Sweden, Norway, Finland, Germany, Holland, Luxembourg."

This is one of the main goals of Burdi and other leaders in the new racist vanguard: to build a global community of young neo-Nazi skinheads. The majority of American skinheads are non-racist and nonviolent, embracing the same working-class pride and punkish style as their racist counterparts—who are responsible, says the Anti-Defamation League of B'nai B'rith, for 34 murders in the United States since 1990. The Southern Poverty Law Center estimates that there are at least 4,000 racist skinheads in the country, the hyper-violent edge of the movement that Burdi is trying to mobilize.

His ideology is hardly new. He holds the conviction that whites must reclaim their Nordic ferocity to protect their interests, that Jews control wide swaths of American life through a secret cabal and that the races are incompatible. "To put black men and

---

[3]Article by Stephan Talty, staff writer for *Time Out New York*, from the *New York Times*, F 25 '96. Copyright © 1996 The New York Times Company. Reprinted with permission.

women in American society," he says, "which is traditionally and essentially established on European traditions, and to say, 'Here you go, you're an equal, now compete,' is just as ridiculous as assuming that you could move white people to the Congo and have them effectively compete." Later, he elaborates via E-mail: "As I have said time and time again, the progeny of slaves cannot live in harmony with the progeny of slavemasters."

"The information highway is the gateway to the future, which makes people like George Burdi particularly frightening," says Wade Henderson, director of the Washington bureau of the N.A.A.C.P. "They are determined to transport the racial divides of today into the world of tomorrow."

The loudest opposition thus far to cyber-racists like Burdi has been voiced in Germany, where one on-line service last month barred its users from accessing the World Wide Web site of a Canadian white supremacist, Ernst Zundel, an early mentor of Burdi's. Meanwhile, Burdi, a Canadian who recently moved to Windsor, Ontario, just across the river from Detroit, has set out to reshape the racist landscape. "In the history of our country, there's been no one more effective in recruiting youth to the white-power movement," says Bernie Farber, national director of community relations for the Canadian Jewish Congress. "When he was active here, the average age of the movement went from 75 to 17."

"...Resistance Records has figured in two of the most notorious recent hate crimes in this country."

Burdi is particularly bullish on the future of electronic racism. "We have big plans for the Internet," he says. "It's uncontrollable. It's beautiful, uncensored."

Rabbi Abraham Cooper of the Simon Wiesenthal Center in Los Angeles says that there are now some 75 hate groups on line. "The point is that all those groups have failed to ignite any significant interest in the mainstream," he says. "Now, suddenly, you have cheap, instantaneous communication through computers. Without the Internet, Burdi would be the equivalent of a one-watt light bulb." "But with it," says Rabbi Cooper, "Burdi has discovered, 'Guess what, you can create your own Columbia House.'"

Already, Resistance Records has figured in two of the most notorious recent hate crimes in this country. The Pennsylvania skinhead brothers who killed their parents in Feb. 1995 fled to the home of a Michigan friend they had met at a concert that Resistance promoted. And one of the soldiers at Fort Bragg in North Carolina who were arrested for murdering a black couple in December had a copy of Resistance magazine in his rented room.

Burdi is the editor of the quarterly magazine, a sort of neo-Nazi life style guide replete with movie reviews (*Pulp Fiction* was "better than a cold beer on a hot Auschwitz afternoon!"), ads for Ku Klux Klan Kollectibles and a roundup of racialist news "suppressed by the mainstream press." "The circulation," Burdi says, "is 19,000 and growing with every issue." Mark Wilson, Burdi's partner and a co-founder of Resistance Records, says that their record label has a distributor or champion in "every white country in the world." Resistance's 12 bands sold about 50,000 CD's in the label's first 18 months of business—a minuscule figure by any measure but, taken with the sum of Resistance's offerings, concrete evidence of a new, coordinated marketplace for virulent ideas. It used to be that such ideas were spread via murky photocopies of obscure books and seventh-generation cassettes that were barely audible. Suddenly, the message, like the messenger, comes in a sleek new package.

The words tattooed on Burdi's right bicep—"To thine own self be true"—tense as he scoops up more Thai chicken in a Detroit restaurant. He is just over six feet tall and weighs 200 pounds, and his high-domed forehead is framed by slicked-back hair and heavy sideburns. Wearing work boots, jeans and a leather jacket, he projects a Brandoesque arrogance. Instead of Brando's vulnerability, though, Burdi displays the tetchy manner of an academic and what he calls an inner rage, which animates him to "do some of my best work."

But he is not a shouting freak in a Gestapo uniform; he can wear a suit without looking ridiculous. His writings may be spiced with the faulty constructions of the overachiever and autodidact, but he is an effective speaker. In fact, until he was about 16, George Burdi was the kind of prodigy that parents dream about.

He grew up in an upper-middle-class family in a suburb of Toronto, the son of an insurance company owner and his wife, neither of whom are racists, says Warren Kinsella in his book *Web of Hate: Inside Canada's Far Right Network*. "As a child," Burdi says, "I read 14 books in two weeks. In grade five, I was tested and given a college-level reading level and a genius-level I.Q. I read everything from Thucydides to Plato to Nietzsche." He got his first computer at age 10 and began programming it. "I made programs for my mother to keep her recipes and track her calorie intake and a whole bunch of other things," he says.

As is often the case with supremacists of every stripe, Nietzsche was Burdi's starting point. "I came to understand his discussion of the Superman," he says. "And Shakespeare's warning about contemporary wisdom, that the common established wisdom of your era is not necessarily absolute truth." He began to see himself as a kind of modern heretic questioning the liberal status quo. His new heroes were Caesar Augustus, Napoleon, Alexander the Great, "anyone with a strong will to assert themselves and expand the territory of their people."

At De La Salle College, a private Catholic high school in Toronto, Burdi was an excellent student. After the school had a Black Pride Month, Burdi lobbied for equal time. "I said, 'How can we have a Black Pride Month and not a White Pride Month?'" he remembers. "And then there was an element of the population that started calling me a Nazi, and I really didn't understand the connection to what I was saying."

Perhaps the connection was strengthened when during history class, Burdi reported on the Holocaust-denial standard "Did Six Million Really Die?" He grew ever more fascinated with white separatism and began lifting weights obsessively, trying to build himself into another kind of Superman. His family was mystified by the change. In *Web of Hate*, Andrew Burdi, George's brother, is said to have told a teacher that George had "gone off the deep end."

At the University of Guelph, some 50 miles west of Toronto, a fellow student handed Burdi a pamphlet about the now-defunct Church of the Creator, an often violent, anti-Christian, white-supremacist group that had followers in dozens of countries, including the United States and South Africa. Immediately, Burdi's thinking jumped from the past to the future, and he became a Creator.

"The parts that appealed to me were the concept of a sound mind, a sound body, a sound society and a sound environment," he says. "In many ways I viewed myself as a racial ecologist. Basically what it says is that every race is primarily concerned with its own growth, its own development, protecting its own culture, having its own piece of land, the welfare of its own young people, so on and so forth."

"He grew ever more fascinated with white separatism and began lifting weights obsessively..."

When he was 19, Burdi discovered a valuable talent: salesmanship. Working at his father's insurance company, he began sending direct mailings to clients who were new parents. "I arranged a deal with Canadian baby photographers to give the parents a free photo of their baby if they let me talk to them about life insurance," he says. Burdi made more than $10,000 in one summer and dropped out of college.

After a trip to the Church of the Creator's headquarters in the Blue Ridge Mountains, Burdi became a full-time white-power agitator. In 1990 he formed his rock band, and by 1992 he had become the Canadian representative of the church's leadership council. He also took up with Wolfgang Droege, leader of a white-supremacist umbrella group, Heritage Front, and he studied National Socialism with Ernst Zundel.

In May 1993 Burdi and several hundred other white-power skinheads were involved in a melee with antiracist protesters in Ottawa. Burdi was arrested for kicking a young woman named Alicia Reckzin; he was convicted of assault and served one month of a one-year sentence before being released on bail, pending appeal.

After his arrest, Burdi looked south. The lack of hate-speech laws in the United States and its roiling racial situation made it the natural destination for an ambitious young white supremacist. He and Mark Wilson, whom Burdi had met through the Church of the Creator, started Resistance Records in Detroit, along with a few other partners.

"I quickly learned that we didn't have to promote it at all," recalls Burdi, "because the demand was so strong. We started signing bands like one a month. It was going like crazy. Phone was ringing off the hook. Mailbox was full of mail every week."

The mail included lots of fan letters to Burdi's band. Concerts by Rahowa and other white-power groups have become vital bonding experiences for the racist faithful, drawing small but ardent crowds to clubs across the United States and Canada. Burdi, with his bare, sculpted torso and army-style pants and boots, is a commanding figure onstage, bellowing out songs like "Race Riot" in a deep, floorboards-shaking voice: "Tremble in fear, White man/the reaper's in the shadowland/Save your children, lock your door/You can't come out here no more." The teen-agers in the mosh pit fling Nazi salutes into the air, and Burdi engages them in racist call-and-response chants.

White-power concerts sometimes give way to violence. The fight in Ottawa for which Burdi was jailed took place after a Rahowa performance; after an Oct. 1994 concert in Racine, WI, by six white-power bands, the lead singer for a Resistance band called Nordic Thunder was shot to death after a confrontation in a convenience store with a small group of black men, one of whom was arrested but not charged and later released for lack of evidence.

In an editorial in Resistance magazine last spring, Burdi explained why music is so essential to his cause: "The reason that the so-called movement has been struggling over the years is because it has operated on a rational—not emotional—level. George Lincoln Rockwell was successful because he could stir people's emotions.... Adolf Hitler is considered one of the best orators in human history, by people that do not even understand German."

Like Burdi, Rabbi Cooper has seen rock-and-roll as the future of white power, and he is worried. "This is a seminal change in how to present racist ideology in a way that will reach middle America," he says. "The idea of utilizing music is of special new concern to us because we can take a half-step back and think of all the wonderful things that have been achieved socially in terms of people in the music field. Music touches the soul, it leaps past the reason."

Most Resistance fans are white teen-agers, some as young as 11. They are often troubled—the eternal awkward youth. "The vast majority of our customers are disenfranchised young people," Burdi says. "More and more, these young people are coming to us and saying, 'They're teaching us in school that to be white is bad, that I should feel guilty for being white.' In many ways now, in tens of thousands of these young people, we have a captive audience."

White-power cliques are often the equivalent of Crips for white kids—the gang's ideology is secondary, at least in the beginning. "Sometimes they feel like an outcast and a loner," says Angela Lowry, an intelligence analyst for Klan Watch of the Southern

Poverty Law Center. "And suddenly, they join a skinhead group and they belong." Once a teen-ager finds his way into a local clique, Resistance and other groups link him up with other white-power followers and give him the sense of belonging to an international and historical movement.

And Burdi, says Remie666, the teen-age skinhead, is probably going to be the main leader of white-power youth in the future. "He has a lot of power in his voice when he speaks. I think he's a very good influence. I see people listening to him more than anyone else."

Such enthusiasm is daunting to hate-group watchdogs. Rabbi Cooper has petitioned Internet providers to adopt a code of ethics that would outlaw hate speech on their services. "Just scrolling through the various racist sites on the Internet, a person can say, 'Look at how many groups there are—I'm not isolated,'" says Rabbi Cooper. "In schools, we're pushing our kids to look at that computer screen to do their homework, to do their research. That's the location where they're going to play their games and that's going to be the main area of engagement, the marketplace of ideas."

"Resistance and other groups...give him the sense of belonging to an international and historical movement."

Not that neo-Nazis go unchallenged on the Internet. Nonracist skinheads in particular attack the Resistance site and other similar ones. They call the racists "boneheads" and consider Burdi a pathetic caricature, citing the time he wore a disguise when he appeared on Geraldo Rivera's talk show. Burdi recently posted a message on the popular news group "alt.skinhead" to advertise the latest Rahowa album, and the response was scathing. "Yay!!!" one person wrote back. "George 'I'm a moron' Burdi admits that all this WP-type"—referring to white power— "[expletive] is just another form of cult...where they convince you they're the only people they can trust, and then they convince you to give them all your money, and then there are the little 'survivalist' camps."

Burdi himself is unperturbed by such responses. He has learned a lesson of direct mail marketing: 10 percent positive response is victory.

At the Resistance offices, crammed into the back of Mark Wilson's house in a working-class Detroit suburb, the faithful wander in and out. There are the somber musicians from Resistance bands, mostly in their 20's, and a handful of teen-agers—shy, eager boys and their shyer girlfriends. They wear midnight-blue nylon bomber jackets, T-shirts, camouflage pants and the de rigueur Doc Marten boots. They sit around, smoke fanatically, drink a few beers and wonder what to do tonight.

"Where's Johnny?" someone asks.

"He's getting a Hammerskin tattoo right across here," another teen-ager calls back excitedly, pulling up his shirt and running his hand just below his chest. Eyes widen in appreciation; a girl laughs softly. The office feels vaguely like a sitcom version of a suburban teen-age hangout.

In a corner, working on a computer, Burdi sighs. He sometimes seems underwhelmed by the quality of his recruits and contemptuous of the very youth he hopes to rally. When the young hangers-on clear out, he asks me, with a rare hesitation, if I might like to hear a song from Rahowa's new CD.

He slips in the disk and clicks the player to track 10, "Racial Holy War." He folds his arms behind his head and tilts back in his chair. The music is actually quite lovely, a moody ballad with an almost formal, Elizabethan air. (White-power bands avoid R & B chords.) Burdi's voice is thick, his accent vaguely British— Pink Floyd is a big influence—and he sings to a purposeful, imaginary stride: "As I march into battle, my comrades I hail/Tonight the White Race prevails/Death by our swords to the vile, alien hordes/Their every resistance shall fail."

Eyes closed, Burdi mouths the words silently, his face gripped with the same precise, naked passion as a rock star singing about the redemption of love. In another room, Wilson is talking with a record distributor about Resistance's sales figures, but it is clear that Burdi hears nothing except his own song. He once wrote, in an article for Resistance magazine: "When our people finally awaken and join the army of the Holy War that is raging in our generation, the feeling will dwarf being amongst 500 saluting comrades. I close my eyes and picture the Nuremberg rallies, in vivid color, in real life right before me." Perhaps he is picturing such a scene right now, with himself onstage, leading a stadium full of middle-class white teen-agers in a throaty salute to their future white homeland.

It is all quite unlikely to happen. Burdi is successful thus far only in relation to the near-total failure of his predecessors: Hitlerites have not been particularly admired—or influential—in America for the past 50 years. What is more likely is that sometime in the future, somewhere in America, a white-power teen-ager will get drunk on beer and George Burdi's songs and will, with his friends, go singing into the night. They might find someone who is different from them, a black man or a Mexican woman perhaps, and go to work with their fists and boots.

Even at the dawn of the 21st century, that is what neo-Nazis do.

Young and Abused[4]

Any young woman can fall prey to an abusive, violent man, no matter how smart or how self-confident she is.

Whenever I talk to my friend Jenny, I get a knot in the he pit of my stomach. Jenny (this name and others have been changed) has this boyfriend Joe who has "mental problems," as she puts it, which is putting it mildly.

Jenny told me recently that one night she casually asked Joe if he was going out, and for no apparent reason he suddenly got mad. He threw her over the sofa, pushed her face into the carpet and pounded her in the ribs. Another time when they were playing around, Joe suddenly pulled off his leather belt and threatened her with it. When Jenny ran into the closet, he promised he wouldn't hit her. But when she came out, he "went off," beating her until her thighs were covered with welts. "I told you not to mess with me," she says Joe told her.

Jenny is afraid of her boyfriend, and I think he likes it that way. I've tried to tell her that he might kill her one day, but she doesn't seem to hear me.

When I read about battered women, I usually think of older married women. But my friend Jenny is only 22. She is one of the many young Black women who are being kicked, smashed and shoved by the same guys who coo about how much they love them—and seem to mean it.

According to a study done by Dr. Anne Flitcraft, codirector of the Domestic Violence Training Project of New Haven, Connecticut, women suffer more black eyes, split lips and other injuries resulting from violence inflicted upon them by boyfriends and husbands than from car accidents, muggings and rapes combined. In fact, national surveys estimate that every year at least 2 million women are abused by their partners.

Although it's difficult to determine who will become a target of violence, research suggests that women under 30 are at greatest risk. The National Resource Center for Youth Services states that approximately a third of all high-school and college relationships turn violent, and those are only the ones that are reported. Actually, that number may be higher, says Murray Straus, Ph.D., author of *Behind Closed Doors: Violence in the American Family*. Straus, who has conducted national studies on domestic violence at the University of New Hampshire since the early 1970's, says that the greatest single factor in predicting whether a person will become abused is age.

"No one knows for sure why [young women are abused], but

---

[4]Article by Jeannine Amber, from *Essence* Ja '97. Copyright © 1997 Jeannine Amber. Reprinted with permission.

one possibility is that for the young, being violent is often viewed as a positive attribute, especially among boys," says Straus. "The image of masculinity is of someone who is ready to show he's a man, and that means ready to fight."

At the same time, a young woman who is getting into her first serious relationship may carry her own set of vulnerabilities. "Young women sometimes have a very powerful sense of the romantic. They're very optimistic," explains Catherine Hodes, director of social services at a Brooklyn shelter for battered women. Hodes says young women often believe either that they can change a violent boyfriend's behavior or that he won't really hurt them. "They often think they can't be made to do something they don't want to do," says Hodes. "And if the relationship becomes violent, young women may not take the time to think things through or seek guidance from an older, more experienced person."

"...the truth is, abuse knows no boundaries; it can happen to any of us."

We Are All Vulnerable

No one likes to be considered a victim. For many of us, the very thought of being smacked around by a man will bring out the fighter in us, often in a barrage of Nubian Queen braggadocio. Recently I witnessed the following scene among a group of twenty-something women in a nail salon. One woman, speaking angrily, explained her reaction when confronted with a threat of abuse from her boyfriend:

"He raised his hand and I said, 'You better not try it unless you're gonna kill me, because if you don't kill me you're gonna be one dead so-and-so,'" she reported. The other women shook their heads in agreement and launched into the usual talk-show explanations of why *other* women end up victims. They blamed everything from violence in hip-hop lyrics, to low self-esteem and growing up with no father.

It was comforting for these young women, as it is for many of us, to believe that abuse happens only to somebody else. We want to believe that violent behavior seeks out a victim because of something about her—how she was raised, how she feels about herself or her socioeconomic status. But the truth is, abuse knows no boundaries; it can happen to any of us.

According to those who counsel battered women, it is virtually impossible to come up with one single characteristic that is common to all potential victims. "Across all studies, there is nothing about a woman's personality, about the way she was brought up or about her living conditions that makes one woman more likely than another to be abused or stay in an abusive relationship," says Jacquelyn Campbell, Ph.D., R.N., who has researched patterns of abuse for more than 15 years and is currently a professor of nursing at Johns Hopkins University. "The only consistent risk factor for being abused is gender. That is, being a woman."

Still, hip-hop, with its often misogynistic lyrics and macho posturing, is frequently blamed for the rise of abuse within young relationships. But many women's advocates, such as Gail Garfield, executive director of the Institute on Violence, which is based in New York City, believe that the hip-hop culture has become a fashionable and easy target for those seeking a tidy explanation for abusive relationships among the young.

"Hip-hop is like one big glass house, it's easy to throw rocks at it. Violence against women is one of those phenomena that have occurred for centuries in every culture and society on earth," Garfield explains. "How do you account for the devastation of Black women's lives in Africa, in the Caribbean, in South America and all over this country in the context of hip-hop music and hip-hop culture? It just doesn't make sense."

Low self-esteem is another factor that many people assume makes a woman vulnerable to entering into and staying in an abusive relationship. After all, only a woman who doesn't think much of herself would "put up" with an abusive boyfriend.

But experts believe that even low self-esteem is not a deciding factor. "I say flip it around," says Hodes. "You have a woman with normal self-esteem, or even high self-esteem, who gets into one of these relationships—obviously not to be abused but to have a relationship. The abuse occurs and as it increases in frequency and severity, she begins to realize that she can't control it; she can't make it stop. Of course her self-esteem is eroded, but it's damaged as a result of the abuse. The abuse doesn't occur as a result of her low self-esteem."

Some people believe that the seeds of domestic abuse are sown by a victim's parents, and growing up without a father makes a woman more vulnerable. But most advocates for battered women say that the absence of a father may cause a child to grow up with economic hardships, but it doesn't necessarily mean she'll be inclined to accept abuse.

There is, however, one factor that most experts agree will contribute to a woman's ending up in an abusive relationship. That factor is growing up with an abusive, violent father.

Children who grow up in a home where abuse and violence are the norms quickly learn that hitting and punching are acceptable ways to relate to other people. Hodes points out that in the battered women's shelters where she works, she often sees both boys and girls exhibiting very aggressive behavior.

"We assume that at some point, while the boys continue to be aggressive, the girls become socialized not to fight back. But as the way we socialize children changes, and as violence increases in our society, I think we are going to see a lot of girls holding on to their aggressive behavior," says Hodes.

Living in an abusive home can also be devastating for children, even before they are born. As many as 50 percent of battered women are beaten while they are pregnant. The March of Dimes reports that battered women are more likely to give birth to low-birth-weight babies. A low-birth-weight baby is more likely to have birth defects and is 40 times as likely to die in the first month of life as a baby of normal weight.

Spotting an Abusive Man

It's rare that a relationship starts out abusive, and in the beginning abusive men are often charming—bringing flowers, calling frequently, buying gifts. Although an abusive man may seem romantic at first, his attentiveness soon turns to possessiveness, which in the end gives way to insults and violence.

Many men who abuse women seem to share certain characteristics. They tend to be excessively jealous, which is often mistaken for love but has nothing to do with it. They tend to keep tabs on a victim by demanding to know her whereabouts every minute of the day. Often they are intensely committed. Sandra Majors, executive director of the District of Columbia Coalition Against Domestic Violence, says many batterers will tell a woman such things as, "You're the only one who understands me," or "The world is so hard on a man like me" to make a woman feel guilty when she considers leaving him. Such statements are a form of control.

"These men can also be sexually coercive; they may force a woman to do things she doesn't want to do..."

Batterers also try to isolate their victim; the abuser cuts her off from her family and friends by insisting they are against her. Abusive men blame others for their failings—his boss made him scream, the world made him lose his temper. These men can also be sexually coercive; they may force a woman to do things she doesn't want to do and even tamper with her birth-control methods.

Abusive relationships follow a pattern. After the violent display comes the calm, with profuse apologies and the promise of redemption. This "loving" period is always followed by more abuse. Nikki, 23, says that was why she stayed with her abusive boyfriend, who once held a knife to her throat. At first, she believed he would change; later, she thought that if she were a "better woman," he would stop punching her. Two years into the relationship Nikki became pregnant, but the beatings didn't stop. Finally she decided to stay with her violent boyfriend because of her child.

Breaking Free

Nikki's decision is a common one. Many abused young mothers hesitate to leave a boyfriend because they fear they'll deprive the child of a father—no small issue in a society in which many see single Black motherhood as pathological.

But even when there are no children, getting out of a violent situation can be far more complicated than just walking away. For women who live in tightly knit communities, leaving a batterer often means leaving family, friends and an entire support system. For a young woman with a limited social network, the prospect of walking away from everyone and everything she knows may be even more frightening than staying with her batterer. And leaving an abusive man does not guarantee safety. Many men stalk their ex-girlfriends, hunt them down and force them to come back. Or kill them.

"It's a fallacy that women don't leave," says Hodes. But many are forced to return because they can't find a place to stay, or they don't have any money or someone to leave their children with while they work. In many instances they are simply afraid.

"For a lot of people not in that situation, it is impossible to imagine how a woman can be in so much fear that she really can't leave," says Warren Price, former director of New York City's Alternatives to Violence, an educational group for abusive men. But fear, says Hodes, is sometimes the very thing that keeps a woman alive.

"Fear can be paralyzing and debilitating; it can also make you face reality. Most batterers who kill women do so after the woman leaves the relationship," explains Hodes. "Leaving can be dangerous, and women know that."

If a woman decides to leave, she may not know whom to trust. Seeking help from what can be a racist and paternalistic law-enforcement and judicial system is singularly unappealing to many Black women. Hodes says, "The message is 'Don't betray your community; don't betray Black men.'" Historically, turning a Black man over to the police, no matter what his violation, has been seen as the ultimate betrayal. "It's an enormous dilemma for Black women," says Hodes, "having to choose between their community and their safety."

Worse, when Black women do decide to seek help, they often don't receive the same level of care as White women, says Garfield, executive director of the Institute on Violence. "If a Black woman and a White woman each gets a broken nose, a broken jaw and multiple bruises, both will internalize their pain, fear and humiliation in similar ways. Any differences will lie in institutional responses to the women's pain. For example, when police enter domestic-violence situations in a Black household, there's often a question as to whether they should view Black women as victims or view the situation as just two Black folks fighting."

Young women may have an even harder time getting help than older victims, because fewer resources are available to them. A restraining order may be difficult for girls under 17 to obtain, and seeking help from social-service agencies usually means getting shuttled into the foster-care system. Young women hate the idea of "being run out of their own home," says Debra Mack-Glasgow, former director of a teen parenting program in Harlem. Mack-Glasgow says approximately a fifth of the women she counseled were beaten by boyfriends.

What We Can Do

Over the past decade, the media has begun to focus attention on the plight of abused women. But little has been said about the men who batter. "You look at the face of a man who's being violent, and it's terrifying. We don't want to deal with him, or his violence, so we expect the woman to change the situation," explains Allan Creighton, executive director of the Oakland Men's Project. "But if we expect men to change, we have to hold them accountable—no minimizing, no bulls—t."

Many experts say we must stop looking to the abused woman to solve the problem of violent relationships and begin to change the climate that accepts abuse. Price compares the climate of tolerance around abuse to that which used to surround drunk driving. When he was growing up, he says, it was considered cool, or at least acceptable, to get drunk and go joyriding. But now, he says, "You're arrested, you get fined, you can lose your license." Price recalls how activists fanned community outrage so that "if your friend is about to drive drunk, you take the car keys. It's not okay anymore."

Price believes we need that same type of coordinated effort in our communities. "We need to tell young men this behavior is not acceptable. We have to tell them that they have to stop."

Getting Out

If your boyfriend or husband hits you, you are in serious danger. Pick up the telephone and call the National Domestic Violence Hotline at (800) 799-7233. It's important to talk to someone who understands what you're going through. It's also important to remember that it may take months before you can make your move.

"People who have never experienced it think a woman can just pack her bags and leave, but it's really not that easy," says Sandra Majors, executive director of the District of Columbia Coalition Against Domestic Violence. Majors was married to an abusive man for seven years; she says a woman should, above all, keep safe and plan for the day shell be ready to leave.

If you find yourself in the middle of a violent episode, stay alert. Think of yourself as a lion tamer. Don't get backed into a corner. Try to keep something between you and your abuser. Also, Majors, stay out of the most dangerous rooms, such as the bathroom and kitchen. They're filled with easy weapons and hard counters on which you might hit your head if you are knocked down. If you're going to run out of the house, have in mind a safe destination, like a convenience store, fire station or anyplace where there are other people.

Once you've decided to leave, be practical. Begin to pack small items, like photographs, and leave them someplace where you can pick them up later. Put money away, as well, either in a separate bank account or somewhere you know he won't find it. Most important, says (continued on next page)

Majors, never boast of your plans to leave; it will only make your abuser watch you more closely and become more controlling.

Often it takes a while for a woman who has been battered to realize that she has to get out. But eventually she will see that no matter how often a man apologizes, he will strike her again. When an abused woman reaches this stage, she will be receptive to information. Says Majors, "She is isolated, and she needs to put herself in a situation where she can see other women who are dealing with the same problem so she can figure out her options." Majors says she can find support groups and counselors at local battered-women's shelters, or she should call the National Domestic Violence toll-free hot line listed above. For the hearing-impaired, the toll-free number is (800) 787-3224.

Why They Stay:
A Saga of Spouse Abuse[5]

Whatever else American culture envisions of petite blondes, it doesn't expect them to end up as social revolutionaries. But just that turn of fate has brought Sarah Buel to Williamsburg, Virginia, from suburban Boston, where she is assistant district attorney of Norfolk County. To a gathering of judges, lawyers, probation and police officers, victim advocates, and others, she has come to press an idea that meets persistent resistance—to explain why and, perhaps more importantly, precisely how domestic violence should be handled, namely as the serious crime that it is, an assault with devastating effects against individuals, families, and communities, now and for generations to come.

Buel, 41, a speed talker—there is, after all, so much to say—tells them what Los Angeles prosecutors failed to explain in the O. J. Simpson case: how batterers cannily dodge responsibility for their own actions, as if other people sneak into their brains and ball their fingers into fists; how they are deft at shifting the blame to others, especially their mates; how they watch and stalk partners, even those under the protection of the court, and especially those who have separated or divorced. Instead of holding up Simpson as the poster boy for domestic violence, the California trial let him get away with doing what batterers almost always do—put on a great public face and portray themselves as victims.

The judges and cops and court officers pay attention to Buel because domestic violence is a daily hassle that takes a lot out of them. And if there's one thing Buel knows, it's how batterers manipulate the law enforcement system. They listen because Buel has that most unassailable credential, an honors degree from Harvard Law School. But mostly they listen because Buel has been on the receiving end of a fist.

"Sometimes I hate talking about it," she confides. "I just want people to see me as the best trial lawyer." But, as Deborah D. Tucker says, "she grabs them by the heart." Tucker, head of the Texas Council on Family Violence and chairman of the national committee that pushed the Violence Against Women Act into the 1994 Omnibus Crime Bill, explains: "She gets people to feel what they need to feel to be vulnerable to the message that domestic violence is not we/they. Any of us can become victimized. It's not about the woman. it's about the culture."

Certainly Buel never had any intention of speaking publicly

---

[5]Article by Hara Estroff Marano, editor-at-large of *Psychology Today* and has completed a book on the social development of children to be published in Sept. 1998, from *Psychology Today* Je '96. Copyright © 1996 Hara Estroff Marano. Reprinted with permission.

about her own abuse. it started accidentally. She was in a court hallway with some police officers on a domestic violence case. "See, a smart woman like you would never let this happen," the chief said, gesturing her way. And in an instant Buel made a decision that changed her life irrevocably, and the lives of many others. "Well, it did happen," she told him, challenging his blame-the-victim tone. He invited her to train his force on handling domestic violence. "It changed things completely. I decided I had an obligation to speak up. It's a powerful tool."

It has made her a star, says psychologist David Adams, Ed.D. By speaking from her own experience, Buel reminds people that law can be a synonym for justice. In conferences and in courts, she has gotten even the most cynical judges to listen to battered women—instead of blaming them. "I am amazed at how often people are sympathetic as long as the victim closely resembles Betty Crocker. I worry about the woman who comes into court who doesn't look so pretty. Maybe she has a tattoo or dreadlocks. I want judges to stop wondering, 'What did she do to provoke him?'" Sarah Buel is arguably the country's sharpest weapon against domestic violence.

Buel finishes her talk, and in the split second before the audience jumps to its feet cheering, you can hear people gasp "Whew!" Not because they're tired of sitting, but because in her soft but hurried tones, the prosecution of batterers takes on a passionate, even optimistic, urgency. It's possible, she feels, to end domestic violence, although not by prosecution alone. Buel does not dwell on herself as victim but transmutes her own experience into an aria of hope, a recipe for change, "so that any woman living in despair knows there's help."

Not like she knew. She herself was clueless.

One of five childern Buel was born in Chicago but moved endlessly with her family from the age of four. Her father, an auto mechanic fond of drink, always felt success lay elsewhere. Her mother, a Holocaust refugee who fled Austria as a children went along selflessly—"she didn't know how to speak up," says Buel, which fueled her own desire to do so.

In the seventh grade, Buel was put on a secretarial track. "I was told I wasn't smart enough. So I refused to learn how to type." When she was 14, her parents divorced. Rather than choose which one to live with (her siblings split evenly), Buel headed for New York.

She went to school—at first—while working as a governess. For the first time, she saw television and while watching Perry Mason decided "this is what I want to do." The next year Buel bounced around to four different schools and families, including her mother's. "I went home for three months, but it was too different," she recalls.

Buel eventually went back to New York, where she had relatives, and began a very erratic course through high school, cutting class and shoplifting with a cousin. By the time she was 22, Buel was an abused woman. It came completely out of the blue. She was listening to a song on the radio, "Jeremiah Was a Bullfrog." "I bet that makes you think of Jeremy [a boyfriend of hers way back when she was 15]," her partner said. Actually what she was thinking was how stupid the song was. "Admit it," he insisted, "it does, doesn't it?" No, she said, it doesn't. He accused her of lying—and slapped her across the face.

The verbal and psychological abuse proved more damaging than the physical abuse. There was endless criticism. "He always said I looked frumpy and dumpy. He was enraged if I bought the *New York Times*." He read the tabloid *Daily News*. "'Isn't it good enough for you?' he demanded. He was extremely jealous. If I so much as commented on, say, a man's coat, he'd accuse me of wanting an affair and flirting. If I wanted to take courses, he insisted the only reason was to flirt with other men. I didn't cook like his mother, clean like his mother. By the time I left I thought, 'The only thing I do well is, I'm a good mother.'"

"...there are half as many shelters for battered women as there are for stray animals—about 1,800—and most do not accept children."

Suddenly, Buel is surprised to find herself revealing this much personal detail. "I never tell other women the details of my own abuse. They'll measure. Was theirs more or less?"

In 1993 and 1994, a coveted Bunting fellowship from Radcliffe College allowed Buel to work only part time as a public prosecutor. Now, in between court appearances, she crisscrosses the country, finally able to accept invitations to train judges and address gatherings such as this, a first-ever assembly of Virginians Against Domestic Violence. She has visited 49 states. She has testified before Congress. She was even asked to introduce the president of the United States at a press conference last spring, when the federal government set up a new Violence Against Women Office.

But no matter who she talks to or what she says about domestic violence, "it always comes down to one thing," says Buel. "They all ask the same question: Why do they [the women] stay."

First she points out that there are half as many shelters for battered women as there are for stray animals—about 1,800—and most do not accept children. For every two women sheltered, five are turned away. For every two children sheltered, eight are turned away.

A Texas study shows that 75 percent of victims calling domestic violence hotlines had left at least five times. Buel herself first went to the Legal Aid Society. There was a three-year wait for help. They never informed her about safety, never told her about alternatives. She did see a counselor at a family center, but her partner wouldn't go; he would only drive her.

Buel left her abuser and got a job in a shoe factory. But the wage was so low she couldn't pay the rent and a babysitter. "I went back because he said he was sorry, it'll never happen again.

When I realized it wasn't true, I left again. I told him I was packing to go to my brother's wedding. I took a bus to New Hampshire, where my mother lived. That didn't work out—she was living on a remote farm, I had no car, and my son was allergic to many of the animals—but I never went back. So 18 years ago I stood on a welfare line with three kids, my own son and two foster children I was raising. But you can't live on that amount of money. We trade our safety for poverty. We go back because we don't know what else to do."

Batterers are expert at portraying themselves as the injured party. The first time her batterer threw her against a wall, Buel's son screamed, "Don't hurt my mom." Then the batterer shouted, "See, you're turning the kid against me."

"I used to think, 'Why me? I must have done something terrible.' Women come to think it was their fault. They feel guilty for not doing a good enough job as a mom because they are unable to protect themselves, or their children."

A major obstacle to leaving, says Buel, is battered women's fear of losing their children or of being unable to protect them. "A Massachusetts study documented that in 70 percent of cases where fathers attempted to get custody of their children, they did so successfully. So when the abuser says to her, 'Sure, you can leave, but I've got the money to hire a good lawyer and I'll get the kids,' he may be right."

"We go back because we think we'll figure out a way to stop the violence, the magic secret everybody else seems to know. We don't want to believe that our marriage or relationship failed because we weren't willing to try just a little harder. I felt deeply ashamed, that it must be my fault. I never heard anyone else talking about it. I assumed I was the only one it was happening to."

One of the biggest reasons women stay, says Buel, is that they are most vulnerable when they leave. That's when abusers desperately escalate tactics of control. More domestic abuse victim are killed when fleeing than at any other time.

Buel has a crystal-clear memory of a Saturday morning at the laundromat with her young son, in the small New Hampshire town where she had fled, safely, she thought, far from her abuser. "I saw my ex-partner, coming in the door. There were people over by the counter and I yelled to them to call the police, but my ex-partner said, 'No, this is my woman. We've just had a little fight and I've come to pick her up. Nobody needs to get involved.' I still had bruises on the side of my face, and I said, 'No, this is the person who did this to me, you need to call the police.' But he said, 'No, this is my woman. Nobody needs to get involved.' Nobody moved. And I thought, as long as I live I want to remember what it feels like to be terrified for my life while nobody even bothers to pick up the phone."

It's time, Buel sighs, to stop asking why they stay and start asking what they need to feel safe. "I'm obsessed with safety now," she confides. "More important than prosecution, more important than anything, is a safety plan, an action plan detailing how to stay alive." And so a first encounter with a victim requires a verbal walk-through of what she'll need to feel safe at her place of work, at home, on the streets, and suggestions about what she'll need for leaving—birth certificates, legal papers, bank accounts—and for dealing with the abuser.

Buel entered Harvard Law in 1987. "I would love to have gone sooner but I had no idea how to get there. I didn't know you had to go to college to go to law school." She imagined you first had to work long enough as a legal secretary. In 1977, after two months on welfare, Buel entered a federally funded job-training program that, despite her awful typing, landed her in a legal services office. Eventually, she became a paralegal aide and began helping domestic violence victims.

In 1980, she started seven years of undergraduate study, first at Columbia University on scholarship, which necessitated "nine horrible months" in a drug-ridden building in New York while on welfare, so that instead of working nights she could spend them with her son. Ultimately she returned to New England and, two nights a week, attended Harvard Extension School, a vastly different world from Harvard Yard. She did well.

Days were spent working as a women's advocate in federal legal services offices, first in New Hampshire, then in grimy Lowell, Massachusetts. Buel started shelters and hotlines for battered women. She helped draft an abuse prevention law. She dreamed about being a voice for the women she represented.

She learned to write. She took classes in public speaking. Toward the end of her undergraduate studies, her bosses asked her where she wanted to go to law school. "Harvard," she replied, "because they're rich and they'll give me money." The lawyers laughed and told her that wasn't how it worked: "They do the choosing, not you." They took pains to point out she just wasn't Harvard material. "You're a single mother. You've been on welfare. You're too old."

Angry and humiliated, Buel began a private campaign that typifies her fierce determination. In the dark after classes, she drove around the law school, shouting at it: "You're going to let me in." Soon she got braver and stopped the car to go inside and look around. Then she had to see what it was like to sit in a classroom. She decided if she ever got accepted, she'd choose one of the orange-colored lockers, because her son was a fan of the Syracuse Orangemen.

Harvard Law not only accepted Buel but gave her a full scholarship. Once there, she was surprised there was nothing in the criminal-law syllabus about family violence—this despite the fact that women are more likely to be the victim of a crime in their own home, at the hands of someone they know, than on the streets. Buel mentioned the oversight to her professor. He told her to take over the class for one hour one day. She thought she'd be educating movers and shakers for the future. "I was amazed when, during the next six weeks, no less than 16 classmates came up to me either because they were in violent relationships or their parents or friends were."

When Boston-area colleagues requested help on an advocacy program for battered women and she couldn't do it alone, Buel put an ad in the student newspaper; 78 volunteers showed up for the first meeting. By year's end there were 215. She started a pro bono legal counseling program. The Battered Women's Advocacy Project is now the largest student program at Harvard Law; a quarter of the participants are men.

In 1990, at age 36, Buel graduated, cum laude. She sent a copy of her transcript to her old junior-high teacher with a note suggesting that she not judge the future of 12-year-old girls.

At first Buel thought it would be enough to become a prosecutor and make sure that batterers are held accountable for assaulting others. But she has come to see it differently. "That's not enough. My role is not just to make women safe but to see that they are financially empowered and that they have a life plan." So every morning, from 8:30 to 9:15, before court convenes, she sees that all women there on domestic issues are briefed, given a complete list of resources, training options, and more. "We surveyed battered women. We asked them what they needed to know. I wanted everyone to listen to them. Usually no one ever does. Most people tell them what to do. 'Leave him.' 'Do this.' 'Do that.' You can't tell women to leave until you give them—with their children—a place to go, the knowledge how and the resources to get by on their own, and the safety to do so. It's all about options."

"The Battered Women's Advocacy Project is now the largest student program at Harvard Law..."

What's more, Buel now sees domestic violence as just one arc of a much bigger cycle, intimately connected to all violence, and that it takes a whole coordinated community effort to stop it, requiring the participation of much more than attorneys and judges. It takes everyone; even the locksmith, so that when a woman suddenly needs her locks changed, the call will be heeded.

Rather than drive her own career narrowly forward, Buel has instead broadened her approach, venturing into places few lawyers ever go. She regularly attends community council meetings in Germantown, a dreary outpost of public housing in Quincy, known for its high crime rate. The council—Head Start teachers, the parish priest, two cops who requested duty in the projects, a few community members—celebrates mundane triumphs. A parents dinner at Head Start. A potluck supper at the church.

Buel is absolutely certain that this is the real answer to crime. It is the prevailing fallacy to assume that big problems require big solutions. First a community has to knit itself together—and from the sound of things the best way is on its stomach. "People here hear that some things are unacceptable," says one. A cop reports, remarkably, there has not been a single incident in a month.

Buel tells the assembled that emergency housing funds are available for battered women whose husbands are not paying support. "This is how I get the dirt on what's going on," she tells me. "These officers will call me when there's a domestic violence problem but the woman isn't ready to enter the legal system. At least we can keep on eye on her, and the children, to make sure she's safe."

Buel is particularly concerned about the children. She knows that children who witness violence become violent themselves. "Some take on the role of killing their mother's batterer," says Buel, who notes that 63 percent of males between ages 11 and 20 who are doing time for homicide have killed their mother's batterer. "We adults have abdicated the role of making the home safe."

Children who witness violence may commit suicide as adolescents, says Buel, pointing to soaring suicide rates among teenagers. Or grow up to soothe the pain with drugs. Or run away from home. A University of Washington study demonstrates that the vast majority of runaway and pregnant teenagers grew up in violent households.

Because she cares so much about the kids, in 1992 Buel started the What Is Your Dream Project in an adolescent center in Chelsea, a depressed community. It grew out of her frustration about pregnant teens, the group at highest risk for domestic violence. "Most of them have no person in their life talking to them about the future. That made me angry. That's how I was stereotyped. There was no assumption I'd be college-bound." The program trains at-risk teens to champion younger kids, telling them about educational and job options, about grants for beautician school or training as electricians or computer technicians, for example. "It was a powerful force for me to name going to law school as a dream. It focused my life," Buel recalls.

For her unusually diversified approach to domestic violence, Buel gives full credit to William Delahunt, her boss, the district attorney. "He has allowed me to challenge the conventional notion of what our job is."

"My boss gets complaints about me all the time," Buel says proudly. There was the batterer who, despite divorce and remarriage, was thought to be the source of menacing gifts anonymously sent to his ex-wife—a gun box for Christmas, a bullet box for Valentine's Day, followed by the deeds to burial plots for her and her new husband. The woman repeatedly hauled her ex into court for violating a restraining order; one lawyer after another got him off. "Finally I got him for harassing her in the parking garage where she was going to college; of course he denied it. The lawyer contended she was making up all the stories. But a detective found a videotape from the garage, which corroborated her charge. In the appeals court, his lawyer, a big guy, leaned into my face and hissed, 'You may be a good little advocate for your cause, but you're a terrible lawyer.'" She won the appeal.

Because the students asked for one, Buel teaches a class on domestic violence to 43 students at Boston College Law School. Over a third of them are males.

And she lectures widely to the medical profession. "Doctors see abused women all the time and don't know it," she says. She is especially interested in reaching family doctors and obstetrician/gynecologists, because in over a third of instances, abuse occurs during pregnancy—as it did for her. It is the primary time for the onset of violence. Her goal is to see that all doctors routinely ask every woman at every visit whether she has been hit or threatened since her last visit, explain that they are now routinely asking the question, state that no woman deserves to be abused, and then provide information and referral if she has. This simple question, by exposing abuse to plain daylight, brilliantly erases some of its shame. It is only when shame is gone that abused women can ask for help.

"...in over a third of instances, abuse occurs during pregnancy..."

You could say that 1994 was the best of times and the worst of times for domestic violence. Spouse abuse was "discovered" by Congress, which passed the Violence Against Women Act. Among its provisions are federal standards that permit enforcement of restraining orders across state lines, the single most important weapon women have to keep abusers from threatening or attacking them or their children.

And spouse abuse was "discovered" by the public at large after O. J. Simpson was arrested for the murder of ex-wife Nicole Brown Simpson and her friend Ronald Goldman. Clear evidence quickly emerged that O. J. Simpson had beaten his wife in the past. To those who know about domestic violence, Simpson fit a well-established pattern—when his partner got serious about leaving him for good, he began a campaign of terror. He began stalking her. He followed her movements. He peeked in her windows. He wouldn't, couldn't, let go.

Despite his ultimate acquittal, O. J., nevertheless, was the answer to some people's prayers. Like Deborah Tucker's. One of those whip-smart, wise-crackin', well-coifed dynamos that Texas seems to breed, who have you howling on the floor while they're stripping your political illusions, Tucker not only heads Texas's Council on Family Violence, she runs the new national Domestic Violence Hotline (1-800-799-SAFE). If the world of action against domestic violence has an axis on which it turns, Tucker is its south pole to Sarah Buel's north.

"Many people worked awfully hard for 20 years to see that violence against women was taken seriously and recognized as a crime. We had seen a law passed, established 1,800 organizations around the country providing services to battered women. We had built an infrastructure to respond to domestic violence and educate about it. Now all that was needed was visibility for the cause. Many of us talked among ourselves that that would happen only when a famous person killed his wife." Of course, no one imagined that person would be black, opening the racial divide. Tucker is now more cautious about what she wishes for.

O. J.'s arrest, says Tucker, "put domestic violence on the map. O. J. and Nicole were wealthy. They were visible. We tend to accept domestic violence in invisible people. We were at a juncture where something like that needed to happen. Social change is slow.

"The murder created a vehicle for common discourse about spouse abuse. The trial was a fiasco. The prosecutor never educated the public about stalking or about patterns of domestic violence. O. J. had followed Nicole and watched her. Everywhere I went, people asked: 'Why would he do that? He was divorced; he even had a girlfriend.' It was a chance to discuss tactics of power and control that do not stop with divorce, a chance to point out that women are in more danger when they leave— though everyone always asks why they stay."

If the Los Angeles D.A.s did little to explain, that is not the case with Buel. She has talked almost nonstop since.

In her travels, Buel has observed firsthand that many jurisdictions have figured out how to reduce violence against women. She sees her mission as spreading the word about them. Buel's considerable charisma stems in no small measure from her conviction that the solutions are out there, if only everyone knew about them. "People are always surprised at my optimism," she says.

"There's no one solution," she insists. "You need a message from the whole community. People point to the policy of mandatory arrest of all batterers in Duluth, Minnesota. But Duluth also has billboards that warn, 'Never hit a child.'" Buel's list of what works includes:

- the end of silence about spouse abuse.
- probation officers sensitive to the safety needs of victims and serious monitoring of offenders.
- mandatory group treatment programs for batterers. Programs must last at least a year, hold them alone accountable, and teach them to respect women.
- sanctions for failure to comply with probation or restraining orders.
- the use of advocates to follow cases.
- training cops in how to investigate and gather complete evidence when answering domestic violence calls.

Buel waves an investigation checklist she got from police in San Diego. If information gathering is done correctly, prosecution can proceed even when the victim refuses to press charges or come to court as a witness. "When a woman refuses to testify, she's not 'failing to cooperate,'" she says. "She's terrified. She's making the statement, 'I want to stay alive.'"

I ask Buel about her working relationships with judges. "In Massachusetts, I'm characterized as too harsh. I simply ask for some mechanism of accountability. Judges here are appointed for life without mandatory training. Many come from the big law firms that represent the batterers. Some do a great job. Others lose sight of the victims and children."

Discrimination against women through the law infuriates Buel. A recent study shows that a batterer who kills his wife typically gets a jail term of two to four years. But a woman who kills her abuser gets 14 to 18 years.

Of course, a great deal of domestic violence never finds its way into the criminal justice system; it's handled by private psychotherapists. "No one wants her husband arrested," especially women from the upper income strata, says Buel. She regrets that she is rarely invited to speak to the mental health community.

"Unfortunately," she charges, "most therapists, including family counselors, have little training in domestic violence. They are often conned by the stories of the batterers, experts at shifting blame. Without realizing it, therapists often put women at greater risk of abuse. There is nothing victims can disclose to them for which there will not be later retaliation. At the very least, therapists don't think in terms of safety plans for the victims.

"Even if the woman gets a restraining order barring her partner from having any contact with her, these guys will make calls or send flowers."

"Batterers are extraordinarily talented in sucking in therapists, the community, even their wives' families. Their whole M. O. is manipulation. They'll get the priest to testify that they're family-loving men, but the priest isn't there during the abuse. They are notorious liars; they'll say whatever makes them look good. Even if the woman gets a restraining order barring her partner from having any contact with her, these guys will make calls or send flowers. They're not really showing love, just proving they can get around the system, showing who's boss." In the toxic world of domestic violence, simply receiving an unsigned birthday card can be a deadly threat.

Yet domestic violence thrives in the best of zip codes, including the bedroom communities for Boston's medical chiefs. "Two of the worst cases I ever prosecuted involved doctors," says Buel, who finds that domestic violence is increasing in severity among wealthier families. "There's a much greater use of weapons. Ten years ago you would never have heard of a computer executive putting a gun to his wife's head."

Because too many victims stay with their batterers, Buel has begun to radically shift her approach to ending violence. "I'm learning new ways to compromise, reaching out to defense attorneys." In this she is crossing a divide most feminist lawyers shun. The defense attorneys, after all, represent batterers, "because they have the money." But they also have some power over their clients. "Some defense attorneys are willing to change their practices, to agree to take on batterers only if they go to a treatment program and stick with it."

This braving of the breach gives the lie to any suggestion that Buel is motivated by vindictiveness. She rolls her huge eyes at characterizations of activists as man haters. Or as do-gooders blind to the "fact" that people don't change.

There are men in her life. First and foremost is her son; he's away—but not too far away—at college. And there is a serious relationship. "He works in another domain, so there's no sense of competition. He is very emotionally supportive and respect the work I do. I had pretty much given up. Most men say I'm too intimidating."

Not David Adams, who runs the first and arguably best counseling program set up in the United States for men who batter. "It's taken someone like her to move the system forward. Only recently have the courts begun to hear women's concerns; they're more attuned to men's perspectives and complaints. She's a tremendous leader widely respected in the criminal justice system. She's become the conscience of the system, always looking at ways victims can be helped and perpetrators held accountable."

Holding men accountable for their violence is a full-time job for Adams, who sees 300 abusers a week at his Cambridge-based Emerge program. "These guys constantly minimize their own behavior. They'll say, 'She provoked me; if she'd only just shut up or respect me more.'" Excuse number two is "I lost control. I just snapped." Observes Adams: "But their 'snapping' is awfully selective; they snap only with the victim, not with their boss or other people."

Battering, Adams insists, "is primarily an instrument of control. It's not anger, though abusers always claim they're impulsive. It is purposeful, though from the outside it looks as if it's irrational behavior. And there's a logic to it; it enforces social rules. It is a learned behavior that's self-reinforcing—batterers get what they want through violence—and socially reinforced through beliefs about women as the social and sexual caretakers of men." He finds it takes at least nine months in the program just to puncture men's denial.

Returning to Boston from Williamsburg, Buel attends back-to-back meetings. First is the board session of a foundation that funds battered-women's shelters. Next comes the Domestic Violence Council, a regional group of private and public attorneys who share information and strategies. Buel started the council in law school. It has grown exponentially since, and now meets at one of Boston's prestige law firms. Discussions this day focus on:

- Lawyers' safety. Being the barrier between a woman

and her batterer sometimes leads to threats, or worse; victims and their attorneys have been murdered-even in the courthouse. A lawyer reports that her tires were punctured.

• A new cultural trend toward what look like organizations for the preservation of fatherhood. Masquerading as involved fathers, members are often batterers who use their kids as a way of stalking or threatening ex-partners. A law student assigned to check out one group's roster reports that 86 percent of the men have restraining orders against them.

• Monitoring the courts. For two years, practicing and student attorneys have been trained to evaluate how the state's judges handle domestic violence cases. Now they're assembling a committee to meet with those doing a bad job—those who, say, don't ask about kids or weapons when considering requests for restraining orders—and inform them how to do better.

The day has no end. Dinner isn't simply a meal, it's an opportunity to give support and advice to two Harvard Law grads who have formed the fledgling Women's Rights Network. Where should they go for funding? Does she know a defense attorney in Edmonton (Canada) for the international information they are putting together on domestic violence?

And Buel whips out some formidable pieces of paper, legal-pad sheets neatly filled with the names and phone numbers of people—73 per side—whose calls she must return. There were, I think, four of them, neatly written, neatly folded, representing two or three days' worth of calls to her office and her home. She keeps her number listed so women in trouble can find her. Somewhere on the list is an Edmonton attorney.

The two young women complain that despite its own budget surplus, Harvard Law has cut funding for law clinics, needed now more than ever as the public sector cuts back. "They'll no doubt use the money to put in more rosewood desks," they scoff.

But all three know it is the very credibility a Harvard Law degree bestows that compels the attention of so many others. And that, says Buel, "also pisses me off. People who wouldn't pay attention to me before suddenly hang on every word."

That seventh-grade teacher, I am certain, the one who almost derailed her for good, is never far from Buel's mind.

III. Violent Images

Editor's Introduction

Sections I and II describe the nature of violent acts as they occur on a personal or local level, i.e., between two, or several people. Hate crimes, spousal abuse, and violent street crimes are all examples of this violence, as they are defined by individual occurrences that are directly experienced. In such instances violence is understood as an act or series of acts, each having a defined beginning and an equally defined end. Violence that is portrayed on television or in the movies is of a vastly different nature. While participation in such violence is indirect, it is witnessed continually by thousands or even millions of people. The focus of this section is the violence the American community watches over and over again, most often as a form of entertainment. The articles contained in this section strive to understand both the nature of the violence that is broadcast to a mass audience, and the consequences of watching such violence.

According to Scott Stossel, in "The Man Who Counts the Killings," renowned television critic George Gerbner essentially views television as a link between its audience and the barrage of violent images Gerbner believes television continually broadcasts. According to Stossel, Gerbner understands television as presenting a vision of the world that is "violent, mean, repressive, dangerous—and inaccurate." The dangers of such a vision lie in the fact that television is a supremely powerful cultural force that many believe is only equaled in history by organized religion. Simply put, most of America watches it on a daily basis. According to studies recalled in this article, the effects of watching violence are quite profound, particularly on children.

Gerbner's protests against the violence he believes to be a fundamental part of television shows have not gone unheard. By the time the new television season begins in September of 1998, all new televisions will be equipped with a "V-chip," a mechanism that "makes it possible to prevent children from seeing shows that carry a rating denoting violence." However, the notion of "rating" shows is not without its difficulties. Mark Landler, in "TV Turns to an Era of Self-Control," discusses the intricacies of attempting to rate the vast number of television shows being broadcast. Landler also examines the often conflicting concerns of network executives who must rate programming without affecting advertising dollars.

The next article highlights some of the effects of the media's continual and unrelenting focus on family violence. Elayne Rapping, in her article "The Family Behind Bars" from *The Progressive*, describes the difference between the portrayals of children in commercials and the portrayals of children on news shows such as *Hard Copy* and *Court TV*. According to Rapping, in commercials, children seem to need little parental guidance, whereas in news shows poor families with violently murderous children populate a world gone out of control. The sensational cases of juvenile violence, rape, and murder highlighted on TV represent only a fraction of juvenile arrests, however, suggesting that the media has contributed to the criminalization of youthful behavior. Rapping believes that the media has instilled in children a lust for attention, which, when combined with economic hardship, makes the impulse to commit crimes even harder to resist.

According to David Thomson in "A Gore Phobia," top-level Hollywood figures should be held responsible for the use of violence as entertainment. The difficulty in assigning such responsibility lies in the fact that a majority of Hollywood leaders do not agree with the American public on the consequences of the media's projection of violence. At the heart of the issue is the question of whether or not the government should intervene when film violence is divorced from the context of actual human suffering. In this article, Thomson reviews the movies that introduced violence, as well as movies that have used it as a crutch or selling point.

The Man Who Counts the Killings[1]

George Gerbner who thirty years ago founded the Cultural Indicators Project, which is best known for its estimate that the average American child will have watched 8,000 murders on television by the age of twelve, is so alarmed about the baneful effects of TV that he describes them in terms of "fascism."

The unlikely event that a major Hollywood studio were to make a movie based on the life of George Gerbner, it might go something like this:

A passionate young Hungarian poet, dismayed by the rise of fascism in his country in the late 1930s, emigrates to America.

Cut to 1942. The ex-poet, motivated by his hatred of fascism, enlists in the U.S. Army. He volunteers for the Office of Strategic Services and ends up in a group of fifteen men trained, like William Holden and his comrades in *The Bridge on the River Kwai*, in the techniques of blowing up bridges and roads.

Cut to January 15, 1945—a sabotage mission gone awry. The young man and his OSS comrades, under heavy fire over Slovenia, parachute into enemy territory. They climb into the mountains and hide in farmhouses, subsisting on emergency rations until they encounter the partisan brigades, with whom they spend the remainder of the war fighting Germans who are in retreat from Greece.

The war takes a bloody toll on the young man's brigade; by V-E Day it has been reduced from 400 men to seventy. But the Allies prevail. And the ex-poet, now a war hero, falls in love. Roll credits: the camera freezes on George and Ilona Gerbner embracing on the deck of their New York–bound ship.

In the more imaginable yet still unlikely event that an independent production company were to make a film based on the life of George Gerbner, it might go something like this:

After the Second World War, in the course of which he has seen enough violence, suffering, and pain to harden even the softest sensibility, and during which he has personally identified and arrested the fascist Hungarian Prime Minister, who is subsequently executed, a brooding Hungarian poet travels with his wife to America. He earns a Ph.D. from the University of Southern California, in the process writing the first-ever master's thesis on the subject of education and television, and begins a long career in academia studying the effects of television on its viewers. In 1964 he becomes the dean of the newly founded Annenberg School of Communication, at the University of

[1]Article by Scott Stossel, from the *Atlantic Monthly* 279/5:86–104 My '97. Copyright © 1997 Scott Stossel. Reprinted with permission.

Pennsylvania, where he builds a curriculum and a faculty from scratch. In 1989, after twenty-five years as dean, George Gerbner retires.

This second film might concentrate on Gerbner's recent activities. Now seventy-seven years old, he is free to pursue more or less full-time what has been a longtime project of his: trying to awaken television viewers from their stupefaction. Television, Gerbner believes, is modern-day religion. It presents a coherent vision of the world. And this vision of the world, he says, is violent, mean, repressive, dangerous—and inaccurate. Television programming is the toxic by-product of market forces run amok. Television has the capacity to be a culturally enriching force, but, Gerbner warns, today it breeds what fear and resentment mixed with economic frustration can lead to—the undermining of democracy.

"Television programming is the toxic by-product of market forces run amok."

Though in general respected within his field, Gerbner is misunderstood, misrepresented, and even mocked outside it. Network executives make what sound like commonsense dismissals of his Cassandra-esque claims. The central question of this film might be, What are we to make of this complex man and his provocative message?

Is Gerbner tilting at windmills? Is he just a mediaphobe with a quixotic message? Or is he a lonely voice of insight, telling us things that are hard to comprehend but that we need to hear if we are to remain free from repression? Right or wrong, is his crusade at bottom a futile one? Do we need to change television programming, and if so, how can we do it? After all, network executives say, viewers are simply getting what they want. The film might end with a shot of a gaunt George Gerbner quoting, as he often does, the toast of Russian dissidents under Soviet rule: "Now let us drink to the success of our hopeless endeavor."

Violence and Television: A History

In 1977 Ronny Zamora, a fifteen-year-old, shot and killed the eighty-two-year-old woman who lived next door to him in Florida. Not guilty, pleaded his lawyer, Ellis Rubin, by reason of the boy's having watched too much television. From watching television Ronny had become dangerously inured to violence. Suffering from what Rubin called "television intoxication," he could no longer tell right from wrong. "If you judge Ronny Zamora guilty," Rubin argued, "television will be an accessory." The jury demurred: Ronny was convicted of first-degree murder.

Although few anti-television activists would agree that excessive television viewing can exculpate a murderer, a huge body of evidence—including 3,000 studies before 1971 alone—suggests a strong connection between television watching and aggression. "There is no longer any serious debate about whether violence in the media is a legitimate problem," Reed Hundt, the chairman of the Federal Communications Commission, said in a speech last year. "Science and commonsense judgments of parents agree. As stated in a year-long effort, funded by the cable-TV industry.... 'There are substantial risks of harmful effects from viewing violence throughout the television environment.'"

The study cited by Hundt reveals nothing new. Researchers have been churning out studies indicating links between television violence and real-life violence for as long as television has been a prominent feature of American culture. Just a few examples demonstrate the range of the investigations.

• A 1956 study compared the behavior of twelve four-year-olds who watched a Woody Woodpecker cartoon containing many violent episodes with that of twelve other four-year-olds who watched "The Little Red Hen," a nonviolent cartoon. The Woody watchers were much more likely than the Hen watchers to hit other children, break toys, and be generally destructive during playtime.

• In 1981 Brandon Centerwall, a professor of epidemiology at the University of Washington, hypothesized that the sharp increase in the murder rate in North America beginning in 1955 was the product of television viewing. Television sets had been common household appliances for about eight years by that point—enough time, he theorized, to have inculcated violent tendencies in a generation of viewers. He tested his hypothesis by studying the effects of television in South Africa, where the Afrikaaner-dominated regime had banned it until 1975. He found that twelve years after television was introduced there, murder rates skyrocketed.

• In 1960 Leonard Eron, a professor of psychology at the University of Michigan's Institute for Social Research, studied third-graders in Columbia County in semi-rural New York. He observed that the more violent television these eight-year-olds watched at home, the more aggressive they were in school. Eron returned to Columbia County in 1971, when the children from his sample were nineteen. He found that the boys who had watched a lot of violent television when they were eight were more likely to get in trouble with the law when older. Eron returned to Columbia County a third time in 1982, when his subjects were thirty. He discovered that those who had watched the most television violence at age eight inflicted more violent punishments on their children, were convicted of more serious crimes, and were reported more aggressive by their spouses than those who had watched less violent television. In 1993, at a conference of the National Council for Families & Television, Eron estimated that 10 percent of the violence in the United States can be attributed to television.

Although Eron's study did not make a special effort to control for other potentially violence-inducing variables, other longitudinal studies have done so. For example, in 1971 Monroe Lefkowitz published "Television Violence and Child Aggression: A Follow-up Study," which confirmed that the more violence an eight-year-old boy watched, the more aggressive his behavior would be at age eighteen. Lefkowitz controlled for other possible variables, directly implicating media violence as an instigator of violent behavior.

Shouldn't the weight of thousands of such studies be sufficient to persuade broadcasters, required by law since the 1930s to serve the public interest, to change the content of television programming? Especially when polls—such as one conducted by *U.S. News & World Report* last year—indicate that 90 percent of Americans think that violent television shows hurt the country? We don't want to become a nation of Ronny Zamoras, do we?

Periods of increasing popular agitation about the effects of television on children (usually inspired by a rising crime rate or by a sensational story like Ronny Zamora's) lead to spasms of political posturing. Studies are commissioned. Imminent legislative or regulatory action is threatened. The broadcast industry filibusters. Within a few months the politicians turn their attention to something new, and the broadcasting industry slips quietly away, barely chastened.

Since 1968, when President Lyndon Johnson convened the National Commission on the Causes and Prevention of Violence, commissions, hearings, and a Surgeon General's report have all found that television is a "major contributory factor" in violent behavior in society.

"A Telegenic Little Gizmo"

The latest burst of activity around the issue of television violence, culminating in the legislating of the V-chip, can be traced to a night in the mid-1980s when a weary Senator Paul Simon, of Illinois, lying in his motel bed, flipped on the television and saw, in graphic detail, a man—being sliced in half with a chain saw—a victim, Simon's staff later surmised, of Colombian drug dealers in Scarface. Appalled that there was nothing to prevent a child from witnessing such grisliness, Simon urged the passage of a law reducing gore on television.

The result, the 1990 Television Violence Act, was a compromise between the broadcasting industry and those who, like Simon, wanted somehow to reduce the violence on shows that children might be watching. Ordinarily, antitrust laws prohibit broadcast networks from collaborating, but Simon's proposal gave the networks a three-year exemption from the laws so that they could jointly work out a policy to curb violence. Though Simon hailed the announcement of the networks (except Fox), in December of 1992, of a set of guidelines governing television violence, this basically toothless bit of legislation had little effect until it was about to expire, at which point network executives promised that they would place parental advisories at the beginning of violent programs ("Due to violent content, parental discretion is advised"). When the act expired, in December of 1993, television was as violent as ever.

Meanwhile, in Canada, the invention of a Vancouver engineer had come to the attention of Keith Spicer, then the chairman of the Canadian Radio-Television and Telecommunications Commission (Canada's FCC equivalent). This invention—in Spicer's words, a "sexy, telegenic little gizmo that fulfills the fantasy of a magic wand" and could solve the problem of television violence without censorship—was the V-chip, the basic rationale for which is by now generally known. Using the chip, which receives encoded information about each show as part of the broadcast transmission, parents can program their television to block out shows that have been coded as violent or sexually explicit. Spicer championed the V-chip and ultimately got a law passed mandating its use in all new television sets sold in Canada.

After the Television Violence Act expired, Representative Edward J. Markey, of Massachusetts, introduced legislation requiring manufacturers to install the V-chip in all U.S. television sets. President Bill Clinton extolled the V-chip in his State of the Union Address last year, and then signed its use into law as part of the mammoth 1996 Telecommunications Act. As of February of next year all new television sets (Americans buy 24 million of them a year) must have the chip. Meanwhile, the broadcasting industry has established a rating system to be employed in conjunction with the chip, age-based like the system used by the Motion Picture Association of America.

Is the V-chip, after all these years, the solution we've been looking for? The "gizmo" that will protect our children from damaging cultural content? Clearly, not everyone thinks so. British opponents of the chip dismissed it early last year, saying it was a "knee-jerk solution" that would impede solving real problems. And criminologists in the United States say that children will circumvent the V-chip—after all, kids are better at programming VCRs than their parents are.

But the real problem, according to George Gerbner, is that all this hullaballoo over the V-chip, and over television violence in general, misses the point. The chip, though it's the result of good intentions, can do nothing to alleviate television's most complex and insidious effects.

"Using the chip...parents can program their television to block out shows that have been coded as violent..."

2,605 Violent Acts a Day

In 1968 President Johnson's National Commission on the Causes and Prevention of Violence appointed Gerbner, who had already been studying violence in the media at the Annenberg School, to analyze the content of television shows. Thus began the Cultural Indicators project, the longest-running continuous media-research undertaking in the world. Gerbner and his team presented findings about both the quantity of violence on prime-time television—that is, how many violent acts are committed each night—and the quality. In analyzing these acts Gerbner's team asked questions like Was it serious or funny? Was it the only method of conflict resolution offered? Were realistic repercussions of violence shown? Who committed most of it? Who suffered the most because of it? The quantity of violence on television was stunning; no less significant to Gerbner, though, were the ways in which this violence was portrayed. But in the first instance of what has since become a frustrating pattern for him, the mainstream media seized on the quantity and ignored his findings about the quality of television violence.

The media continue to be fixated on the amount of violence the Cultural Indicators Project finds, because the numbers are staggering. Today someone settling down to watch television is likely to witness a veritable carnival of violent behavior. On average there are more than five violent scenes in an hour of prime time, and five murders a night. There are twenty-five violent acts an hour in Saturday—morning cartoons—the programs most watched by children, usually without any supervision. And that's only network television. A survey by the Center for Media and Public Affairs that looked at all programming—including cable—in Washington, D.C., on April 7, 1994, tallied 2,605 acts of violence that day, the majority occurring in the early morning, when kids were most likely to be watching. By the reckoning of the Cultural Indicators Project, the average American child will have witnessed more than 8,000 murders and 100,000 other violent acts on television by the time he or she leaves elementary school. Another study, published in the *Journal of the American Medical Association* in 1992, found that the typical American child spends twenty-seven hours a week watching television and will witness 40,000 murders and 200,000 other violent acts by the age of eighteen. Ellis Rubin's defense of Ronny Zamora begins to sound plausible.

> *"Today someone settling down to watch television is likely to witness a veritable carnival of violent behavior."*

"Never was a culture so filled with full-color images of violence as ours is now," Gerbner wrote recently. This is an assertion he makes often, in his writings and speeches and interviews.

> Of course, there is blood in fairy tales, gore in mythology, murder in Shakespeare, lurid crimes in tabloids, and battles and wars in textbooks. Such representations of violence are legitimate cultural expressions, even necessary to balance tragic consequences against deadly compulsions. But the historically defined, individually crafted, and selectively used symbolic violence of heroism, cruelty, or authentic tragedy has been replaced by the violence with happy endings produced on the dramatic assembly line.

The Cultural Indicators Project has since 1968 amassed a database of reports on the recurring features of television programming. Today its archive contains observations on more than 3,000 programs and 35,000 characters. In looking at characters, coders record, among other characteristics, sex, race, height, level of aggressiveness, and drug, alcohol, or tobacco use. For every conflict the coder records how the character acts: Did he get angry? How did he resolve the conflict? If a character is part of a violent act, the coder records whether he suffered or committed it, and whether it was committed in self-defense. The results are then analyzed statistically to try to account for differences in the behavioral trends of the characters. Are there statistically significant differences in the percentage of, say, victimhood or alcohol abuse by sex? By level of education? By race? By social status?

In addition to this "message system analysis," Gerbner's researchers do "cultivation analysis," which tries to measure how much television contributes to viewers' conceptions of reality. Cultivation analysis asks, in other words, to what extent television "cultivates" our understanding of the world. Gerbner believes this to be the most important aspect of his research. It is also the part routinely ignored by the mainstream press and attacked by the broadcasting industry.

One of the basic premises of Gerbner's cultivation analysis is that television violence is not simple acts but rather "a complex social scenario of power and victimization." What matters is not so much the raw fact that a violent act is committed but who does what to whom. Gerbner is as insistent about this as he is about anything, repeating it in all his writings and speeches. "What is the message of violence?" he asks me rhetorically over tea in his office at the University of Pennsylvania, a cozy, windowless rectangle filled with books, pictures, and objets d'art. "Who can get away with what against whom?" He leans forward intently, as though confiding something, although he has already said this to me several other times, during several other conversations. His eagerness to make me understand is palpable. "The media keep focusing on the amount of violence. But concentrating on that reinforces the message of violence. It concentrates on the law-and-order aspect of violence. Harping on this all the time makes people more fearful—which is the purpose of violence to begin with."

"The Mean World Syndrome"

So what, exactly, has nearly thirty years of cultivation analysis shown? Among other things, the following: Americans spend fully a third of their free time with television. This is more than the next ten highest-ranked leisure-time activities put together.

- Women make up a third or less of the characters in all samples except daytime serials.
- The "lower classes" are almost invisible on television. According to the U.S. Census, at least 13 percent of the population is "poor," with a significant additional percenage being classified as "low-income wage-earners." Yet the lower classes make up only 1.3 percent of prime-time

characters.

- For every white male victim of violence there are seventeen white female victims.

- For every white male victim there are twenty-two minority female victims.

- For every ten female aggressors there are sixteen female victims.

- Minority women are twice as likely to be victims as they are to be aggressors.

- Villains are disproportionately male, lower-class, young, and Latino or foreign.

"The more violence one sees on television, the more one feels threatened by violence."

What is the significance of all this? First, the sheer quantity of violence on television encourages the idea that aggressive behavior is normal. Viewers become desensitized. The mind, as Gerbner puts it, becomes "militarized." This leads to what Gerbner calls "the Mean World Syndrome." Because television depicts the world as worse than it is (at least for white suburbanites), we become fearful and anxious—and more willing to depend on authorities, strong measures, gated communities, and other proto-police-state accouterments. Discounting the dramatic increase in violent crime in the real world, Gerbner believes, for example, that the Mean World Syndrome is an important reason that the majority of Americans now support capital punishment, whereas they did not thirty years ago. "Growing up in a violence-laden culture breeds aggressiveness in some and desensitization, insecurity, mistrust, and anger in most," he writes. "Punitive and vindictive action against dark forces in a mean world is made to look appealing, especially when presented as quick, decisive, and enhancing our sense of control and security."

The more violence one sees on television, the more one feels threatened by violence. Studies have shown direct correlations between the quantity of television watched and general fearfulness about the world: heavy viewers believe the world to be much more dangerous than do light viewers. Thus heavy viewers tend to favor more law-and-order measures: capital punishment, three-strikes prison sentencing, the building of new prisons, and so forth. And the fact that most of the heavy viewers are in low-income, low-education families means that the most disenfranchised in our society—and, it should be said, the people most exposed to real violence—are making themselves even more so by placing their fate in the hands of an increasingly martial state. Politicians exploit this violence-cultivated sensibility by couching their favored policies in militaristic terms: the War on Crime, for example, or the War on Drugs. "We are headed in the direction of an upsurge in neofascism in a very entertaining and very amusing disguise," Gerbner told a lecture audience in Toronto two years ago.

The first time I talked to Gerbner after reading his writings, I asked him if this wasn't all a bit Big Brotherish. "TV images are complex," he told me. "The disempowering effects of television lead to neofascism. That kind of thing is waiting in the wings. Nazi Germany came on the heels of a basic sense of insecurity and powerlessness like we have here now. I don't want to over-simplify, but that is the direction we might be heading."

Violence, Gerbner says, is all about power. The violence on television serves as a lesson of power that puts people in their place. Members of minority groups grow up feeling that they're more vulnerable than others. Television cultivates this view. But, I counter, minorities *are* more vulnerable. They are victims more often than middle-class white Americans are. Improving the depiction of minorities on television will not change this social fact. Gerbner strives to clarify: "Television doesn't 'cause' any-thing. We're wary of saying television 'causes' this or that. Instead we say television 'contributes' to this or that. The extent of contribution varies. But it's there."

Elsewhere Gerbner is less circumspect. "The violence we see on the screen and read about in our press bears little relationship either in volume or in type, especially in its consequences, to vio-lence in real life," he has written. "This sleight of hand robs us of the tragic sense of life necessary for compassion." No doubt a victim of the Mean World Syndrome myself, I was surprised to learn that Gerbner is absolutely right, at least about the volume of violence. Scary and crime-ridden though the world is these days (violent crime has more than doubled over the past thirty years; an American is six times as likely to be the victim of assault with a weapon as he or she would have been in 1960), prime-time television presents a world in which crime rates are a hundred times worse.

Why Sex Doesn't Interest Gerbner

The Cultural Indicators Project does not generally publish statis-tics about sexual encounters on television. But the aggregate number of sexual references or images on television rivals the number of violent acts. The Center for Population Options, for example, determined that the typical teenager sees nearly 14,000 sexual encounters on television every year. And few of these encounters can be said to promote traditional family values. A study by the conservative Media Research Center found that por-trayals of premarital sex outnumber portrayals of sex within mar-riage by eight to one. Why isn't this sort of thing of greater inter-est to Gerbner?

Given that Gerbner's background is European (in particular the Frankfurt School tradition, which taught the dangers of the control of the masses by ideological cultural content), and given that his outlook is in many ways political, it is unsurprising that sex is not his overriding concern. While deploring the mechan-ical, passionless athletic contortions that pass for sex in Hollywood movies these days, Gerbner believes that the politics of sex in culture (except when force or violence is also involved) are less sinister than the politics of violence. "Most countries have codes about violence, not about sex," he says. "For us it is the other way around. We have a rather prudish and misguided sense of ratings."

Though other countries share our concerns about violence in culture (France, for example, strictly regulates shows that combine violent and erotic content and might be psychologically disturbing to children), Europeans generally have more-liberal attitudes toward sex than Americans. Cultural theorists and policymakers from Europe and Canada see it as an irony—and, given what they consider America's proclivity for gunboat diplomacy, as appropriate—that the United States is relatively easygoing about violence while being fairly uptight about sex. Consider *NYPD Blue*, the critically acclaimed show that has distressed citizens and legislators in both Canada and the United States—but for different reasons. Ronald I. Cohen, the national chair of the Canadian Broadcast Standards Council, explains, "In the United States the problem is over sexual content. In Canada the only issue was with violence, not with the number of bare posteriors." In fact, one of the challenges facing those standardizing V-chip ratings is this discrepancy between the cultural concerns of the two countries, across whose borders broadcast transmissions freely move.

"...by the time children reach school age, they will have spent more hours in front of the television than they will ever spend in college classrooms.

What seems to concern most Americans about sex on television (and sex in the culture at large) is that it makes it impossible for parents to control what the self-proclaimed Luddite Neil Postman, the author of *Technopoly: The Surrender of Culture to Technology* (1992), has called "the content and taboos of adult life." Parents, in other words, no longer have the opportunity to teach their children about the birds and the bees gradually, in a manner they consider appropriate; everything is exposed—so to speak—to kids all at once. The old system of moral socialization breaks down.

The New Religion

Whoever tells most of the stories to most of the people most of the time has effectively assumed the cultural role of parent and school," Gerbner says, "...teaching us most of what we know in common about life and society." In fact, by the time children reach school age, they will have spent more hours in front of the television than they will ever spend in college classrooms. Television, in short, has become a cultural force equaled in history only by organized religion. Only religion has had this power to transmit the same messages about reality to every social group, creating a common culture.

Most people do not have to wait for, plan for, go out to, or seek out television, for the TV is on more than seven hours a day in the average American home. It comes to you directly. It has become a member of the family, telling its stories patiently, compellingly, untiringly. We choose to read *The New York Times*, or Dickens, or an entomology text. We *choose* to listen to Bach or Bartók, or at least to a classical station or a rock station or a jazz station. But we just watch TV—turn it on, see what's on. And in Gerbner's view it is an upper-middle-class conceit to say "Just turn off the television"—in most homes there is nothing as compelling as television at any time of the day or night.

It is significant that this viewing is nonselective. It's why Gerbner believes that the Cultural Indicators Project methodology—looking at television's overall patterns rather than at the effects of specific shows—is the best approach. It is long-range exposure to television, rather than a specific violent act on a specific episode of a specific show, that cultivates fixed conceptions about life in viewers.

Nor is the so-called hard news, even when held distinct from infotainment shows like *Hard Copy* and *A Current Affair*, exempt from the disproportionate violence and misrepresentations on television in general. The old news saw "If it bleeds, it leads" usually prevails. Watch your local newscast tonight: it is not unlikely that the majority of news stories will be about crime or disaster—and it may well be that all six stories will be from outside your state, especially if you live far from any major metropolis. Fires and shootings are much cheaper and easier to cover than politics or community events. Violent news also generates higher ratings, and since the standards for television news are set by market researchers, what we get is lots of conformity, lots of violence. As the actor and director Edward James Olmos has pointedly observed, "For every half hour of TV news, you have twenty-three minutes of programming and seven minutes of commercials. And in that twenty-three minutes, if it weren't for the weather and the sports, you would not have any positive news. As for putting in even six minutes of hope, of pride, of dignity—it doesn't sell." The author and radio personality Garrison Keillor puts it even more pointedly: "It's as bloody as Shakespeare but without the intelligence and the poetry. If you watch television news you know less about the world than if you drank gin out of a bottle."

The strength of television's influence on our understanding of the world should not be underestimated. "Television's Impact on Ethnic and Racial Images," a study sponsored by the American Jewish Committee's Institute for American Pluralism and other groups, found that ethnic and racial images on television powerfully shape the way adolescents perceive ethnicity and race in the real world. "In dealing with socially relevant topics like racial and ethnic relations," the study said, "TV not only entertains, it conveys values and messages that people may absorb unwittingly—particularly young people." Among viewers watching more than four hours each day, 25 percent said that television showed "what life is really like" and 40 percent said they learned a lot from television. African-Americans especially, the study showed, rely on television to learn about the world.

Television, in short, tells all the stories. Gerbner is fond of quoting the Scottish patriot Andrew Fletcher, who wrote to the Marquise of Montrose in 1704, "If I were permitted to write all the ballads I need not care who makes the laws of the nation." Fletcher identified the governing power of, in Gerbner's words, a "centralized system of ballads—the songs, legends, and stories that convey both information and what we call entertainment." Television has become this centralized system; it is the cultural arm of the state that established religion once was. "Television satisfies many previously felt religious needs for participating in a common ritual and for sharing beliefs about the meaning of life and the modes of right conduct," Gerbner has written. "It is, therefore, not an exaggeration to suggest that the licensing of television represents the modern functional equivalent of government establishment of religion." A scary collapsing, in other words, of church into state.

Is *I Dream of Jeannie* Violent?

Portentous talk like this gets the network executives rolling their eyes. Isn't this all a bit dire? Many in the broadcasting industry find Gerbner's work incomprehensible or ridiculous. His research has come in for scathing criticism over the years. Though usually soft-spoken and reasonable, Gerbner can be unyielding and strident; he is known, even among his closest disciples, for sometimes believing that people who disagree with him are motivated by personal animosity or vested interest. A letter from two screenwriters to *The Pennsylvania Gazette*, the alumni magazine of the University of Pennsylvania, in March of 1982 read, "We and many of our colleagues find ourselves wishing, perhaps in vain, that Gerbner will eventually recognize that many people of good will may disagree with him, not because they're misinformed but because they simply think he's wrong."

Gerbner's methodology draws fire mostly for its supposed insufficient emphasis on context. For years he has been ridiculed for a single example he cited as part of a routine Cultural Indicators Project profile: network executives have never ceased to bring up the *I Dream of Jeannie* episode from 1968 that Gerbner deemed excessively violent. ("It had a really violent dream sequence," Gerbner says.) Frustrated by incidents like this one (more recently the project classified the *Laugh-In* twenty-fifth-anniversary special as very violent owing to pratfalls and slapstick), Gerbner will no longer willingly discuss the content of individual shows, insisting that it is the overall pattern that matters most.

In 1983 ABC published a critique, "A Research Perspective on Television and Violence," that took particular issue with Gerbner's findings. Gerbner's inclusion of accidents, slapstick comedy, acts of nature, and cartoons within his definition of violence, the study said, "results in tallies that distort the amount of realistic violence." Though ABC's critique was dismissed by academic researchers as self-serving, an ABC vice-president, Christine Hikawa, reflected the sentiment prevailing among broadcasters at the National Council for Families & Television Conference in 1993 when she said, "When researchers equate *Tom and Jerry* with *I Spit on Your Grave*, their credibility goes right out the window."

Most people, I think, would agree with Hikawa. A cartoon is surely more appropriate for and less damaging to young viewers than a verisimilitudinous movie like *Silence of the Lambs*. Road Runner's depredations against Wile E. Coyote lack the visceral effect of the gorier violence committed by, say, the serial killer in the 1995 movie *Seven*, in which the rabidity is clearly meant to be disturbing.

But a cartoon's lack of brute visceral impact, Gerbner says, is precisely what makes it so insidious. "Violence in our studies is overt, physical demonstration of power that hurts or kills. Whether it is done in a so-called serious way or a so-called humorous way has no functional significance." He continues, "Humor is a sugar coating that makes the pill of violence go down much more easily—so it gets integrated into one's framework of knowledge." "Pratfalls are dangerous," Gerbner told me when I asked how his studies could implicate my beloved Three Stooges. "To make pain seem painless is sugarcoating power, sugarcoating the message of power. People don't understand that humor can be very violent and very cruel."

"Swift, Painless, Effective"

When George Plimpton recently asked why, if television violence causes violence in the streets, television comedy doesn't cause comedy in the streets, he was with trademark wit making a commonsense observation: we don't directly replicate in our lives most of what we see on TV. But Gerbner doesn't say that we do. The reason that even apparently innocuous comedy can be so dangerous, he says, is that it reinforces viewers' perceptions of how the world works. No, comedy doesn't cause comedy in the streets. But TV violence indirectly contributes to our understanding that there is violence in the streets, typically wrought by a stronger entity against a weaker one. "Humorous stories are easier to digest," Gerbner says, "easier to absorb. But basically they are all messages of power. Messages of who can get away with what against whom."

Gerbner has coined a term that describes most of the screen violence we see. "We are dealing with the formula-driven mass production of violence for entertainment—what I call 'happy violence.' It is swift, painless, effective...and always leads to a happy ending." Happy violence appears both in cartoons and in action movies like *True Lies* and *Die Hard*, wherein all problems can be solved by violence and violence has no serious consequences. Movies, it should be noted, are an important part of the

"No, comedy doesn't cause comedy in the streets."

constant violent fare on television and in the culture in general. They must become more and more graphic if they are to penetrate our violence-hardened sensibilities. Gerbner points out that body counts always rise in action sequels: the first *Die Hard* movie had eighteen deaths, and the second had 264; the first *Robocop* movie had thirty-two deaths, and the second had eighty-one; and the three *Godfather* movies piled up twelve, eighteen, and fifty-three corpses respectively. "Escalating the body count," he has written, "seems to be one way to get attention from a public punch-drunk on global mayhem." What, Gerbner asks, does this cultivate in our kids, in society? "We live in a world that is erected by the stories we tell...and most of the stories are from television. These stories say this is how life works. These are the people who win; these are the people who lose; these are the kinds of people who are villains. It's a highly stereotypic world day after day. It doesn't matter whether it's serious or humorous. The main difference is that cartoons can go further. There is no more serious business for a culture or a society than the stories you tell your children."

Of course, stories have always been used to teach and control. The use of violent stories as moral tales is older than Hansel and Gretel. What is new is that the stories are standardized and commercialized. "For the first time in human history," Gerbner says, "the stories are told not by parents, not by the school, not by the church, not by the community or tribe and in some cases not even by the native country but by a relatively small and shrinking group of global conglomerates with something to sell. This changes in a very fundamental way the cultural environment into which our children are born, grow up, and become socialized." It used to be that scary stories were told to children face-to-face, so they could be modulated, softened, individually tailored by the parents or the community depending on the situation and the desired lesson. Children today, in contrast, grow up in a cultural environment that is designed to the specifications of a marketing strategy.

Media Monopolies and Censorship

Television violence, Gerbner has written, "is but the tip of the iceberg of a massive distortion in the way in which we make cultural policy in this country. [Cultural decision-making] is drifting dangerously out of democratic reach." In his view, television violence is just one symptom of a serious underlying problem that threatens to stifle democracy: the very structure of the culture industry.

Most of the debate about acceptable television programming is cast, especially by those in the industry, in terms of censorship versus free speech. But Gerbner says this is misleading: although censorship is unquestionably a problem (there's altogether too much of it), it is not the usual culprit, government, that is doing the censoring. It is private corporations. Gerbner writes,

The Founding Fathers did not foresee the rise of large conglomerates acting as private governments. Nor did they envision their cultural arms, the mass media…forming a virtual private Ministry of Culture and Established Church rolled into one, influencing the socialization of all Americans. In licensing broadcasters and then letting the marketplace take its course, Congress has made law respecting the establishment of the modem equivalent of religion and has given a few giant conglomerates the right to abridge freedom of speech.

The market, Gerbner says, is a plutocracy, not a democracy. And the largest market interests use the First Amendment as a shield while denying it to the disenfranchised. Censorship! Censorship! broadcasters cry when anyone suggests that their programming has deleterious social effects, that they might try distributing something different. Yet these interests exercise de facto censorship themselves: in co-opting all programming (as recently as 1986 ABC, CBS, and NBC controlled 70 percent of the television market) a media monopoly has consolidated the diversity of human experience into a few basic formulas. A concentrated marketplace puts distinct limits on the range of views represented. The people have no say in what gets broadcast. This, in Gerbner's view, is plainly undemocratic. But we have become so accustomed to the dominance of a market-driven, advertiser-sponsored media system that we don't realize it doesn't have to be this way.

"Whereas in the United States the federal commitment to public broadcasting is less than $1.50 per capita, other countries typically pay about $25 to $30 per capita."

Alternatives to the American system of broadcasting do exist. Britain, for example, requires all television owners to pay a yearly license fee, which goes into a fund to subsidize independent productions on the BBC. In France proceeds from a tax on entertainment fund private and public producers, ensuring that a range of perspectives gets represented. Whereas in the United States the federal commitment to public broadcasting is less than $1.50 per capita, other countries typically pay about $25 to $30 per capita. Aside from the establishment of the currently besieged Corporation for Public Broadcasting (which runs PBS), in the 1960s, the only serious attempts to legislate federal protection of the public interest in broadcasting were made in the 1930s. Herbert Hoover, who presided over the original Communications Act, for example, called for a two percent tax on radio-set sales to "pay for daily programs of the best skill and talent."

In most truly democratic countries television is subject to the electorate; the public interest is upheld. In the United States, however, the few laws requiring broadcasters to serve the public interest have never been enforced. This is in large part because federal policy for U.S. broadcasting, set in the 1930s, heavily stacked the deck in favor of a market-driven system. During the Depression policymakers hoped that a commercial broadcasting model would ensure sufficient programming diversity. But when the commercial model was codified in the Communications Act of 1934, its only—albeit important—concession to a broader civic responsibility was the stipulation that holders of broadcast licenses agree to serve the "public interest, convenience, and necessity."

The vaunted 1996 Telecommunications Act is the first significant update of the 1934 Communications Act. It has many elements, but one of its basic goals is to restore "competition" in the broadcasting market through further deregulation. Robert W. McChesney, a professor at the School of Journalism and Mass Communication at the University of Wisconsin at Madison, spoke in blunt Gerbnerian terms at the founding convention of Gerbner's Cultural Environment Movement, held in March of last year in St. Louis. "The 1996 Telecom Bill is truly one of the most corrupt pieces of legislation in American history," he said. "It has basically covertly handed over all communications to a few conglomerates. And it's all based on a big lie that Goebbels would have been impressed by: that the bill is meant to focus competition." By deregulating the industry, the Telecommunications Act has ensured that it will be consolidated still further. A rash of mergers has already taken place.

McChesney and Gerbner believe that it is structurally impossible for advertising-based television programming to represent the range and diversity of positions in our society. The problems, McChesney wrote in *Telecommunications, Mass Media, and Democracy: The Battle for the Control of US. Broadcasting, 1928–1935* (1993), are that "US political culture does not permit any discussion of the fundamental weaknesses in capitalism" and "corporate media have encouraged the belief that even the consideration of alternatives was tantamount to a call for totalitarianism."

According to Gerbner, a 1974 House committee report on television, suppressed by the broadcasting lobby before it could reach the House floor, suggested that the very organization of the network industry led to violent programming. Gerbner has long believed this to be true. Look at lists of the ten top-rated shows each year, he urges. Most of them are not violent; they're more likely to be comedies or nonviolent dramas. Yet producers still make scores of bloody shows. If network executives are merely obeying free-market forces, how can it be that they're making lots of shows that aren't in the highest demand?

Because, Gerbner told me, "there is no free market in television." It is well known in the industry that few television programs will break even in the domestic market. According to Todd Gitlin's book *Inside Prime Time* (1983), it costs more to produce one minute of your own programming than to buy an hour's worth from the world market. A programmer in Copenhagen, for example, can lease an old episode of *Dallas* for under $5,000, less than the cost of producing one minute of original Danish drama. The high cost of production means that producers must sell their shows into syndication or abroad—from which more than half the receipts come—if they wish to make a profit. Selling shows abroad requires a proven story formula that, in distributor lingo, "travels well." The most common formulas are obvious: sex and violence.

The Simple, the Naked, and the Bloody

Sex travels well. A Parisian or a Warsawian can delectate in Pamela Anderson in her bikini on *Baywatch* as well as a New Yorker can—hence *Baywatch* is the most-watched show in the world. Violence travels well. When Sylvester Stallone rains bullets on the bad guys, who duck or spew blood, a viewer in Beijing can understand what is going on as well as a viewer in Peoria. Grunting is easy to translate. That's why *Mighty Morphin Power Rangers* is watched by 300 million children in eighty countries. Violence and sex are naturally televisual genres: they're image-driven. Humor, subtlety, complex dialogue, and culture-specific idiosyncrasies don't translate so well. Thus there's an overwhelming global marketing imperative in favor of the simple, the naked, and the bloody. Cheap to produce, easy to distribute—violence is the surest road to profit. It becomes part of a global formula that is, in Gerbner's words, "imposed on creative people and foisted on the children of the world."

Polls show that the creative people in Hollywood don't like this. Formulas constrain them. Television-station managers don't like it either: 74 percent say they do not like the violent shows they program. But bound by the bottom line, the cost per thousand viewers (CPM), they are obliged to buy them. Advertisers have no vested interest in pitching goods during violent shows; in fact, they worry about tainting their products with unsavory associations. But advertisers, too, bow before the almighty CPM. Market forces (high demand) make top-rated shows too expensive for many advertisers. According to Gerbner, some of the highest-rated programs have gone out of existence because they became too costly for advertisers. Finally, viewers—what they say in polls notwithstanding—do watch violent shows. Yes, there are so many of these shows that it's hard to avoid them. And yes, viewers have been conditioned to accept the corporate violence doled out to them. Still, viewers, too, are implicated in the culture and media structure, along with executives, producers, station managers, writers, and advertisers. If television violence is a problem, and most agree that it is, then it is a systemic problem.

What needs to be addressed, then, is the whole structure. Each of its constituencies, Gerbner believes, if given a chance to escape the repressive market-dictated strictures that bind it, would do so. What is needed is an alternative model. But in a political environment where, as the journalism professor Robert McChesney points out, alternatives to a market system cannot be entertained without ridicule, this is a challenging need to meet.

How do we escape from the trap? That is largely what the Cultural Environment Movement was conceived to do.

The Cultural-Protection Movement

After he retired from the deanship at Annenberg, George Gerbner became, as he puts it, "a part-time researcher, full-time agitator" and continued to lecture all over the world on television violence. At the end of his speeches people would ask, What can we do? He would answer, Write your politician or broadcaster. Teach your children about television formulas. But this, Gerbner came to realize, was "feeble and humiliating— why should we have to ask for something that ought to be a right?" In other countries people had a right and a voice equal to those of conglomerates and broadcasters. Why couldn't people in the United States? So in late December of 1990 Gerbner and some likeminded friends got together in a borrowed conference room in Washington, D.C., to launch the Cultural Environment Movement (CEM). A quarter century earlier Rachel Carson's *Silent Spring* awakened readers to the perils of pollution and stimulated a generation of environmentalists to action. Gerbner's Cultural Environment Movement would do the same for media culture.

> *"In other countries people had a right and a voice equal to those of conglomerates and broadcasters."*

The movement yielded its first significant fruit a year ago, when it held its founding convention. Hundreds of delegates (left-leaning academics, progressive activists, former TV-industry people, and cultural policymakers from all over the world) assembled in a Holiday Inn on a bland commercial strip along Highway 366 in St. Louis. Their mission, as articulated in a draft of CEM's Viewer's Declaration of Independence, was to "dissolve the cultural bands which have tied human development to marketing strategies, and to assume an active role in making policy decisions about the cultural environment into which...children are born." A serious mandate, and an ambitious one.

Too ambitious? The convention, a three-day affair jampacked with working groups, cultural events, and plenary sessions, throbbed with activity and optimism. It had much of the tone of a civil-rights rally, swollen with the revolutionary fervor and progressive rhetoric of the sixties. Sumi Sevilla Haru, a four-foot-ten-inch, ninety-pound Filipino labor leader full of compressed energy, spoke in the language of the labor union when she told the convention, "We have to do something about the media massacre. We don't want to agonize—we need to *organize*." When *The Washington Post* columnist Dorothy Gilliam entreated delegates in an after-dinner speech to "think of your work as civil-rights work CEM can be part of the civil-rights movement" (for which she got a standing ovation), she was making explicit the broader mission by which most of the delegates defined themselves. The general effect of the idealistic enthusiasm was inspiring. But there was in all this an element of Pollyannaism, of preaching to the converted. No one was there to disagree. As one sober-minded delegate, a former television writer and producer and now a retired professor of media studies, confided to me, "These people are zealots. They're naive. Notice that there are no network people here. Things would be different if there were."

The last night of the convention I asked Gerbner how he thought this sometimes radical progressivism would play in the mainstream cultural arena, which is in general fairly moderate, even conservative. He replied that CEM should perhaps be seen not as radical or leftist, or even as liberal, but as "liberating." Americans have been responding to the rhetoric of family-values conservatives who, Gerbner says, really are on to something. The specific example Dan Quayle chose to use—Murphy Brown's getting pregnant out of wedlock—may have been unfortunate, but in Gerbner's opinion he made a good general point. "Fundamentalists have pre-empted the cultural issue," Gerbner says. "They're appealing to legitimate concerns of American families and organizations who resent dependence on media." This is precisely why CEM is so important: "The culture wars are heating up, and we need a liberating alternative to stop fundamentalists from expropriating the issue and taking it in a repressive direction."

CEM intends to fight for alternatives both to censorship and to the old-fashioned pieties of the cultural conservatives. But, I asked Gerbner, aren't we just talking about competing visions of cultural reality, of morality—one on the left, one on the right? Each side wants to impose its vision on the country, and therefore naturally favors whatever cultural products advance it. Gerbner replied, "We are not just providing a single alternative cosmology to, say, the religious right. We're advocating diversity." But "diversity" is weak tea, protest some of those who deplore today's violent television. Censorship is dangerous, Gerbner would be likely to reply. Conditioned by his dislike of fascism to distrust any kind of concentrated power (governmental, corporate, or otherwise), Gerbner cannot abide censorship, which can be both a means to and an end of such concentrations. Thus he can be very explicit about the sorts of programming we should and should not have—up to a point. We *should* have shows that depict minorities and women more favorably; we *should* have fewer mindlessly violent shows; but we *should* not use censorship to attain the programming we want.

The Cultural Environment Movement's basic mission, in other words, is to see that more stories by more different kinds of people are broadcast. Stories by people with something to tell, as Gerbner likes to say, rather than stories by people with something to sell. Think of a cafeteria, he says. When you enter a cafeteria, you feel that you have a right to choose what you will consume. But although some would argue that the choices in the cultural cafeteria are better now than they were for a parochial customer of the past, the choices remain limited: you have to choose from what's there. As a citizen, Gerbner believes, you have a responsibility to ask, What are the possibilities? How do we make this into a much richer and more nourishing and more diverse cafeteria? People don't realize that they have a say in what gets served here. CEM's mission is to make them aware of this fact, so that cultural choices get pushed into the political realm, where they belong.

"The Commons Is Needed"

Of course, one problem with this mission is that when culture is subsumed under a political rubric, debates about artistic values become debates about political values. The notion of aesthetic taste gets pushed aside. Taste, to be sure, can be a dangerous concept, a smokescreen to obscure political designs; Keyan Tomaselli, a combative South African media theorist who spoke at the CEM convention, points out that "good taste" can be its own form of censorship. For years in South Africa it was considered in "poor taste" to bring up certain aspects of race relations in middle-class white society; standards of "decency" ensured that art depicting these issues would be rare and marginalized. Clearly, "decency" and "poor taste" were bourgeois prettifications conjured to dress up (and thereby protect) outright racist attitudes. Nevertheless, art in the Western tradition is generally founded in some sense on taste, maybe even on elitist taste. When CEM tries to make political values interchangeable with cultural ones, it risks junking the critical standards we do have, many of which can be and are used as arguments against the quality of Hollywood's standard violent schlock.

"From the 1950s to the 1970s the three television networks provided considerable common cultural ground for the United States."

And then there are those, conservatives in particular, who will argue that what Gerbner is advocating when he speaks of diversity is really "identity politics," or quotas applied to culture. The implications of total diversity, these people will say, will be total fragmentation. True, in the ideal CEM imagining, shows would represent minorities more accurately and in truer proportions relative to the overall population.

But taken to its logical extremes, that might mean accepting Pat Buchanan's *No Way José* show (exploring the lives and views of xenophobic white male economic protectionists) and the *Ralph Reed Family Values Show* (with nary a homosexual or nonbeliever in sight), not to mention Madonna's *S&M Hour* (for those who find their taste in sexuality inadequately represented by current programming). The pursuit of diversity, if overzealous, leads to proliferating factions and subgroups. The result is tribalization, as each group retreats to its own set of stories.

A nation, almost by definition, must have some stories its citizens hold in common. From the 1950s to the 1970s the three television networks provided considerable common cultural ground for the United States. Everybody watched the same programs and televised events and was in some sense linked by this shared experience. But in the 1970s, with the spread of niche marketing and cable television, channels proliferated. The audience fragmented. America lost its common hearth.

"To recognize diversity," Todd Gitlin wrote in *The Twilight of Common Dreams: Why America Is Wracked by Culture Wars* (1996), "more than diversity is needed. The commons is needed." The danger inherent in CEM's using cultural diversity as a political tactic is that the idea of the commons gets lost. Of course, without this tactic we're in danger of being stuck with a limited set of master narratives favored either by conservative absolutists or by corporate conglomerates whose first concern is profit, not public interest, and for whom the universalist principle means appealing not to a common humanity but to the lowest common denominator. The trick for CEM will be to navigate between the Scylla of standardized, noninclusive, corporate-conglomerate-produced, market-strategy-conforming formulas that at least provide much of the nation with common cultural capital and the Charybdis of more-inclusive, more-diverse, less-formulaic, community-produced stories and programming that isolate each subgroup behind its respective cultural bulkhead. Gerbner believes that the Cultural Environment Movement can develop a mosaic that will to some extent incorporate ideological differences while representing the cultural claims of a larger cross-section of society than existing mainstream culture represents. In fact, he says, CEM can be the forum for all those who want to regain some say in what culture gets produced, in what they and their children consume.

At the convention's invocation, a slightly weird, touchy-feely affair with Jewish, Muslim, Christian, and Navajo prayers and progressive exhortations, Gerbner said his standard piece about returning cultural decision-making from the invisible Ministry of Culture to the people. To me, the most interesting words he spoke were these: "Our task now is to assemble a coalition like the anti-fascist coalition of the 1940s, with the partisan brigades."

Fighting Fascism

Fascism is the specter that looms, tenebrous, over all of Gerbner's life and work. There are at least two ways to interpret the shadow it casts. The first is to grant his warnings about creeping fascism all the more authority for his having lived under fascism, and for his having risked his life to fight it during the Second World War. The second is to discount everything he says on the subject because his significant early experiences under fascism have unduly colored his world view: since the war he has seen everything in terms of it.

My initial instinct was to incline toward the second interpretation. In my early conversations with Gerbner, I sometimes had to stifle the urge to say, Lighten up. My own cultural experience—watching violent cartoons when I was little, and violent action movies when older—has yet to produce any obvious violent or fascist impulses. And I am by no means alone in believing that, disproportionate quantities notwithstanding, violence in culture generally reflects the violence that is already present in real life. Family-court prosecutors scoff at the notion that television causes violent children; bad living conditions or bad genes do. Art since ancient times has depicted violence, and even tried to use it as catharsis. (Though Greek plays, Gerbner points out, never showed violence onstage; it was almost always reported by a messenger.) Moreover, although the studies that find the most-dramatic correlations between television and violence get the most publicity, there are other respectable studies whose conclusions are more restrained. "Television in the Lives of Our Children," for instance, one of the first major undertakings in the field, was published in 1961 after people became concerned about violent new shows like *The Rifleman* and *The Untouchables*. Researchers examined ten North American communities from 1958 to 1960, scrutinizing in great detail many aspects of television's effects. Their conclusion was a model of common sense.

> For *some* children, under *some* conditions, *some* television is harmful. For *other* children, under the same conditions, or for the same children under *other* conditions, it may be beneficial. For most children, under *most* conditions, most television is probably neither harmful nor particularly beneficial.

Beyond this, CEM's criticisms of "the market" will not be popular. If the flip side of freedom, innovation, comparative material prosperity, and global leadership is some crass commercialism, philistinism, and formulaic television shows, wouldn't most people say, So be it? It is easy to imagine the bafflement of free-market conservatives—and of the viewing public in general—at the phenomenon of CEM: What's wrong with television? What's fascist about *I Dream of Jeannie*? What's bothering the leftist malcontents this time?

But CEM has at least as many relatives on the right as on the left. In fact, one of CEM's closest older cousins grew out of the Moral Majority. In the 1980s Jeffy Falwell's Coalition for Better Television complained, as CEM does today, that the industry's commerce-at-all-costs ethos adversely affected programming. In advocating television that strictly reflected the cultural values of the Moral Majority, CFBT was more a predecessor of Dan Quayle than of CEM. But today people of all political persuasions are insecure. They worry about their safety and their future, and about the safety and the future of their children. This insecurity is aggravated, if not actually caused, by the cultural environment. Conservatives have recognized the insecurity and speak to it. Gerbner's view is that conservatives exploit it, and use it to push the country in a repressive direction. If this is true, then it may be that CEM does have a role to play as a guardian against fascism. Only it is less television per se that CEM is guarding against than the tendency of fundamentalists to favor absolutist measures in both the political and the cultural realm.

The Hollywood version of Gerbner's life would probably be a great movie. It tells a heroic story. And I don't think it would do most people any harm to watch it. But I do understand why Gerbner might say that the movie would contribute in a subtle way to neofascist impulses. In its simplicity, its glorification of violence as a means of resolving conflict, and its glossing lightly over the suffering and tragedy of violence, the movie would add to an aggregate that fosters the Mean World Syndrome and greater acceptance of martial measures. Maybe Gerbner could afford to lighten up a little anyway. But I can see why he might find the independent film version of his life (its less straightforwardly heroic portrayal of him notwithstanding) superior to the Hollywood version in a way that is more than just aesthetic.

Television, in Gerbner's view, is by no means inherently bad. It does much that is good. For many people who would otherwise be just plain bored, television represents an enrichment of cultural horizons. It has gone a long way toward diminishing isolation and parochialism and has given us cultural capital to hold in common. No modern state can govern without television; it is the social cement that religion once was, holding disparate groups and subgroups together. But, Gerbner firmly believes, so potent is television's power to inform and control, so strong is its power to teach us who gets away with what against whom, that a democratic people that cedes control of television to a nonelected few will not remain a democratic people for long. The more one contemplates the pervasiveness of stereotypical patterns in television, the more one perceives the inaccurate picture of reality it cultivates in viewers—and the more one inclines toward a charitable understanding of Gerbner's fears about fascism.

TV Turns to an Era
of Self-Control[2]

It is September 1998, and in flickering family rooms around the country, viewers are tuning in for their first glimpse of the new television season. Situation comedies dominate the prime-time schedules of the six networks, but there is bold drama as well. *N.Y.P.D. Blue*, in its sixth season on ABC, is more provocative than ever.

Parents can rest easy because their television sets have the V-chip, which makes it possible to prevent children from seeing shows that carry a rating denoting violence or sexual content.

And despite the cries of Hollywood's Cassandras, the rating system has not destroyed television but has burnished its new golden age, which some critics say started a few years back. As the American film industry did after adopting a ratings system in 1968, television has responded with its most inventive work; creative producers like Steven Bochco (*Hill Street Blues*, *N.Y.P.D. Blue*, *Murder One*) feel free to push the envelope without worrying that young children will sneak a peek.

This, at any rate, is how some network executives and media scholars view the near-future of television. The only trouble is, practically no one in Hollywood agrees.

As the television industry begins the daunting task of creating the ratings system it promised to President Clinton at a White House meeting late last month, most producers and writers are predicting disaster. They say that ratings will be ruinous for a host of reasons, not the least of which is that few parents agree on what is or isn't suitable fare for children.

Dick Wolf, who produces the NBC crime drama *Law and Order*, does not allow his 2-year-old son to watch *Mighty Morphin Power Rangers*, the hugely popular children's show on Fox, because he believes that its cartoonlike violence is more dangerous than the real-world mayhem depicted on his series. "After my son watched *Power Rangers* one day," Mr. Wolf recalled, "he came out and started giving me pretend karate kicks."

Haim Saban, who produces *Power Rangers* and eight other children's shows, including the often criticized cartoon *X-Men*, says he encourages his 5-year-old daughter to watch *Power Rangers* but draws the line at *60 Minutes*. "If V stands for violent, they better slap a V on *60 Minutes*," Mr. Saban said.

These men have their own agendas, of course. One is a leading creator of true-to-life adult dramas. The other is the television

[2]Article by Mark Landler, from the *New York Times*, Mr 17 '96. Copyright © 1996 The New York Times Company. Reprinted with permission.

industry's most prolific producer of children's shows. But the fact that they disagree so profoundly on what's suitable for children suggests just how difficult it will be to develop a television ratings system.

How Do You Rate 1,640 Hours a Day?

In pledging to adopt such a system for everything from *Power Rangers* to *Picket Fences*—and in promising to do it by 1997— television has taken on a task that producers, network executives and advertisers liken to catching lightning in a bottle. The stakes are breathtaking because the Government has mandated that in two years all new television sets must be equipped with the V-chip, a microchip that's encoded to block selected broadcast signals (the V stands for violence).

"No matter what we do, we're going to be virulently criticized," said Jack Valenti, the president of the Motion Picture Association of America, who last month brokered an agreement between the four broadcast networks and the cable industry to adopt ratings for sex and violence. At the meeting between President Clinton and a delegation of media barons on Feb. 29, Mr. Valenti announced that he would lead the effort to devise the ratings for television. Much has been made of how the television industry has capitulated to political pressure in agreeing to rate its programs. Most network executives acknowledge that with the passage in early February of the Telecommunications Act of 1996 and its V-chip provision, the broadcast and cable networks recognized they faced a stark choice: they could either rate their own shows or let the Government do it for them.

What is less understood, though, is that it may be well-nigh impossible for television to create a viable ratings system. Mr. Valenti notes that the average 70-channel cable system shows 600,000 hours of programming a year, or 1,640 hours a day. For the purposes of rating, that is the equivalent of 821 feature films per day; the M.P.A.A. rates only 600 films per year.

Moreover, many shows are delivered to the networks only hours before they are broadcast. And unlike theatrical releases, network television shows are underwritten by advertising. Already, some major advertisers say they may feel compelled to pull commercials from series or specials that have ratings indicating sex or violence.

Mr. Valenti must also persuade the networks and the cable industry to agree on a common ratings system. That would be hard enough given the subjective judgments that people bring to issues like sexual content, harsh language and violence. But also, the broadcast and cable industries approach the question of ratings from very different perspectives. CBS, NBC, ABC and Fox are loath to scare off advertisers; the USA Network, HBO and other cable services, less dependent on ad revenue, are less worried about the impact of ratings.

Whatever scheme he ends up devising, Mr. Valenti must proceed with the knowledge that he will probably never satisfy producers like Mr. Saban, who thinks ratings are simply unworkable, or Mr. Wolf, who contends they will drive sophisticated dramas off network TV and onto cable.

To Barry Diller, the former chairman of Fox who now runs Silver King Communications, the whole issue seems as unreal as a Saturday morning cartoon. "It is a terrible thing for this industry to promise the public something that we cannot, even minimally, deliver," he said.

Still, Mr. Valenti is assembling a task force of 19 to 25 people from all corners of the television industry, and it will meet weekly over the next eight months to research, debate and fashion a ratings system. He said the group would use the movie association's ratings as a template. Those familiar codes range from G (General audiences), PG (Parental guidance suggested) and its tougher cousin PG-13, up to R (Under 17 requires accompanying parent) and NC-17 (No one under 17 admitted). Network executives said the television ratings would probably be more specific about age suitability—PG-8 or PG-10, for example—but would be fuzzy about actual content.

"It is a terrible thing for this industry to promise the public something that we cannot, even minimally, deliver..."

As Hollywood's emissary to Washington, the 74-year-old Mr. Valenti is no stranger to the spotlight. He led the effort to rate movies 28 years ago under intense public scrutiny and pressure from theater owners. He has honed his pitch in years of after-dinner speeches and testimony before Congressional committees. "Is it a flawed system? You bet," Mr. Valenti said by telephone from Los Angeles, "But like Churchill said about democracy, 'It is the worst of all forms of governments, except for every other form of government.'"

Mr. Valenti has been drawing on his skills as a lobbyist to sell the idea of ratings to some of Hollywood's leading producers. Recently he had dinner with Mr. Bochco to plead his case. Mr. Bochco's *N.Y.P.D. Blue*, the highly rated Tuesday night show on ABC, has become a bellwether in the debate over ratings. The network has placed a parental advisory on the series throughout its three seasons because of its steamy sexual content. "I don't approve of ratings," Mr. Bochco said last week. "But given that we have to live with them, I don't want to bury my head in the sand."

The Economic Costs, and the Political

For all his talents as persuader, Mr. Valenti will have a hard time bringing around much of Hollywood. Mr. Wolf, for example, noted that advertisers routinely cancel commercials on *Law and Order* when it plumbs sensitive topics like abortion or assisted suicide. In that show's first season, he said, NBC lost $800,000 in advertising on a single episode that explored the bombing of abortion clinics.

ABC was forced to discount commercial time on *N.Y.P.D. Blue* deeply for its first two seasons. In fact, while the series has consistently placed in the top 10 in the Nielsen ratings, several advertising executives said ABC was still selling commercials on *N.Y.P.D. Blue* at a slight discount.

Mr. Wolf and others said that placing ratings on these series would only aggravate the situation. With a PG-13 rating, he said, *Law and Order* and *Murder One* would become easy marks for special-interest groups that already go after companies that buy commercials on these shows. "I've yet to meet the CEO of a major corporation who has the intestinal fortitude to face down that kind of attack," Mr. Wolf said.

Pressure on advertisers has often generated more publicity than results. But the Rev. Donald E. Wildmon, president of the American Family Association, a conservative political organization in Tupelo, MS., that has put pressure on advertisers, said a ratings system could make it easier to scare sponsors. "Advertisers are becoming a little more leery about the programming they support," Mr. Wildmon said, "It could play out that if a program has an R rating, they won't want to be on it."

For at least one big advertiser, the prospect of ratings is unsettling. Philip Guarascio, the president of marketing and advertising at General Motors Corporation, said G.M. would have to give extra scrutiny to a show that carried a rating denoting violence or sex. G.M. already submits television series to episode-by-episode scrutiny before it advertises on them, but Mr. Guarascio said that an R rating would be a "red flag," which could make sponsors a target for pressure groups. "We want to sell our cars and trucks to a broad audience," Mr. Guarascio said, "but you cannot ignore external forces. We're a highly visible company, so we're under a magnifying glass."

Top network executives say they are unruffled. ABC loses roughly $20 million in advertising revenue every year because of sponsors' rejecting controversial programs, said Robert A. Iger, the president and chief executive of Capital Cities/ABC. But he believes that adding ratings to shows will barely affect the network's prime-time schedule. It won't lead ABC to ask for less provocative programming, he said.

As an example, Mr. Iger recalled that when Mr. Bochco proposed *N.Y.P.D. Blue* to ABC four years ago, he referred to it as an "R-rated" series. Mr. Iger told Mr. Bochco that if he created a high-quality adult-oriented series, ABC would schedule it—and stick by it. "Let's say that it's a year from now, and we have a ratings system," Mr. Iger said. "If Steven came to me with the same request, I would give him exactly the same charge."

Indeed, some observers argue that a ratings system will create more ambitious programs and weed out the dross. "Ratings will probably be salutary from an esthetic point of view," said Mark Crispin Miller, a professor of media studies at Johns Hopkins University. "A mild inducement to clean up your act can actually work to the betterment of the product."

Where the Networks and Cable Diverge

Whatever new products come along, few children between the ages of 2 and 11 tend to watch the shows that will receive adult ratings. In the case of *N.Y.P.D. Blue*, only 4 percent of its audience is between 2 and 11, according to the A. C. Nielsen Company. For *Law and Order*, the number is 3 percent. When young children watch prime-time television, they gravitate toward situation comedies, which dominate the 8 PM to 10 PM period. For ABC and its rivals, the question is, Does losing 4 percent of a program's audience make it unprofitable?

Common sense would say no, but network television is an odd beast. It makes its money by delivering the largest possible audiences to advertisers. Advertising executives said that even losing a small percentage of viewers could force some shows off network television and onto cable.

"Advertising executives said that even losing a small percentage of viewers could force some shows off network television and onto cable."

Cable networks are less vulnerable to swings in viewership and ad revenue because they get half their revenue from subscriber fees. That difference has stoked a protracted feud between the networks and cable. The networks contend that they have been unjustly tarred as purveyors of sex and violence when cable services like USA, TNT, Showtime and HBO show far more lurid material.

Even more galling to the networks, the cable industry has taken the lead in publicizing the depth of public anger about television violence. Most recently, the National Cable Television Association released a major study of television violence that found that the amount of mayhem on television—both network and cable—had escalated in recent years. "They get to posture on the side of truth, virtue and ratings when by far the most violent programming is on their channels," said one senior network executive, who would speak only anonymously.

Remembering the Children

Squabbles between broadcasters and cable executives obscure the central underlying issue: How can the industry improve television for children?

Given that so few young children watch television from 10 PM. to 11 PM, some people argue that Mr. Valenti should start by focusing his energies on daytime television, including talk shows and Saturday morning fare like *X-Men* and *Power Rangers*. Animated series are particularly controversial because they are loaded with violence, though it is often of a stylized or fantastical nature. "As a parent, I am much more irritated by the violence in *X-Men* than I am by the violence in an adult movie," said Peggy Charren, a longtime advocate of better children's programming.

Mr. Saban, not surprising, argues that his *Power Rangers* should receive a G rating because its violence is so clearly a fantasy. "We fight turtles with traffic lights on their heads," he said.

For all their spirited defense of prime time, network executives are oddly silent on children's programming. In part, this is because they acknowledge that they have no idea how sponsors would react if animated shows carried violence warnings.

Of all the issues that face Mr. Valenti, perhaps the most bedeviling is whether ratings can actually make television better for children. Several executives contend that "graduated" ratings will not work for television because viewing is a passive act, not a deliberate one like going to the movies. Others note the obvious: that ratings have done little to stem the flood of violence in movies. "Ratings will in no way influence the kind of programs that get made," said Michael J. Fuchs, the former chairman of HBO, "They'll put electronic barriers around certain kinds of shows."

For that matter, some experts point out that the M.P.A.A. ratings have flaws that would be magnified if they were adopted by to television. Barbara Wilson, a professor of communication at the University of California, Santa Barbara, and a researcher on the cable-sponsored violence study, said movie ratings tended to be restrictive on sexual content but lenient on violence. "The ratings focus more on what might be offensive to parents, as opposed to what poses risks to kids," she said.

Mr. Valenti has been listening to these arguments for nearly three decades. "I've stepped on many of these land mines in the past," he said.

Even people skeptical about the whole enterprise said that Mr. Valenti's experience would be a benefit as he leads the television industry through the ratings thicket. But given the complexity of the issues, the scope of the challenge and the shortness of time, it still may not be enough.

The Family Behind Bars[3]

In the spirit of the current publishing trend of tell-all memoirs recounting family dysfunction, perversion, and abuse, I'd like to share some painful moments from my own family history. When my daughter was less than two years old, she cold-bloodedly attempted the murder of her infant brother, only two days home from the hospital. In a fit of jealous rage at the attention the little intruder was getting, she snuck into his room and attempted to drag him from his cradle and commit unspeakable acts of violence against him. Luckily she was stopped in time. Somehow she managed to grow up and become a productive citizen, despite her early criminal tendencies. For this we all thank our (then) Higher Power, Dr. Spock.

This was not the only incident in which one of my children revealed violent or anti-social tendencies during childhood and adolescence. I'd forgotten about these occurrences, but they were brought to mind recently, after an evening of CNN and *Court TV* that left me trembling at my family's narrow escape from the jaws of the criminal-justice system and the glaring spotlight of media infamy.

In one news story and trial report after another, I saw terrifying "there-but-for-the-grace-of-God-go-I" examples of an alarming media trend: the criminalization of the American family. Or, to be perfectly accurate, the criminalization of the poorer, more downwardly mobile elements of the American family.

First came the stories about children in the single-digit range being arrested for acts of violence. There was an update on a six-year-old who had killed a smaller child, followed by one about an even younger child who attempted a similar act. Should these children be tried as adults, we were asked? Certainly the Republicans, prosecutors, and police officers interviewed thought so. And the Democrats who were interviewed also concurred, evidently following the lead of the White House, which these days strikes a tone more sorrowful and less fire-breathing, but adopts a policy every bit as punitive as the Republicans'.

I watched in horror the *Court TV* trial of a white, middle-class couple named Provenzino that had, it was alleged, failed to keep its sixteen-year-old from committing various crimes: a series of burglaries and the growing of an illegal marijuana plant. The son, who was already serving a year in juvenile detention, testified for his shell-shocked parents. But to no avail; they were convicted of irresponsibility after failing to convince a jury that they had done everything they could to keep the kid in line. A collective shiver must have passed through all of Middle America that

---

[3]Article by Elayne Rapping, author of "The Culture of Recovery," from *The Progressive* 60:37–8 S '96. Copyright © 1996 The Progressive, Inc., 409 E. Main St., Madison, WI 53703. Reprinted with permission.

night. "It's eleven o'clock; do you know where your kids are?"

There is a rage across the land, and unless you are very highly placed, or have wisely committed your kids to a tough military academy or convent, you had best be looking over your shoulder for the cops and *Hard Copy*.

How did this happen? Why the growing demonization of kids and relatively powerless parents, while the rich and powerful are allowed to get away with murder—mass murder, quite often, in the case of corporate and government crimes that endanger or destroy millions at a shot?

The media have a lot to do with it. For while this trend begins in Washington politics, it is television's role in framing political issues that has ensured the emotional effectiveness of this targeting of families and kids as the source of all evil.

From the start, TV has focused attention on family life and "family values" as the basis for morality and social order. It has willfully distracted us from the larger political and economic arenas. It rarely lets us see who determines the policies and who provides (or doesn't provide) the funds for the jobs and services that make properly functioning family life possible.

Of course, TV's motives have been primarily economic, not political: The main point of commercial television is to sell things. And in a consumer-driven market, in which most shopping is done for family consumption, it is not surprising that television has always addressed its audience as *essentially* family members.

"There is little that families, and especially kids, on commercials and sitcoms don't have, or don't easily get."

We in Television Land are always assumed to be a mom, a dad, or a kid. And our main job is always assumed to be consuming. Buy this cereal; buy that soap; buy this home computer so your kids can go to college; buy that car so your family can vacation in style and comfort. The popular bumper sticker that reads I SHOP, THEREFORE I AM aptly reflects the bearer's exemplary internalization of this most basic demand of consumer society.

But there is a politically revealing contradiction between the ways families and kids are portrayed in commercials (and in the sitcoms and soaps and dramas that commercials fund) and the way they are portrayed in news and tabloid shows.

Family-based TV programming since the 1950s has been based on a view of human nature that is sunny, benevolent, and, apparently, effortlessly self-regulating. Because of this, the guiding rules of family order and discipline are excessively permissive. There is little that families, and especially kids, on commercials and sitcoms don't have, or don't easily get. Nor is this unchecked impulse to instant gratification seen as problematic, either morally or practically. Needs are filled easily—without resorting to crime—because money, it seems, grows on trees.

Kids on these shows, and in most commercials, need little parental guidance. Indeed, they are often, and annoyingly, prone to give their parents advice and to cutely—always cutely—disrespect and contradict them. They are angelic, cleans-scrubbed, smiling, and seem to stay happily on track.

And why not? The track they travel is so easy and pleasant to navigate. When they do go astray, it takes little more than a brief parental word—always in the final moments of the segment—to remind them of the wisdom of the title of their generic ancestor: *Father Knows Best*.

This permissive, narcissistic image of human nature as endlessly and effortlessly in search of easily attained pleasure is in perfect sync with the media's ultimate goal: to prime kids to want, strive for, and buy, buy, buy the things hawked in commercials.

Thus, in "family-viewing" hours, the line between commercials and shows blurs confusingly. The shows themselves are powerful models of the consumer lifestyles and aspirations that the commercials tout only more blatantly. (That's why Procter & Gamble, in the 1950s, was so quick to put a stop to shows like *The Life of Riley*, *The Goldbergs*, and *The Honeymooners*—that idealized working-class and immigrant life—and replace them with fathers who knew best and earned and consumed in appropriate corporate style.)

Bill Cosby's Heathcliff Huxtable—who headed one of the rare black sitcom families—exemplifies this model of family life and the assumptions about human nature that drive it. Cosby easily jollies his kids into obedience in a way that can only make most parents do a resentful double take. He and his kids are always on the same wavelength, living and striving for ever more up-to-date and fashionable clothing, furniture, and gadgets.

"No fourteen-year-old needs to have a $95 shirt, unless he is onstage with his four brothers!" says Cosby to his son as he demands that such a shirt be returned to the store. But all the kids—and Cosby himself—are already wearing clothes that cost at least that much. And they are so happy, and seem to do so little, to acquire it all. Adam Smith must surely be smiling down on these characters and admiring the work of his *Higher Power, the Invisible Hand*.

But there is a flip side to this sunny media message about families and kids. The other, darkly demonic version of kids and families is the one on the news, on crime shows, and more recently on the tabloids, filled with poor families who could never *legally* enjoy the bounty of consumer society, and so were never pictured in the sitcoms and commercials that pushed it so hard.

On these shows we see a more Hobbesian vision of families and youth and human nature in which kids, and increasingly parents, are out of control, inherently antisocial, and prone to unprovoked violence. *These* kids and families live in a world where life is indeed nasty, brutish, and short, and the lust for things needs to be kept in check by ever stronger and more inhumane methods.

There is a far-from-subtle color and uniform code in the media to help viewers figure out which images and messages apply to them. Except that lately the lines and codes seem to be blurring. For the media—following the lead of politicians—now feel compelled to broaden their warnings to an ever-greater demographic range, as more and more people are finding it harder and harder to keep up with the program of work, clean living, and consumption that drives the wheels of progress.

Now many white and middle-class kids and parents, like the poor Provenzinos, are depicted being dragged off to jail or subjected to humiliating interrogations in Kafkaesque courtrooms.

This is a real media contradiction, which would be funny if it weren't so scary: The media primes us to lust unrestrainedly after things seen on television, even as the political and economic forces have been making it harder for even the middle classes to gratify those desires.

Bill and Hillary Clinton, my old comrades of anti-Vietnam-war days, would probably have little sympathy for parents like me in today's political climate.

She is fast losing patience with those of us who couldn't make our marriages stick. She urges cracking down on divorce now, in an effort to preserve family values and so drive down youth crime.

And he has a whole laundry list of youth-oriented ideas to solve our social crisis. Kids like mine will wear uniforms and be home by eight. They won't smoke. They won't drink or do drugs. They won't listen to rock or rap. They won't watch TV. Or, if they must, they will be monitored by a V chip. And they certainly won't have sex or produce kids of their own before they are properly married and employed. For kids unfortunate enough to have parents on welfare, there is a more draconian, even Dickensian, list.

Nor will age be an excuse (and here is where I see visions of my infant daughter, diapered and drooling, with nothing but a pacifier to comfort her, as she rots in prison as a hard case). Even kids too young to have any conception of right or wrong, much less "crime," will be rounded up and placed in twenty-three-hour lockdown with mass murderers, it seems. And if the current "Dr. Spocks" don't help parents avoid such mishaps, they, too, will find themselves on the evening news, being dragged off to the slammer.

Will this solve the problem of juvenile crime and the breakdown of family values? Dole and Clinton are in eerie agreement that it will. The trouble is that the media version of juvenile crime is grossly misrepresented. According to *The Real War on Crime*, the newly released report of the National Criminal Justice Commission, most kids who land in juvenile courts and detention centers have committed an offense neither violent nor serious. Only six out of 100 juvenile arrests are for violent crimes of any kind. And only one-half of 1 percent are in for rape and murder, the acts most often, and most sensationally, thrown at us by the media.

"The media primes us to lust unrestrainedly after things seen on television..."

Kids don't do well behind bars. A full 11,000 of the 65,000 kids incarcerated engaged in "suicidal acts" while in "protective custody." Which leads one to wonder just who should be brought up on charges in this system.

It is unsettling to think that so much that is problematic in family and youth behavior is now being deemed "criminal" and dealt with by the law. And it is worth looking a bit more closely at the media's role in this, before swallowing whole their version of the problem, which demonizes kids and parents while letting corporations and policymakers off the hook.

As the National Criminal Justice Commission's study shows, most crime—juvenile *and* adult—is against property, and only tangentially, and far less frequently against persons.

Perhaps it would be more reasonable to run massive campaigns against images of glamorous, expensive consumer goods on TV, and skip the jeremiads against media violence and family and moral breakdown, which sound so good and accomplish so little.

As this eye-opening study demonstrates, most crime is rooted in the need or greed for *things* in an age when the pressures of growing economic uncertainty and hardship, combined with an ever-intensifying push by the media to instill insatiable commodity lust, make the impulse to commit such crimes harder and harder to resist.

A Gore Phobia[4]

If you live in the dark, you have an instinct for when the gotchas are coming. You can feel the movie getting aroused. You know you have a serious chance of seeing something terrific, or something you'd rather not see—like the dawdling, merciless preamble to ear removal in Tarantino's *Reservoir Dogs* or the pulping and live burial of Joe Pesci in *Casino* or even the blitzing of the White House (another Clinton deal?) in *Independence Day*. Sometimes, you can even imagine entire motion pictures being made to justify such startling visions—rather in the way Abraham Zapruder's life must have been recast by those frames of super-8 he shot in Dallas on November 22, 1963. And he never knew he was filming a scene.

When Jean-Paul Sartre was a kid, he went to the movies. Born in 1905, he could see Charlie or *Birth of a Nation* when they were up-to-date. Years later, he recalled those compelling sights as "frenzies on a wall." I've always loved that phrase and its sense of the wild excitement movies can give you, the sheer wonder and peril in sudden movement and cuts that come too fast for you to close your eyes. That dread and delight cover Dr. Caligari and Hannibal Lecter, Fred Astaire and Roger Rabbit; they even go as far as the flash of Sharon Stone in *Basic Instinct*.

With movies, the function of seeing was sucked out of the brain and isolated; it was further pressed on by surrounding darkness and a screen that might be larger than life. Only a little more than a hundred years ago in the history of human sophistication, Parisians (no less!) are said to have jumped from their seats and run screaming from the dark when the Lumière brothers projected a shot of a railway locomotive coming (very slowly) toward the camera.

We smile at such naïveté. Yet maybe we should retain some wonder still for the ghost of Lecter, the impact of *Crash,* or the next graphic first that goes home in our eyes. Don't we believe in bacteria? Don't we credit the notion that Sigourney Weaver might nurse within her some alien seed with bite? So why are we not stricken carriers of some terrible sight—sprung on us before we were ready—that we regret having seen?

From the outset, movies gave us violence and loveliness till we hardly knew which was which. In *The Great Train Robbery* (1903), a gun was fired into the camera with reckless aplomb and promise of things to come. The screen was also full of beautiful faces. We forget that before photography and film, a person might live a long life without seeing anyone that beautiful. Today, we have beauties everywhere—on the screen and on the

---

[4]Article by David Thomson, from *Esquire* 127:48–9 My '97. Copyright © 1997 David Thomson. Reprinted with permission.

page—as listless as Kate Moss, and we mistrust the attribute. We find it hollow, superficial, and "glossy," the start of a lie. But we are also drugged by "beauty," or glamour, so that we hate the drug and our weakness—and the mere word *beauty* can often prompt a sneer or a sigh.

Still, for decades movies thrived on showing us things we had not seen. The western rode on urban society's dream of wide-open spaces; and it declined as Monument Valley became a cliched site for automobile ads. There was a time when poor people got great satisfaction from the houses, the clothes, the ease, and the shine of wealth: That's a vital part of the Hollywood comic romance of the 1930s, just as screwball is the first hint that, somehow, those blithe people don't quite deserve their luxury, because they are crazy as well as lovely.

Throughout its history, the medium has known the marvel in new personalities: We cannot rekindle the first frenzy for, say, Gloria Swanson (Norma Desmond took her over) or Clark Gable. But we may appreciate the freshness that Vivien Leigh brought to *Gone with the Wind*, the debut of James Dean (doubly blessed in that it was all there would be), and even the glee of Julia Roberts in *Pretty Woman*. You could hear the silent "Wow!" in the dark. And we long to be wowed, to believe in the new, the unattainable but surely existent happiness that beckons pursuit.

But there is a darker side to seeing, and it consists of being shown something more violent, more cruel, more disturbing, and more outrageous than we have ever seen before. We seem to be in just such a fearsome season again: with *Crash* and its unflagging interest in sexual situations that involve damaged people and wounded vehicles; with *Lost Highway* and its studied, floor-level shot of a heavy glass tabletop embedded in a man's head, the joint sealed with bubbling blood. There's that grisly moment in *Blood & Wine* when a desperate Jack Nicholson, in search of a lost stolen necklace, thinks to feel inside the blood-soaked panties of Judy Davis (his wife in the story), who is at that moment dying in a crashed car. I'd never seen that before or heard anything like the sound Davis makes. Her moan at the unkind touch is true to the dramatic situation and proper protest from a fine actress that she should have to make such junky films. And all this is to say nothing of what we can expect in the upcoming film of James Ellroy's *L.A. Confidential*, directed by Curtis Hanson (*The Hand That Rocked the Cradle* and *Bad Influence*) and starring Kim Basinger and Danny DeVito.

The "backlist" to these moments is a very rich one, I fear. It starts with the gunshot in *The Great Train Robbery*, and it includes the many deformities invented by Lon Chaney and his makeup box; the face of Kong gazing upon Fay Wray and breathing so heavily that her last flimsy clothes might be wafted away; the grapefruit that James Cagney squeezes in Mae Clarke's face in *The Public Enemy*; Richard Widmark throwing the old lady down the staircase in *Kiss of Death* and laughing his laugh; the corpse getting out of the bath in *Les Diaboliques*; and—coming to a moment of real historic importance—the shower killing in *Psycho*, about which the fastidious, polite malice of Alfred Hitchcock could boast that no one ever actually saw a single frame of Janet Leigh's (or her shower-in's) flesh being broken.

Psycho is relevant not just because of the tour de force visualization and editing with which Hitchcock made an idiot out of the 1960 censor's attitude toward violence. Far more important is the way in which it is a movie about the character who cuts Janet Leigh to pieces. The thirty or so minutes before Leigh enters the shower is a kind of test-case grilling of the character she plays and of the actress's skin. She is put up there on our wall for us to inspect; she undresses several times; she is poked, prodded, and hounded by the lens. Then comes a voyeur in the plot (Norman Bates), who flinches at the sight of so much skin and...comes back as his fierce mother to off the temptation. Norman may not be a hero; you may not choose to see him as "sympathetic." But he is, in curious ways, the most humane and sensitive character in the film. What I'm seeking to suggest is that we are subtly enlisted in his act of murder. The psycho is the "I" and the eye in this study of schizoid division and dissociation—in which, more or less, the murderous arm doesn't quite know what's driving it.

That's what's crucial to the impulse of "dangerous" spectacle in so many films: It is being offered duplicitously, to seduce us, with something cruel or evil in mind. An intricate torture is being made available. Don't misunderstand me. I love the "Wow!" in movies and the danger. Shocking effects, violence, and horror don't regularly trouble me. I approve of everything from the sliced eyeball in Luis Bunuel's *Un Chien Andalou* to the severed ear in David Lynch's *Blue Velvet* (a real masterpiece, I think, just as *Lost Highway* is a travesty of genius). I hate censorship, and I love the wicked zest audiences feel for forbidden spectacle.

But I'm wary. And I have a wife who, it seems, married a film critic so that she could get advance warning on films not to see. She holds the firm view that there are certain depths of violence and outrage that she doesn't want to watch. She is a photographer, I should add, not a person reluctant to witness. But she regrets having seen the rape scene in *A Clockwork Orange*. Few American moviegoers may realize that the film's maker, Stanley Kubrick, is similarly rueful. Kubrick owns, or controls, *A Clockwork Orange* in Britain because of some contractual nicety, and for many years now he has banned the movie—in theaters and on video—in the country where he lives.

Apparently, he feels the picture may have inspired some real-life violence—what we call copycat action. I don't know the details, and I don't begin to support any theory that the risk of copycatting in a crowded, jittery society amply equipped with disturbed people and worse should deter artists or even showmen from their work. But only a fatuously optimistic movie lover

"I hate censorship, and I love the wicked zest audiences feel for forbidden spectacle."

can continue to live in this society without feeling that there are connections between things seen and things done.

Copycatting worries me a great deal less than something I will call alienation. For just as moviemakers have pursued the unspeakable, the impossible, and the hitherto unshowable, so they have begun to develop technologies of mayhem. That includes everything from Hitchcock's meticulous cutting to Peckinpah's outfitting actors with sachets of blood and "flesh-like material" so that when they are shot, their very bodies seem to break up. And now it has reached as far as the digitalization whereby fingers, limbs, and heads can be lopped off and relocated to our dreams.

More or less, we "know" the craft and have become people who watch with one eye on the drama and the other on its making. (*Psycho* may have been the first popular movie in which the director could be watched that way.) But I was shaken recently by a conversation about *The English Patient* in which a friend told me he had been agonized and horrified by the many shots of Ralph Fiennes's terribly burned face. The film had been spoiled for him: He couldn't watch. Whereas I had seen only makeup and the concept of the character. And I loved the movie. But my sophistication had carried me away from human reality and a tasteful treatment of suffering. I missed something. And the fact is, surely, that many of us (movie buffs especially) have become blase about these appalling sights; that's why the movies must strive ever harder to shock us. We see, but we don't always register the pain or the horror. We are too smart any longer to believe. Add that loss to the one involving beauty and we're two down.

IV. Stopping the Violence

Throughout this issue of *The Reference Shelf*, the point has been made that while violence is an undeniable aspect of modern society, quests to understand it and alleviate its effects are equally important. Such is the focus of this section. Here, authors discuss violence as it exists on a national scale and as it is manifest in communities throughout the country. These articles also convey past attempts to counter the threat of violence, and what has been learned from the successes and failures of those attempts.

In an article from *U.S. Catholic*, Patrice J. Tuohy discusses an array of measures taken to prevent violence. According to Tuohy, effective solutions that address the perceived root causes of violence include gun control, legal reform, criminal rehabilitation, equalization of school funding, extra educational help for at-risk children, universal health care, job training, low-cost housing, decent wages, and family assistance. In this article, Tuohy includes a detailed questionnaire, which essentially asked an assortment of *U.S. Catholic* readers both how they perceive violence in the present day, and what they believe can be done to alleviate it. Answers to the questionnaire range from training individuals in conflict meditation involving nonviolent principles, to ensuring that young people have access to organized, constructive activities after school.

Along with the many pragmatic attempts to prevent violence, many Americans are concerned with the moral questions that are inevitably invoked by discussions of violence. In a survey from the *Wall Street Journal*, Ellen Graham and Cynthia Crossen review what many perceive to be a general decline in overall values and morality that is most directly manifest in violent behavior. Based on the answers to the survey, the authors conclude that if people were to correct their own behaviors, independent of external law or authority, the fight against violence would be far more successful. The authors further assert that the burden of correcting violent behavior falls primarily on parents.

Research financed by the Harry Frank Guggenheim Foundation and the U.S. Census Bureau has revealed that, in general, adolescent delinquents and persistent adult criminals have no desire to find legal jobs or stop using drugs and alcohol. Mark S. Fleisher, writing in *USA Today*, responds to the findings of this research and examines the patterns of the criminal lifestyle. According to Fleisher's findings, the lives of persistent criminals share certain characteristics, most notably childhoods filled with chaos and a lack of solid parental control. To remedy this situation, Fleisher believes neglected and battered youngsters should be permanently distributed to small residential homes that are funded and regulated by the federal government.

According to sociologist Amitai Etzioni, director of the Center for Communication Policy Studies in Washington, D.C., the American public feels quite strongly that the United States is enduring far too much violence. In an article entitled "How You (Yes You!) Can Stop Violence in Your Town," from *Redbook*, Michael D'Antonio examines ways that communities can counter their frustration with the persistent problem of violence. On the individual/local level, increased community policing, monitoring the levels of violence children watch on television, and training children to resolve conflicts without resorting to violence are all, according to the author, proven deterrents against increases in community violence.

Marc Kaufman, writing in *Parents*, describes the fear of violence that he believes is rampant among parents. Their fears are not without basis. According to The Council on Crime in America, a third of all crimes committed in America are undoubtedly of a violent nature. Moreover, the involvement of children in violent crimes, either as victim or as perpetrator, is notably on the rise. Kaufmann reports that as the police and the criminal-justice system cannot stem the tide of violence, millions of parents are banding together and joining neighborhood and town watches, or embracing a more aggressive neighborhood activism.

In the final article of this issue of *The Reference Shelf*, Marilyn Sherman asserts that school systems should be involved in violence prevention programs. The problem of violence in schools of all types—from the grammar school to the university—is attracting the attention of administrators throughout the nation. According to the Children's Institute International, 41 percent of teenagers simply do not feel safe at school. The author believes that schools, law enforcement agencies, parents, and religious leaders must combine their efforts and create a unified violence prevention program. Sherman outlines the essential components of such a program.

Violent America[1]

One in five homicides occurs in families. More than 1 million Americans are in jail or prison. There are more gun dealers in the United States than gas stations. America is the violence capital of the industrialized world. It is our problem, but what can any one of us do to solve it?

She was an attractive, intelligent woman, mid-40s, good job, nice new rehabbed condominium in a changing-for-the-better big-city neighborhood. She had lots of friends and a loving family. On a crisp autumn evening, she sat quietly on the train home from work turning over the day's events and planning what she was going to have for dinner. She debated about whether to stop at the grocery store but decided she had enough food. It was 6 PM—time for a workout before dinner.

As she neared her building, a young man approached and passed. Two seconds later he was grabbing at the purse slung around her right shoulder. She was yanked around and then pushed facedown to the ground. She cried out, "Please don't hurt me!" She felt an excruciating stinging in her back. Her attacker fled down the street. It took her a moment to realize that she had been stabbed. She struggled to stand and began yelling for help as she made her way to the front door of her building. She was getting weaker. She pressed the first buzzer, then the second, then all the buzzers. She could not speak any more. She was found minutes later by a neighbor lying in a pool of blood at the entrance to her condominium.

This woman survived her violent attack but not without physical and mental scars. She had a severed spleen and colon and a punctured and collapsed lung. She was in the hospital for a month. Her parents sold her condo for her and she moved to the suburbs where she feels safer. She has a hard time trusting people.

A few years earlier, another woman, after years of beatings and verbal abuse from her husband, finally chose to flee with their daughter and find safety. She left the East Coast suburb where she had spent her entire life and sought refuge at an urban shelter for battered women in a city 1,000 miles away from her husband. She feels safer now, but she doesn't trust people.

Safety, it seems, is relative in America's violent culture, and trust is a scarce commodity. No one can escape the violence in our society. Although we tend to view strangers with more suspicion, most violence occurs between people who know each other. Everyone becomes the "other" in our crime-laden, individualistic society, and the other is the enemy. How can Christians, including *U.S. Catholic* readers, adhere to the biblical

---

[1]Article by Patrice J. Tuohy, managing editor of *U.S. Catholic*, from *U.S. Catholic*, 61:6–15 F '96. Reprinted with permission of *U.S. Catholic* published by the Claretians, Chicago, IL 60606.

admonition to welcome the stranger, when the stranger is likely to blow their heads off?

Of course, statistically this last statement isn't true—danger doesn't lurk around every corner. Yet who can deny that some corners are more dangerous than others, and corners of the world we thought would be safe—our quiet neighborhoods, our secluded suburbs, our churches, our homes—are within the ugly reach of violence. Regardless of race, creed, color, or natural origin—who we are or where we live—we are all directly and indirectly affected by violent America.

When I look at my own life, I say, "Thank God, I have never been assaulted or beaten or abused." Yet the two women I described above are people I know. And a guy from my high school—we sat together in algebra—was murdered by serial killer John Wayne Gacy. And the sleepy Chicago suburb where I grew up, Addison, Illinois, where nothing much seemed to happen, is now the scene of one of last year's most gruesome crimes—the murder of a pregnant woman for the sake of the baby she was carrying, who was cut out of her womb after she was shot in the head. It is all so awful and overwhelming and numbing.

"...the United States is now the most violent nation in the industrialized world."

According to the Federal Bureau of Investigation, the United States is now the most violent nation in the industrialized world. More than 20,000 homicides are committed each year, and in 1993 there were 7,864 hate crimes identified. The Children's Defense Fund reports that in the U.S. 100,000 children carry guns to schools, 700,000 carry knives, and 160,000 students skip school every day for fear of violence.

Homes are the most violent places in America: more than 50 percent of the women murdered are killed by partners or ex-partners, and 2.7 million children are reported to be victims of neglect, physical abuse, sexual abuse, or emotional maltreatment.

For the average, law-abiding citizen, the situations that give rise to violence seem far removed. It's other neighborhoods that have gangs and drive-by shootings. It's other families who physically and verbally abuse their children, beat their spouses, or abuse drugs and alcohol. It's other people who are filled with bigotry and hate and intolerance.

But, then again, most Americans have been or know someone who was the victim of a violent crime. And on any given week, many Americans, including 17 percent of *U.S. Catholic* readers surveyed, fear for their safety at least once.

No Easy Answers

The statistics are frightening, and most Americans are begging for solutions. Some Americans, though very few *U.S. Catholic* readers, believe that getting tough on crime, increasing the use of the death penalty, allowing citizens to carry concealed weapons, stricter sentencing, and drastically cutting welfare will solve the problem of violence.

Others, both in and out of our readership, believe that gun control, substance-abuse prevention, stronger family and community ties, improved education, and more jobs would help reduce violence in our society. Eighty-one percent of *U.S. Catholic* readers believe that the government should give more attention to preventing crime than building more prisons.

U.S. Catholic reader Carolyn Torrance of Harrisburg, Pennsylvania believes the solution lies in working for "economic, racial, gender, and class justice and teaching all persons that they have a right and a responsibility to contribute to the work and arts of a community."

Several other readers, including Sister Mary Beatty of Flint, Michigan and Donna Acquaviva and Robert Naylor of Gerrardstown, West Virginia, suggest supporting and participating in peace-and-justice organizations. Reader Rosemary Luckett of Manassas, Virginia stands up to prejudice and bigotry when she encounters it and "adopts conservation and recycling activities to lessen the violence done to the earth."

Overall, readers, like many Americans, believe it is important to vote their consciences and try not to get sucked into accepting the unrealistic either-or solutions politicians offer them (it's either up to individuals to solve the country's problems, or it's up to the government).

But when it comes to systemic, comprehensive strategies, no one is sure of what to do. Because there is no one cause for the violence in America, there is no one solution.

Bad Connections

One culprit that's become the target of a lot of the blame for violence is the media. Ninety percent of *U.S. Catholic* readers believe that television, movies, and music lyrics encourage children to be more violent. When I was a kid, we sat around as a family and played educational games put out by World Book Encyclopedia. Now kids I know spend hours by themselves playing Doom—a high-tech, sci-fi, 007-type of shoot-'em-up game—and other simulated warfare games on their computers. I haven't noticed behavior that could be termed violent among these children, but studies show that violent images desensitize viewers and increase their aggression.

I don't see my own behavior as particularly violent, yet there was a time when, after taking a two-year hiatus from TV, I found all of its kicking, punching, and killing very disturbing. Now 12 years later, I watch the explosive, horrific violence in films like *True Romance* and *Pulp Fiction* and barely flinch. My immune buildup worries me.

Dr. Deborah Prothrow-Stith of Harvard School of Public Health says in her book *Deadly Consequences* (HarperCollins, 1991, written with Michael Weissman) that "in the media world, brutality is portrayed as ordinary and amusing," and its excessive depiction leads to overestimating the amount of violence in the real world. Prothrow-Stith refers to this as the "mean-world syndrome," which "fills a person with feelings of danger, mistrust, intolerance, gloom, and hopelessness."

More and more children are spending their evenings alone playing Mortal Kombat, while seniors are locked up in their homes terrified to step outside. And the "busyness syndrome" among working Americans leaves them with little time for anyone. The more people are disconnected from the community, the more frightened and fearful they become of their neighbors.

Americans are losing their ability to relate to one another—let alone trust one another. In everything we do, we are encouraged to avoid or dispense with human contact—cash stations, computer home shopping, voice mail. At my grocery store, a computer voice tells me the price of an item as it is scanned by the cashier. It announces the total, the amount tendered, and the change due. In an emotionless tone it says, "Thank you" and "Have a nice day," while the cashier hands me my change and receipt. On more than one occasion, unless I initiated conversation, the cashier has not said a word to me. He or she was simply at the service of the computer—providing it with human hands when necessary.

"The more people are disconnected from the community, the more frightened and fearful they become of their neighbors."

It is so much easier to be indifferent and uncaring when we reduce human beings to disembodied voices or, worse yet, abstractions. Violence thrives on abstraction. That was the evil genius of Nazism. Jews were isolated and restricted from any interaction with other citizens. Once people lost sight of who individual Jews were, the collective Jews could become the "they" who stood at the root of all social and economic problems; soon it started to make sense to "dispose" of them.

The Red-baiting of the McCarthy era brought with it, on a smaller scale, a similar kind of abstraction, and this is the kind of abstraction that we see in our current political debates. "Liberal" and "conservative" have become hate-filled, divisive labels, as have "prolife" and "prochoice" and "white male" and "welfare mother."

What You Can Do

This type of cynicism and labeling is one of the leading preventable causes of violence. There are others. Despite the overwhelming nature of the problem and while we are in need of grave social changes, each person can do something to stop the violence in our society. It begins in little ways. It begins with asking ourselves such questions as:

Do I use derogatory, degrading, or offensive terms when describing others? Do I insist on having my own way and force or intimidate others into complying? Do I allow myself to express my anger in irrational ways? Do I use vulgar or abusive language? Do I prejudge people? Do I fear people who are different from me? Am I cynical and suspicious? Do I distance myself from others? Do I hold grudges? Do I allow injustices to be done to me or others? Do I fail to stand up for myself? Do I abuse myself through addiction?

In a commencement address last year, Milwaukee's Archbishop Rembert Weakland shared this advice to students: "Watch the tendency toward excessive self-centeredness. Violence begins when the lives of others have no longer any value but become cheap and expendable. Watch anger. The trick one must learn is to turn valid anger into true passionate concern that is under rational control."

U.S. Catholic reader Cathy Hagen of Blountstown, Florida says that the best way to curb violence in one's personal life is "to strive to act in love and not react in anger. Keep asking yourself, 'What would Jesus do?'" Reader Frank Zolvinski of Gary, Indiana recommends "taking stock of one's life and one's flash points."

These are simple measures, but they can make a difference. After that, we must get to know our neighbors, as Mr. Rogers has told us time and again. Ask any law-enforcement officer and he or she will tell you that community awareness and involvement is essential in curbing crime. Neighborhood-watch programs and community policing are far more successful in preventing crime than hiring more cops or building more prisons. "The gangs don't go away," says Ian Jipp, a Chicago resident who staged a candle-light march in his North Side community after being mugged, "but they'll move on if they know they're being watched."

Communities are beginning to discover that gangs work on the divide-and-conquer principle. The more united a neighborhood is, the less chance gangs have of taking over. "I knew the march was a success," says Jipp, "when I went out to breakfast the next morning and saw neighbors talking who had never talked to one another before. People in this diverse neighborhood learned more about who they could trust and who they could go to for help."

Gang activity, which has been a longtime problem in inner cities, is now infiltrating suburban areas around the country at a rapid pace. Sam Rivera, a seasoned security guard, has witnessed an increase in violence and gang activity in his South Chicago community. "They use Mafia tactics now—threatening to harm the family members of anyone who tries to leave or inform on the gang."

Rivera, who refuses to wear a gun on his job, has a long list of what the average person can do to reduce violence—first on that list is community involvement. "When I was a teenager, I used to get in fights, hang around, and act like a punk," he says, "but then I saw a lot of bad things going down in the neighborhood. Me and my buddies decided to do something about it."

They formed a community group that sponsored dances and neighborhood cleanups and worked with the local priests, politicians, and police to get youth involved in positive projects.

Ultimately, though, for Rivera, the key is "to train your mind to ignore people's hostility." Weakland offers similar advice: "The temptation to answer in kind, especially when it comes to verbal abuse, is strong. But I have to say constantly to myself that verbal abuse is not conquered by more abuse."

U.S. Catholic reader Dotty Nittler of Denver, Colorado simply tries "talking softly to the angry person," and William Cofell of St. Joseph, Minnesota attempts to remain calm and keep communication open, while still respecting people's anger.

U.S. Catholic reader Mary Lennard of Cincinnati, Ohio compares controlling her anger to whitewater rafting: "If you control the raft to go faster or slower than the river, you stay afloat. However, by letting the river carry you along, the water will dash the raft against the rocks."

Teach Your Children Well

"Children need role models—not only national celebrities but local heros."

Naturally the best way to counter violence is to start with our children—teaching kids right from wrong, bringing them to church, getting them involved in worthwhile activities—before they have learned the lessons of violence. Everyone agrees on this point, which makes local and federal cutbacks directed at educational and violence-prevention programs all the more incomprehensible.

Children need alternatives to the apathy and violence of the streets. As Kevin Clarke writes in "How violence is robbing our children" in the November/December issue of *Salt of the Earth* magazine, "It's an idea as old as 'idle hands make the devil's work,' but it's a notion repeated time and time again by people who work with young people: if teens have nothing better to do, they will find ways to get into trouble."

With school violence on the rise (a 38 percent increase in the past five years, according to the National League of Cities), working to keep children out of trouble makes sense, but experts say we must be careful not to blame violence on "kids today." In a 1994 article in *Parade,* Children's Defense Fund director Marian Wright Edelman notes that:

> While we decry rising youth violence, drug use, and antisocial behavior, the plain truth is that we adults have preached moral and family values we have not practiced consistently in our homes, religious congregations, communities, and national life.
>
> It is adults who have financed, produced, and performed in the movies, TV shows, and media that have made violence ubiquitous in our culture. It is adults who manufacture, market, and make available guns to anybody who wants one, including our children. It is adults who have taught that hate, racial and gender intolerance, greed, and selfishness are family values.

Children need role models—not only national celebrities but local heroes. They need to see the adults in their lives taking action against violence. My father became a legend in our neighborhood for breaking up a rumble between a group of tough guys from the town's rival high schools—Addison Trail and Driscoll Catholic. He walked up to the gang of 20 or so kids, saw one kid he knew, and said, "Come on, you don't want to fight. You'll give Catholics a bad name." Enticing them with a barbecue in our backyard, he got half the crowd to follow him, leaving the rest of the group with no one to fight.

It was a small victory, but it had a positive influence on a lot of young people, including his children. Years later, my sister was driving down a city street with two young teenage boys in her car when they were horrified to see on the opposite side of the street another teenage boy being beaten by 12 teenagers on bikes. In a split second she made the decision to turn her car around and drive up into the middle of the fray with lights flashing and horn honking. The kids in the car thought she was nuts. "What are you doing!" they yelled, "This is not our problem. Don't get involved!"

Later, when the attackers scrambled away and she made sure the beaten boy was okay, she explained to her young charges that, in fact, it was their problem: "It would have been wrong for us not to help."

I'm not recommending such dramatic or risky intervention for everyone, but the point is: we must do something, and our children have to witness our concern and action.

In their pastoral letter "Confronting a Culture of Violence," the *U.S. Catholic* bishops conclude:

> Above all, we must come to understand that violence is unacceptable. We must learn the lesson of Pope Paul VI, 'If you want peace, work for justice.' ...Society cannot tolerate an ethic which uses violence to make a point, settle grievances, or get what we want. But the path to a more peaceful future is found in a rediscovery of personal responsibility, respect for human life and human dignity, and a recommitment to social justice.

Hard-earned Hope

Most *U.S. Catholic* readers are involved in or financially support violence-prevention programs. There are numerous programs in parishes and dioceses and communities across the country that deal with violence in our communities. Advocacy groups lobby for gun control, funding for violence-prevention programs, and neighborhood cop-on-the-beat programs. Youth groups create educational and recreational alternatives to gang involvement.

The most effective programs try to get at the root causes of violence by:

- repairing broken communities;
- compensating for the missing male presence in many children's lives;
- dealing with the anger, sense of powerlessness, and

> lack of self-esteem that lead to addiction, physical abuse, or violent crime;
> - providing children with real opportunities so that they will know they have a future;
> - promoting responsible TV viewing and helping parents develop nonviolent skills in their children;
> - assisting children in acquiring empathy, impulse control, and problem solving;
> - teaching that racism, sexism, and abusive behavior are always wrong;
> - counseling the witnesses or victims of abuse and violence so that the cycle of violence will not continue.

These nationwide efforts serve as beacons of hope in what often seems like an unstoppable wave of brutality engulfing our world. And hope is the best antidote of all to violence. Sixty percent of *U.S. Catholic* readers surveyed even go so far as to state that it is possible for us to create a nonviolent world. But it is an arduous, exhausting task, and often it is hard not to lose heart.

That is the time many people resort to prayer—prayer not only for the safety of loved ones and neighbors but for the strength not to be overcome with grief and despair. Many *U.S. Catholic* readers recommend meditating on the Prayer of St. Francis as a way to curb their own violent behavior or renew their sense of hope for an end to the violence in our society. "Make me a channel of your peace"—it is such a simple request. As I write these words, I have just learned that the son of family friends was shot and killed during an attempted carjacking. He was 21, a college senior studying English literature. He volunteered his time to serve as a coach, tutor, and mentor to inner-city, at-risk kids. He was doing all the right things to help stem the tide of violence, but he was swallowed up nevertheless. His parents, I fear, are going to have a tough time trusting people.

But that isn't the end of the story. Violence and death never have the last word—not for Christians, nor any people of God. I'll let this young man, Ethan Kane, have the last word—the last line of one of his poems: "I lie on my back and dream of the day/Enemies place their arms on the ground."

Reader Survey Response

I REACT TO VIOLENT SITUATIONS IN THE FOLLOWING WAYS:
Violence is just one of many reactions. The solution is to teach people the difference between reacting to any situation according to how they feel and responding according to how they believe. Racism and sexism are examples of the belief in "us against them." The solution is to teach what it means to say that every person is made in the image and likeness of God.

John Brennan
Newburgh, NY

Seek help and safety, pray for God's intervention, and attempt to stop violence with words.

Gregory N. Kuhn
Cambridge, MN

With fear, anger, and frustration.

Maureen R. Gervais
Lowell, MA

I feel a sense of helplessness—I just freeze and do nothing. Only later do I imagine how I could have reacted.

Mary K. Okapal
Findlay, OH

I HAVE HELPED DECREASE VIOLENCE BY:
Teaching my students conflict management.

Janice Saggio
Colis, OH

Volunteering my home as a safe home for victims of domestic violence.

Scott Sweeney
Lewistown, MT

Teaching my children values of right and wrong and the law.

Mary Blake
Menominee, MI

Setting an example to family, friends, and acquaintances.

G. B. Weber
Wasilla, AL

I have tried to support legislators and other public officials who have tried to decrease violence in what I believe is a safe and sane manner and who have not gone along with the crowd in support of more prisons and longer or mandatory sentences, which do not do any good except further harden and educate prisoners in more violence.

Cecil R. White
Menlo Park, CA

Not allowing my children to watch violent cartoons. I donate to causes that assist women and children who are victims of violence.

Name withheld
Missoula, MT

Not owning a gun.

Debby Filla
Twinsburg, OH

By my personal example in difficult situations and by my preaching on this subject.

> Father William L. Travers
> Fairfield, CT

Suggesting to my children and grandchildren that a violent reaction usually accomplishes nothing.

> Aggie Kunzman
> Alliance, NE

IF I CATCH A CHILD REACTING VIOLENTLY, I DO THE FOL-LOWING:
Have them think about how the other person felt when they used violence on them and what their alternatives are. Realistically, they are going to feel this way again, but it is never okay to hit or degrade someone else.

> Debby DelCiello
> Janesville, WI

I would try to reason with them and explain the uselessness of violence.

> Name withheld
> Springfield, MA

As an elementary school teacher, I would ask him or her how Jesus would have acted in such a situation and also why he or she is reacting in a violent way. Finally, I would try to teach the child strategies that are useful in resolving conflict peacefully.

> J. Thompson
> Fullerton, CA

Have them take some time out.

> Name withheld
> Cambridge, MN

Help them identify their feelings, their needs, and the resources available to them that will result in a successful conclusion.

> Charlotte Weisenhorn
> Des Moines, IO

THE THINGS MY FAITH HAS TAUGHT ME ABOUT VIOLENCE ARE:
The use of violence is never acceptable except in defense of yourself or another. If everyone accepted this, violence would disappear because the first punch would never be thrown, shot fired, or bomb dropped.

> Peter Andre
> Clearwater, FL

God is bigger than the violence in our world. We may not understand why or the psychological motivations behind violent acts, but God is in control of our lives.

> Name withheld
> Manitowoc, WI

I must become a peacemaker in my sphere of influence. I must work to stop the injustices that may lead to violence in others.

> Candace Wegerson
> Duluth, MN

Not much if you are talking about priests, nuns, and the church. Some of the actions of nuns were nothing less than abominable toward children. I never remember hearing a priest address the subject of violence against wives and children or talk about prejudice.

> Name withheld
> Winfield, WV

That it is wrong to grow angry with our neighbor, wrong to raise a hand against them, wrong to judge them, and wrong to kill them.

> Michael Kleshock
> Cincinnati, OH

Violence does not solve problems. Peacemakers are blessed, they shall be called children of God.

> Sister Marie Anatrella
> Brooklyn, NY

I try to understand the motivation of some people creating violent acts such as gangs, but it is hard because it all seems so senseless.

> Betty Annecharico
> Pacific Palisades, CA

IF VIOLENCE WERE DIMINISHED OR ELIMINATED, MY LIFE WOULD BE DIFFERENT IN THE FOLLOWING WAYS:
I would feel freer to walk through any neighborhood, but most important, I would be freer to teach my students without the distractions caused by the effects of violence in their lives.

> Germaine R. Wieman
> Houston, TX

I wouldn't worry about my daughter working at night. I would feel free to offer help to strangers without wondering if it was a setup. I would waste less energy on worrying.

> Name withheld
> Neenah, WI

There would be less stress; it would be easier to raise a family; and life would be more enjoyable.

Ernie Gawili
El Paso, TX

I would still have my mother who was killed violently.

Charlene Sanders
Hereford, TX

I would be less uneasy in certain locations and in certain situations.

Donald L. Perry
Buffalo, NY

I'd pray differently in Mass, and I'd see more happy faces around me.

Sister Helen Borszich
St. Francis Mission, SD

I feel bad for the little ones who have to be so strictly cautioned not to talk to strangers. We walk six blocks to church every day and usually meet children who are on their way to school in the opposite direction. These children rarely meet our eyes or say good morning. I have to think it's because of the warnings they have received.

Name withheld
Appleton, WI

Since I work as a news reporter and producer, I'd probably be unemployed.

Michael Voris
Farmington Hills, MI

Children and women would suffer less abuse. The general public would be more trusting.

Name withheld
Bettendorf, IO

The majority of my time would be spent on the teaching process versus conflict resolution.

Ken Mohr
St. Louis, MO

My children would grow up in a better world. I worry every day that they could be victims of violence.

Deborah Mittelman
Peachtree City, GA

I'd be a more outgoing person.

Albin Kuzminski
Clinton, MI

THE BEST WAY TO CURB VIOLENCE IN ONE's PERSONAL LIFE IS:
To be accountable for my own behavior, limit violent TV programs and movies, encourage children to participate in sports and vent their energies, and learn patience.

> Margaret Ransone
> New Orleans, LA

Live the gospels.

> A. Keller
> Evergreen Park, IL

Be smart, be cautious and aware, live peacefully, and pray for peace and for our brothers and sisters.

> Karen Doughan
> Green Bay, WI

Limiting exposure to excessive media coverage of violence.

> Steve Koenig
> Loveland, CO

Accept and learn that violence solves nothing.

> Sandy Bahe
> Elburn, IL

Discuss violence with family and friends, especially children and how it permeates our lives. Don't allow put-downs, severe criticism, offensive jokes, or mean-spirited behavior in the family.

> Connie Meixner
> Oakdale, MN

Take a look at the life of Saint Francis of Assisi.

> Bruce Snowden
> Bronx, NY

...AND IN SOCIETY IS:
Gun control. A comprehensive look at what to do about urban poverty. A consensus that terrorism and antigovernment extremism are not noble. I have America Online and people in there praise Tim McVeigh, Randy Weaver, and David Koresh—can you believe it?

> Thomas Farrell
> Santa Clara, CA

Community-based policing and strong neighborhood-watch programs.

> Dave Heney
> Arcadia, CA

Stronger families and belief in the teachings of Christ. A more healthy respect for other people's lives and their value to each of us.

Richard F. Schieler
York, PA

To improve the lives of the poor and ensure good schools for their children and to see that social services are not eliminated, depriving those in need.

Mrs. George Beck
Glenview, IL

Do something to eliminate the causes of enmity and violence. Promote justice and strive to overcome all dehumanizing factors existing in our culture. It is an impossible task, but still a valid objective to work for.

Father Donald Lund, C.S.V.
Bourbonnais, IL

Less sex and violence on TV. More family planning at the teenage level so babies brought into this world are wanted and brought into a great family atmosphere.

Name withheld
Janesville, WI

A PERSON WHO HAS DONE A LOT TO MAKE THE WORLD LESS VIOLENT IS:

Martin Luther King, Jr.	Mother Teresa
Mahatma Gandhi	Dorothy Day
Nelson Mandela	Thomas Merton
Jimmy Carter	Cardinal Joseph Bernardin
Pope John Paul II	Father Daniel Berrigan
Billy Graham	Oscar Romero
Jesus	Bishop Thomas Gumbleton

GENERAL COMMENTS:
Children learn and imitate what they see. Fractured families and neighborhoods invariably produce fractured people. Future violent people can be derailed from that path in early youth only by being truly loved by gentle people.

Teresa Matthews
Harrison, AR

The question on the military concerns me. I considered my 25-year military career a commitment to try to make the world a safer place. The most peaceful people I know are military; we're the ones that must face the violence our elected representatives choose.

Mark C. Miller
Indianapolis, IN

The prison system has diluted its efficiency since it has attempted to become a correctional institution. Prisons can only be penal facilities. Meting out penalties, as prescribed by law, is what they've always done best.

Sam Munafo
Philadelphia, PA

Give people the tools to choose alternatives to violence and this world will be a better place for all. Put those who sell guns to kids out of business. Try to educate adults and children about the abuse of drugs and alcohol.

George F. Reczek
Roundup, MT

Having seen the effects of violence in my own life, I really feel strongly that families are too busy to teach proper morals and ethics, and kids have too much free time.

Kathy Carleton
Olmsted, OH

Violence is one of the most disturbing aspects of our society. It destroys trust, which is the foundation of all healthy relationships and communities. We must all strive to eliminate this disease which afflicts our country and world.

Michele Jack
Pasadena, CA

Traditional Values Aren't All Good

"Violence is habit forming, and America is addicted," says Julian Bond, the narrator in the 1995 HBO special "Violence: An American Tradition." America has carried violent traditions through the centuries. What we now call the cycle of violence started when Columbus landed on America's shores and continued through the violent subjugation of Native Americans, slavery, the guntoting psychopathic outlaws of the Wild West, the Civil War, gangsters, the Ku Klux Klan, lynchings, race riots, drug dealers, gangbangers, grisly tabloid journalism, an all-time high in domestic abuse. "Violence is learned," says Bond. "It can be unlearned. But that can't happen until America deals with the roots of its violence."

The Catholic Church has a violent past that must be dealt with as well, but, as the *U.S. Catholic* bishops point out in their pastoral letter "Confronting a Culture of Violence," Catholic tradition offers much wisdom in finding ways to end the cycle of violence:

What we believe, where we are, and how we live out our faith can make a great difference in the struggle against violence. We see the loss of lives. We serve the victims. We feel the fear. We must confront this growing culture of violence with a commitment to life, a vision of hope, and a call to action. Our assets in

this challenge include:
- the example and teaching of Christ;
- the biblical values of respect for life, peace, justice, and community;
- our teaching on human life and human dignity, on right and wrong, on family and work, on justice and peace, on rights and responsibilities;
- our tradition of prayer, sacraments, and contemplation which can lead to a disarmament of the heart;
- a commitment to marriage and family life, to support responsible parenthood and to help parents teach their children the values to live full lives;
- a presence in most neighborhoods—our parishes and schools, hospitals and social services are sources of life and hope in places of violence and fear;
- an ethical framework which calls us to practice and promote virtue, responsibility, forgiveness, generosity, concern for others, social justice, and economic fairness;
- a capacity for advocacy that cuts across the false choices in national debatejails or jobs, personal or social responsibility, better values or better policies;
- a consistent ethic of life which remains the surest foundation of our life together.

I express myself more violently than I used to.
7%   agree
88% disagree
5%   other

I would call the police if I witnessed domestic abuse or criminal violence in my neighborhood.
98% agree
1%   disagree
1%   other

I have moved because of violence where I lived.
12% agree
84% disagree
4%   other

Men are more likely than women to react violently in a stressful or confrontational situation.
79% agree
15% disagree
6%   other

Sexist and racist jokes constitute violence.
60% agree

31%   disagree
9%   other

I consider swearing at someone to be a violent act.
72%   agree
22%   disagree
6%   other

Television, movies, and music lyrics encourage children to be more violent.
90%   agree
6%   disagree
4%   other

I believe the most serious source of violent behavior is:
17%   availability of weapons.
12%   substance abuse.
3%   racism and other forms of intolerance.
30%   fragmented families and lack of role models.
1%   government budget cuts affecting the poor.
1%   insufficient law enforcement.
5%   boredom from poverty and lack of opportunities.
20%   loss of values and community support.
2%   child abuse.
9%   other

To protect myself from violence, I:
48%   don't walk alone at night.
3%   have taken a self-defense class.
17%   installed tighter security in my home.
4%   carry pepper spray or mace.
1%   carry a knife or other weapon.
3%   keep a gun in my home.
24%   other

Catholics should practice Jesus' command to turn the other cheek, even when their personal safety is jeopardized.
24%   agree
66%   disagree
10%   other

I am often afraid of strangers.
27%   agree
68%   disagree
5%   other

During any given week, I fear for my safety at least once.
17%   agree
80%   disagree
3%   other

I often pray that my loved ones will not become victims of violence.

61% agree
32% disagree
7% other

I don't think I could forgive someone who committed a violent act against me or a loved one.

27% agree
56% disagree
17% other

Our government should give more attention to preventing crime than building more prisons.

81% agree
11% disagree
8% other

Prisons make people more violent, not less.

66% agree
19% disagree
15% other

I think measures such as mandatory sentencing requirements and "three strikes" policies will deter people from committing crimes.

36% agree
54% disagree
10% other

Capital punishment is a justifiable form of violence.

24% agree
69% disagree
7% other

Our country's tradition of using military force to solve international problems has sent a message to Americans that violence is an acceptable response to confrontation.

41% agree
52% disagree
7% other

Violence has gone too far in our society for grassroots organizations to really help.

10% agree
86% disagree
4% other

It is possible for us to create a nonviolent world.

60% agree
23% disagree
17% other

American Opinion
(A Special Report)[2]

A Quarterly Survey of Politics, Economics and Values;
God, Motherhood and Apple Pie: Most Americans Believe
That the Nation's Values Are a Disgrace; But That Doesn't
Mean They Are Giving Up Hope

All around them, Americans see a decline in values and morals. They deplore the diminished authority of the four great repositories of their values—religion, the law, schools and families. Yet despite their pessimism, Americans passionately believe in the importance of values, and they have given them a lot of thought. Of the four American Opinion poll topics this year—time, health, money and values—this one, concerning religion, the family and the moral issues confronted in daily life, elicited the most heartfelt comments.

"I have a gut feeling that we all wish we could just get along," says Dan Burgess, a 53-year-old spare-parts salesman in Boerne, Texas. "The Bible teaches love, and I think it's there, and it just needs to be brought out."

Pamela Sue Howard, an Oconto Falls, WI, mother of three, at one time worked 89 hours a week after her husband had lost his job. "Believe me, I know what struggle is," she says. Nevertheless, her sense of values remained strong. "We have to do something, not just sit and whine," she says. "You have to set an example, make a difference. It starts at home and spreads."

David Ivie of Dallas believes that "most Americans don't realize how good they have it here."

A uniquely American hopefulness underlies many of their comments, but the majority of the poll's 2,003 respondents believe that America's morals are shaky and getting shakier. Almost two-thirds of them, or 61%, said the state of morals in America today is "pretty bad and getting worse." Contrast that to 1964, just a little more than two decades ago, when only 41% of people thought morals were bad and getting worse. In 1964, 16% thought morals were pretty good and getting better; today, only 7% express that kind of optimism.

Morals and values are the underpinnings of people's choices—the reason they get jobs, raise children, vote and don't rob banks. They are set down in the scriptures and in documents like the Constitution, but they also evolve as society changes. Despite the growing complexity and diversity of the nation, Americans still share two central values: individualism and freedom. But conflict

[2]Article by Ellen Graham and Cynthia Crossen, staff reporters, from *The Wall Street Journal* D 13 '96. Reprinted by permission of *The Wall Street Journal*, © 1996 Dow Jones & Company, Inc. All Rights Reserved Worldwide.

arises when those values are applied to difficult social problems, such as immigration, the death penalty or divorce.

Most of the talk about values today concerns "family values," a term that is embraced by politicians of every stripe. To Republican Robert Dole, family values meant cutting taxes so both parents wouldn't have to work. To Democrat Bill Clinton, it meant signing into law the Family and Medical Leave Act, which ensured job security for working parents, among other things. "Clinton has been very effective in blocking Dole from making any foothold in the family-values issue," a Republican pollster said during the presidential campaign, reflecting the growing use of the term strategically rather than idealistically.

Yet the politicians are right that Americans are deeply concerned about the state of the family. When the polling firms of Peter D. Hart and Robert Teeter asked which area of American society most needed improvement in the next few years, the No. 1 choice—of 27%—was strengthening the family. The sometimes cynical political rhetoric taps into a yearning in people for something that's larger than themselves.

"That kind of rhetoric appeals to people who worry that without some kind of course correction, we'll lose the bonds that hold people together and make life tolerable," says Mark Hanson, associate for religious ethics at the Hastings Center in Briarcliff, NY.

> "The term 'family values' is often used as shorthand for the simplicity, homogeneity and unity of the 1950s and before."

The term "family values" is often used as shorthand for the simplicity, homogeneity and unity of the 1950s and before. Many Americans hark back to the nostalgic portrayals of the traditional family that were burned into the nation's collective memory through that era's television sitcoms and magazines like the *Saturday Evening Post* and *Life*. More than 80% of the respondents to this poll said the nation's morals and values in the 1950s were higher than those of today. Judith Stacey, a professor of sociology at the University of California at Davis, observes that it's no coincidence that the 1950s were also the time when America was at the height of its global political and economic power.

"So in the popular unconscious you get this mixture of images that go together—a strong United States, economic growth and a particular *Father Knows Best* family system that actually was not as widespread as people think," she says.

Perhaps most of all, parents today worry about how the decay in values is affecting their children—and how they can protect them from drugs, crime and school violence. One man confesses that his 16-year-old daughter "has hardly ever played outside—and we don't live in a bad neighborhood." A mother of four recalls how, after her daughter was pushed down a stairwell at school by gang members, she waited outside the principal's office for a week to discuss the incident with him—and then felt that by reporting it, she had endangered her daughter further. "You shouldn't have to live with that for your child to get an education," she says.

For all their anxiety, however, most parents report with relief that their own children have weathered unsavory influences to become solid citizens—and also friends. "I know you must be a parent first, but they are also my best friends," says an Arizona mother of her grown children.

The poll shows once again how emphatic Americans are about the importance of religion in their lives. Almost a third of the respondents said that beyond having a good family, a strong religious faith was the best indicator of personal success. When it comes to issues of right and wrong, 37% of respondents said they should be decided based on God's law. Only 25% thought they should be decided by society as a whole; 33% said they should be a matter of personal conscience.

Today it is the media, and television specifically, that many parents believe is thwarting them from passing their own values along to their children. Indeed, 46% of the respondents strongly or somewhat favor imposing more government controls on television, the movies and on-line services. "I wish I could unplug all the TVs in the world—really I do," says Ms. Howard of Wisconsin. "Except maybe the Weather Channel."

The Rev. Ted Hoskins is a 63-year-old "boat minister" who ferries among isolated island fishing communities off the coast of Maine. Until a couple of years ago, he had spent his entire pastoral life in an affluent Connecticut suburb. At bottom, Mr. Hoskins says, the people in these two disparate communities are more alike than different. In both, the paramount concerns are holding families together and making a living. Whether plying choppy waters in lobster boats or jammed onto crowded commuter trains, he says, "we all just want life to work."

Which of the following do you think would make the biggest difference if Americans made an effort to do better in that area?

Strengthening the family	27%
Independence and personal responsibility	19%
Religion and faith	16%
Service to others, sharing and helping others	11%
Traditional values	9%
Work ethic	6%

What is your approach to raising children?

Pretty much the same as my parents	57%
Fairly different from my parents	40%

Are you raising your kids just like mom and dad raised you? And even if you don't have kids now, would you follow in your parents' footsteps?

Americans aren't of one mind when it comes to the knotty issue of parenting—and their answers to these questions clearly reflect that. While 57% say their approach to parenting is or

would be "pretty much the same" as their folks', 40% say their
style is or would be "fairly different."

For several respondents, discipline is the issue that determines
whether they are carrying on their parents' traditions or parting
company with them. "Discipline in the home is where it all
starts," says Linda Sue Johnson, 49 years old, an assembly-line
worker from Russellville, KY, who says she is raising her children
just as strictly as she was raised. "You have to teach them right
from wrong."

But John Liss, a 41-year-old truck driver and father from
Glendale Heights, IL, says he doesn't believe that sparing the rod
necessarily spoils the child. When he was growing up, "punishment came in the form of hitting or spanking with a belt," he
says, "and we don't believe in those methods. Growing up, I just
didn't see the point in it."

Ken Scannell, 65, a salesman from El Paso, TX, says he raised
his three sons with as firm a hand as his father used. "If they get
away with too much, they end up being a menace to society," he
says.

Joy Merrell, a 59-year-old part-time worker in Sparta, TN, has
had the chance to experiment with two generations. As a teenager, Ms. Merrell wasn't permitted to wear shorts or date until she
was 16. She decided to allow her four children to date when they
were 15, to do few chores around the house and to get lots of
spending money from her.

Ms. Merrell thinks that was a mistake. "I don't think they used
good judgment in who they dated and what they did when they
dated," she says. "they got careless about taking care of their
possessions because they figured mom would just replace them."

After her 38-year-old son's marriage broke up, Ms. Merrell
became surrogate mother to four grandchildren, who now live
with her. She says she is much stricter with the grandchildren
than she was with her children. They do chores, don't get as
much spending money and have to wait an extra year before
being allowed to drive.

"I don't think they are more responsible than my children
were," Ms. Merrell says. "But I think they try harder in school
and have greater expectations for themselves."

—Timothy L. O'Brien—

**What kind of impact do you feel these social movements
have had on today's values?**

	+ IMPACT	− IMPACT
Civil-rights movement	84%	12%
Environmental movement	81%	13%
AIDS-awareness movement	80%	12%
Women's movement	76%	19%
Family-values movement	69%	18%
Right-to-life movement	50%	41%

The social movements that have turned America into an ideological battlefield for the past 30 years have actually made this country a better place to live, said the majority of this poll's respondents.

By margins of about four to one, Americans say the civil-rights movement, the environmental movement, the AIDS-awareness movement, the religious or family-values movement and the women's movement all have had positive effects on society.

"They have all raised consciousness levels," says Rick Balestreri, 44 years old, an executive at a Sacramento, CA, home-building company. When people are "down" about the state of the country, movements that promise "change" look good, says John Hartman, a professor of sociology at Columbia University. "Even just the word 'movement' conjures up the idea of some change."

Many of the causes included in the survey strove to change people's values and behavior rather than to address the kinds of bread-and-butter issues people care about most today, Dr. Hartman says. Movements like organized labor, involving pocketbook issues of wages, job security and health care, might have provoked stronger responses on both sides, he says, but the flagging labor movement "hasn't been on the radar screen."

Only their reactions to the antiabortion movement revealed deep divisions, with an almost equal number responding positively and negatively.

The 10-year-old effort to increase awareness about AIDS received more approval than the "religion and family-values movement," despite the fact that criticizing "family values" is like disparaging motherhood. Even among people who identify themselves as very religious, 78% said the AIDS-awareness movement has had a positive impact on society.

The most highly praised movement was civil rights, which has now become more of a cultural icon than a topic of political debate. About 84% of people said the movement has had a positive impact, while only 12% thought it had changed things for the worse. An overwhelming 84% of whites said its impact had been positive.

Morris Harper, a 55-year-old Houston real-estate investor who was a high-school student in Little Rock, AR, during the city's vicious desegregation battle, blames the movement for "spreading anger in the populace to other groups and creating a white backlash." Mr. Balestreri, who voted for the California referendum rolling back affirmative action, calls the movement's impact extremely positive. "All Americans should pull together as a team," he says. Both men and women said the impact of the women's movement had been positive—79% of men approved, compared with 76% of women.

—David Kirkpatrick—

"Even among people who identify themselves as very religious, 78% said the AIDS-awareness movement has had a positive impact on society."

Rate your own morals and values on a scale from one to 100 (100 being perfect).

96 to 100	21%
90 to 95	29%
80 to 89	26%
75 to 79	11%
0 to 74	11%

Saints or sinners? If you can believe them, most Americans are closer to canonization than damnation, even though they say that in general, Americans' morals are poor and getting worse. When asked to rate their own morals and values on a scale of one to 100, with one being totally depraved and 100 being pure as the driven snow, exactly half gave themselves a score of 90 or above. Only 11% rated their morals below 75.

Men were less likely than women to rate themselves high in morals; 57% of women, but only 43% of men, gave themselves a 90 or above. A sense of morality also seems to grow with age. Among the respondents who are 18 to 34 years old, 41% rated themselves above 90. Among those 65 and over, 63% rated themselves that high.

While it isn't surprising that most people believe they are above the halfway point, the clustering at the top was even more dramatic than pollster Peter Hart had expected. Part of the reason may simply be the way the question was posed. "Given the opportunity to make a quick evaluation, you remember all your best points," says Mr. Hart. "But if you had them sit down and write an essay on why they gave themselves that rating, or to tell the ways they don't live up to their rating, my guess is the number would come down significantly." Edward Petry, a retired general building contractor in Mendota, CA, rated himself a 95. "We had morals in my family when I was a kid," says Mr. Petry, 67 years old. "My parents were strict."

Dan Burgess, a spare-parts salesman in Boerne, Texas, gave himself a perfect score—100. Yet he, too, believes the country's morals are in terrible shape. "The moral of the world today is money," he says. "I really believe that's wrong."

Mr. Burgess, 53, says he often thinks about morality and religion. "I think age has a lot to do with it," he says. "You see a little bit better than you did when you were 20. You slow down, look at the full picture of life instead of what's happening today and what's going to happen tomorrow."

—Cynthia Crossen—

Most serious problems in our society stem from:

A decline in moral values	51%
Financial pressures on families	37%

By a healthy margin, Americans believe the roots of crime and other social ills stem from a fundamental decline in moral values rather than economic pressures on families.

Many seem to regard a claim of hardship as a poor excuse, despite the long-held belief that there's a connection between poverty and crime. Only 37% blamed society's problems on economic factors, versus the 51% who cited a breakdown in moral standards. To 11%, both factors are equal.

The moral-decline explanation gains favor as people age. Of those 18 to 34 years old, only 45% blamed morals, whereas 66% of the 65-and-over group did.

The adversity argument cuts no ice with Mary Beth Wilson of Tempe, AZ. She grew up one of four children of a single mother who worked as a seamstress and never made more than $40 a week. Now 56 and the owner, with her husband, of an investment and real-estate business, she says she and her siblings kept to the straight and narrow despite their poverty. The difference between then and now? "If I had to pick one word, it's respect," she says. "Growing up, I couldn't do anything really bad, out of sheer respect for mom and all my elders—teachers, clergy, politicians, doctors. They were revered." Television has helped undermine such respect in today's youngsters, she says. "Bart Simpson is a smart-alecky, disrespectful little brat."

Christine Walters, who lives in a suburb of Birmingham, AL, also grew up poor, but she sees the issue differently. In her view, the seeds of social problems are sown when economic woes distract parents unduly, and when mothers have to take jobs outside the home, "leaving the kids alone to raise themselves."

In her job as a waitress, she has a lot of contact with teenage co-workers. "Their main complaint is that no one is listening," she says. "Their parents are too busy just trying to survive." She herself raised four kids alone, without child support. But her children, now 19 to 24, came through unscathed; one is even studying for the ministry. She regrets that she couldn't provide more materially. "I would have liked to give them a roof that didn't leak, a car that would actually get them to school," she laughs. Instead, she says she gave them a lot of attention—what she terms "something to hold onto that wouldn't slip away."

—Ellen Graham—

For each of the following decades, were the nation's morals and values higher or lower than now?

	MUCH HIGHER	SOMEWHAT HIGHER	SOMEWHAT LOWER	MUCH LOWER
The 1950s	59%	23%	4%	3%
The 1960s	20%	50%	14%	5%
The 1970s	8%	48%	27%	4%
The 1980s	6%	41%	23%	11%

Ah, for the good old days: the 1950s. Families—working dad, nonworking mom and a couple of kids—were strong. Americans went to church. They believed in the power and authority of their country. And their children had the chance to get, at no cost, a good public education.

Many Americans wish they could turn their clocks back to those days. More than 80% of the respondents to this poll said the nation's morals and values were much or somewhat higher in the 1950s than now.

Belief in the 1950s as a golden decade was consistent among most demographic groups, although people 65 and over were the most likely to hold that opinion. Yet there was less nostalgia for the '50s among blacks than whites; among white respondents, 86% said the morals in the 1950s were higher than today; among blacks, only 66% agreed.

Judith Stacey, professor of sociology at the University of California at Davis, suggests that as fondly as many remember that decade, it couldn't have been as perfect in reality. If America's values were so universally accepted and respected, why did the baby boom reject so many of them? "Because for an awful lot of people," says Dr. Stacey, the traditional family "was stultifying and phony."

Yet during the '50s, '60s and even into the '70s, Americans shared a belief that they were making progress in solving the country's problems. Today, many people say they feel helpless in the face of a high crime rate, the growing inequality between rich and poor and a diminishing sense of financial security—regardless of how hard they work.

Saladine Huntley, a Chicago nursing student and the 35-year-old father of four, yearns not for the 1950s, but for the idealism of the 1960s. "The loyalties today are more to self and family," he says. "Back in the 1960s, the loyalty was to a cause." Still, Mr. Huntley is cheered by what he sees around him in his own community, where, he says, long-time residents "rally to help each other." Scott Wernimont, a 26-year-old contractor-relations representative in Carroll, IO, is also cautiously optimistic. "There's a resurgence in the '90s to go back to ethics, traditions and a moral code,' he says. "When you start thinking of having kids, you start thinking more about how you want to live your life and what you want to pass on to your children."

—Cynthia Crossen—

If you were hiring a new employee, which would you consider a strong reason for rejecting someone's application?

Past record of drug abuse	49%
Past record of alcoholism	18%
Having a homosexual relationship	11%
Having committed adultery	10%
Arrest in protest rally	3%

Live and let live. For all their dismay about slipping moral standards, Americans are still tolerant of those who stray from conventional behavior.

Or so it would seem from their responses to a hypothetical question, in which they were asked whether any of the following would be a strong reason for rejecting a job applicant: past drug use or alcoholism, adultery, a homosexual relationship or an arrest for participation in a protest rally.

With the exception of drug use—which disqualified a job candidate in the eyes of 49% of the respondents—most of these behaviors drew a yawn. Fully 23% replied that none of these considerations would be strong grounds for rejection.

The replies were fairly consistent across all demographic groups—even among a subgroup that tends to be most conservative on social issues: evangelical Christians. On only one issue —homosexuality—did fundamentalists' responses differ sharply, with 20% saying they would turn down such an applicant.

"People are relatively nonjudgmental and pretty tolerant in America," says Alan Wolfe, a professor at Boston University and author of a forthcoming study on middle-class morality. "They believe in virtue and morality, but they don't believe in shouting it from the rooftops." They also, it seems, believe in second chances. "The past is the past," says Christine Walters, a waitress in Springville, AL.

For many, forgiveness doesn't extend to drug users, however. So incensed are Americans about the nation's drug culture that some are willing to accept modest limits on their own freedoms to help stop drug abuse. Pamela Sue Howard of Oconto Falls, WI, was asked to take a drug test recently when applying for a job. She says it didn't bother her, comparing it to the precaution of locking her car. Besides, she says, "I don't want to be working with someone pushing drugs."

—Ellen Graham—

"So incensed are Americans about the nation's drug culture that some are willing to accept modest limits on their own freedoms to help stop drug abuse."

How do you feel about each of the following proposed changes?

	FAVOR	OPPOSE
Increase programs for the poor, elderly	74%	23%
Reduce the number of immigrants	72%	25%
Impose the death penalty more	71%	24%
Tighter handgun control	69%	27%
Stricter divorce laws	46%	45%
More media controls	46%	51%

We're out of control. That's a fear shared by many Americans today. Feeling vulnerable socially and economically, a majority of respondents to this poll said they favor stricter limits on immigration and handguns and greater use of the death penalty. By a smaller margin, many Americans also favor more restrictions on the media and divorce.

"They want rules, though they don't want any authoritarianism that will interfere with their freedoms. They want soft rules," says Alan Wolfe, author of a forthcoming study on middle-class morality.

Here is how the poll's respondents felt about some of the difficult moral issues facing Americans today:

Immigration: Almost three-quarters, or 72%, believe the number of immigrants allowed into the U.S. should be reduced. Compare that with 1965, when only 33% of the respondents to a Gallup poll said immigration should be curbed. One worry now is that immigrants will overwhelm the country's social-service programs. "We have some very poor people who are citizens," says Mae Irene Shanahan, 77 years old, of Powell, WY, "and we are obliged to get them on their feet. We can't take care of the world."

Death penalty: While 71% of respondents think the death penalty should be imposed more often, the figure is highest among those who say they are fairly religious: 79% of them favor it, compared with 63% of those who say religion is not very important and 70% of those who consider themselves very religious. "Being nice about things like this doesn't get results," says Charlene Adams, a 57-year-old Catholic mother of five from Marysville, CA.

Divorce: Most Americans say the breakdown of the family is at the crux of America's values crisis, but they're split on whether laws should make it more difficult to divorce. While 46% say divorce laws should be tightened, 45% say no. "Once you decide you don't like each other, all the laws in the world can't keep you together," says Pete Marjon, 47, a divorced machine operator in Phoenix.

Media: Men and women split on the issue of whether the government should exercise tighter controls on television, movies and on-line services. More than half of women, or 53%, would like to see more restrictions, compared with only 38% of men.

Guns: A resounding 69% either strongly or somewhat favor making it more difficult to own handguns or assault weapons. A huge percentage of women, 79%, want these gun controls, compared with 58% of men. "I don't like going to a shopping mall at night. I think about kids carrying guns," says Debbie Lingl, a homemaker and mother of two.

Spending on poor and elderly: Almost three-quarters, or 74%, believe government spending on programs for the poor and elderly should be increased. Of those with incomes under $20,000, 85% favor an increase, while only 66% of those with incomes of more than $50,000 do.

—Andrea Petersen—

Can We Break the Pattern of the Criminal Lifestyle?[3]

Crime control policies are failing, despite optimistic statistics to the contrary. Crime control refers to the use of imprisonment as punishment for unlawful acts committed and a deterrent to their commission, as well as rehabilitation programs that include, but aren't limited to, education, vocational training, and treatment for alcoholism and drug addiction. Policymakers who pander for votes by alleging that getting tough on criminals will curb street crime are wrong. These threats have little effect on behavior-hardened street criminals.

During my years of research among "hard-core" adolescent delinquents and persistent adult criminals who cycle between sidewalks and cellhouses, we hung out together on street corners and in alleys and bars, missions and flophouses, jail and prison cells, and places where drugs were sold. This research, funded by the U.S. Census Bureau and Harry Frank Guggenheim Foundation, revealed that these criminals do not want to find legal jobs and stop using alcohol and drugs. Moreover, they do not interpret their lifestyles as lawful citizes do.

Persistent criminals see an unlawful lifestyle as relatively care-free and morally acceptable. Living a lawful lifestyle, however, would force them to relinquish the freedom of social irresponsibility. These criminals have little interest in society's rules and have learned to use the criminal justice system to their advantage. To them, prisons are sanctuaries that deliver social, medical, and recreational services. A system of effective crime control measures can be developed, but to do that, policymakers must learn more about the lives of street criminals.

The lives of persistent criminals have a trajectory or path which has its inception in early life. I call this trajectory a "street lifecycle." It has four sequential stages, each one linked to and establishing the conditions for the next.

My subjects' childhood homes were angry places. They were born into families where parents were alcoholics, most smoked marijuana, and many used heroin or cocaine. Fathers were criminals, often drug dealers. Mothers (and sometimes grandmothers) were involved directly in criminal activities with their husbands, brothers, sons, and nephews. Sometimes, these women were passive observers, but they always were active consumers of the money and goods brought about by crime.

Parents usually did not get along well with each other, especially when they were drunk. Women were beaten by their

---

[3]Article by Mark S. Fleisher, author of *Beggars and Thieves: Lives of Urban Street Criminals* and associate professor of criminal justice sciences at Illinois State University, from *USA Today* 125:30–3 My '97. Copyright © 1997 *USA Today*. Reprinted with permission.

mates' fists or slashed with a knife; men were cut by knives wielded by women. Fathers and mothers assaulted their sons and daughters. Children were whipped with belts, punched with fists, slapped with hands, and kicked. I have witnessed mothers striking their sons and daughters repeatedly with heavy leather straps, then looking at me and saying, "It's for their own good."

In these homes, no one read to their children; no one cautioned them about the dangers of alcohol and drugs; no one said school was important; no one encouraged youngsters to read; no one bought school supplies; no one encouraged kids to write stories; no one helped children with arithmetic; and no one cared.

In their teenage years, these youngsters abandoned home life for street life. At first, they stayed away for a few days or a week, but as they adjusted and became part of the street's action, stints away from home grew longer and longer, until these youths never returned. They wandered city neighborhoods and banded together into loosely knit social groups (gangs), which afforded them some modicum of safety and protection, but at the same time exposed youngsters to drugs and violence and cut them off from social relationships to children and adults who might have helped them. By junior high school, nearly all were chronic truants and drug addicts, indulging freely in alcohol, marijuana, crack cocaine, heroin, or a combination of these drugs. They apprenticed at burglary, car theft, drug selling, pimping, and armed robbery—occupations that soon landed them in juvenile detention and then, as adults, in prison.

"State and Federal spending on inmate medical care exceeds $3,000 per inmate annually."

For adolescent and young adult criminals, a stint in prison often proved an acceptable alternative, offering them goods and services unavailable on the street. Prison is stable and provides plenty of food, a clean bed, recreation, and access to medical and dental services. State and Federal spending on inmate medical care exceeds $3,000 per inmate annually. Research shows that most inmates leave prison healthier than when they entered. Social life in prison is good, too. Some inmates continue criminal activity, such as drug dealing, while others just "lay up" and enjoy the safety and pleasures of not hustling for money and food every day.

Eventually, the easy life inside ends. Nearly all prison inmates are released and go back to home neighborhoods. As criminals age, they return to find that social ties have been broken from years in prison. Going home gets harder. Some former street companions still are behind bars, others were killed on the street, and some have died from drug overdoses, developed AIDS, or become ill from chronic alcoholism and/or hepatitis. They must compete against younger, more active criminals for the street's limited bounty. The harshness of street life never ends. Many aging hustlers prefer to return to the secure world of prison; others panhandle and commit petty crimes to support chronic alcohol and drug habits. These men and women sleep on cardboard boxes on concrete sidewalks, in empty cars and abandoned buildings, and under bushes in city parks.

Decades of research in social science have shown that intimate face-to-face interactions in early life are crucial in the molding of an individual's basic personality, the formation and perpetuation of attitudes toward the world, and the determination of socially acceptable behavior and personal self-control. Adolescent behavior is the single most important indicator of bad parenting. A 15-year-old runaway girl in Kansas City, MO, understood the link between parenting and street crime: "My mother's six kids are drug addicts, alcoholics, runaways, violent, and gangbangers. What kind of mother do you think she was?"

Where were the parents of the teenage boys and girls I watched prostitute themselves to earn cash for drugs and alcohol? At two in the morning, I was the only adult among adolescent gang members. No parents kept these children out of harm's way.

There are mothers and fathers who are awful parents, and no amount of scapegoating, expensive family therapy, and excuses can compensate for the damage inflicted on kids by years of parental abuse and neglect. To transform violent and drug-addicted, neglectful parents into loving and kind caretakers would be as expensive and risky as rehabilitating the deviant youngsters reared by them. There are no documented cases of family therapy programs that can transform hundreds, if not thousands, of brutal parents into kinder and gentler mothers and fathers. Would you allow your children to be cared for by a former cocaine addict and convicted felon? How much tax revenue are you willing to invest in high-risk programs for people with proven histories of violence toward kids? What will be the return on your investment?

There is only one sure way to protect battered and neglected youngsters. They must be placed permanently in small residential homes funded and regulated by the Federal government. Local foster care programs may be well-meaning, but they often are poorly funded, suffer from inadequate administrative oversight, and do not provide stable, long-term homes for children. A system of Federal residential homes can be effective with adequate funding, well-trained adults, and high-quality care.

Kids deserve safe and stable places to live. Such residential homes must receive line-item Federal funding, with firm financial support from states. These facilities never must become pawns in political battles. Church groups, volunteer organizations, schools, and other community agencies can assist by identifying at-risk youngsters of all ages and developing community facilities for them. Decreasing the escalation of socially destructive behavior means ending child abuse. Protecting children is not just another remedy for breaking the street lifecycle—it is the *only* remedy. Everything else is very expensive damage control.

The cost of these residential homes is paltry compared to the annual price of crime and victimization. One study estimates health care costs associated with violent acts over a three-year period were approximately $179,000,000,000. America must be intolerant of interpersonal violence by keeping offenders in prisons for very long terms. Discontinuing "second chances" and keeping violent inmates imprisoned will reduce the number of victims and lower the cost of street crime.

Let us stop apologizing for imprisoning violent criminals. Research shows it is cheaper to house persistent criminals in prison than it is to release them every few years, then to arrest and convict them again and to pay for the damage they left behind. What is more, the nation can afford to build more and more prisons. State and Federal expenditures on adult correctional facilities nearly always are less than four percent of total budgetary expenditures. Ironically, spending money on prisons boosts the economy. The cost of prison construction and the annual operating budgets of correctional facilities are paid to contractors and staff members who spend salaries on shopping, vacations, houses, cars, etc.

"Taxpayers are told that educated inmates will change their lifestyles."

If more and more prisons are to be built, they must be used in a more cost-effective manner. Operating budgets can be cut by examining rehabilitation costs. The centerpiece of criminal justice rehabilitation is education. Taxpayers are told that educated inmates will change their lifestyles. If alcoholics and drug addicts were treated for addictions and understood the destructiveness of alcohol and drugs, they would stop drinking and using drugs and the crime linked to substance abuse would end. If delinquents and adult criminals received vocational training, they would find legitimate jobs and stop selling drugs, firearms, and stolen property. Criminals sentenced to prison would learn a "lesson" and, when released, acquire a job and live a lawful lifestyle. The education model of social change assumes, of course, that criminals gladly would meet society's lawful expectations once given a chance to do so. That is a foolish assumption, though.

Education as a remedy for a criminal lifestyle for the most part has been a failed experiment in social engineering, but this lack of success has not dulled its popularity. Government administrators design, implement, and oversee education-based crime control programs and, when they fail, bureaucrats report "modest success" and request more money for improved, expanded, and intensified initiatives.

Before diverting another dime of tax revenue to education-based programs, taxpayers should demand proof they have economic value. The public needs an answer to this question: How many former state and Federal inmates who were recipients of education-based programs filed a Federal and/or state income tax return within one, three, five, or 10 years after release? A similar question should be asked of community-based rehabilitation programs. These data should be easily obtainable. Inmates and probationers should have a Social Security number, which could be checked against state and Federal income tax databases.

If taxpayers do not break even on the cost of rehabilitation programs, the bureaucracies that support them must be pared down and the money invested in worthwhile projects. These might encompass rehabilitating dilapidated schools, buying computer equipment for children who stay in school, providing low-interest loans to college students, and rebuilding inner cities.

Work is the standard community activity everywhere in America. We should expect no less from prisoners. In *Warehousing Violence,* I showed that, in a maximum-security Federal penitentiary—the United States Penitentiary (USP) at Lompoc, Calif.—skilled administrators transformed a prison into a revenue-generating "factory." Products created by inmate employees in Federal Prison Industry (Unicor) were valuable commodities that garnered revenue which exceeded the USP Lompoc's annual operating budget by about $25,000,000.

What is more, the inmates said that monthly salaries earned in Unicor, which averaged about $220 each, markedly improved their quality of life. Inmates shopped at the commissary for name-brand products and favorite snacks and in early evening could be seen walking on the prison compound, eating quarts of ice cream. This lifestyle, said many of the prisoners, "beats sleeping under bridges."

"State inmate workers earn $6-8 an hour and their wages are garnished for room, board, and restitution."

The benefits of inmate work do not end there. The Federal prison system's financial responsibility program requires convicts to pay court-ordered child support, alimony, and court-imposed fines. The more they earn, the more they pay. State correctional agencies have caught on. Oregon Prison Industries manufactures a line of clothes, "Prison Blues," and exports them to Italy, Japan, and other countries. California prison industries export prisoner-made clothing to Japan and Malaysia. State inmate workers earn $6-8 an hour, and their wages are garnisheed for room, board, and restitution.

Every inmate should have a full-time job manufacturing valuable goods or supporting the production of those items. American union leaders fuss about inmate labor taking away union jobs. What are the alternatives? The nation can spend billions more tax dollars on prison construction and operating budgets with little financial relief in sight, or develop prison-based industrial programs that reduce the cost of Federal and state imprisonment. Realistically, those who are locked behind secure walls and fences can't do many jobs available to free citizens, but inmate workers may be the lower-paid, lowskill American labor force that is needed to compete against Third World workers. If the skills of imprisoned felons displace union workers, the latter ought to seek more education and get better jobs.

There are felons who do not need to be imprisoned. Offenders whose past behavior does not include arrests and/or convictions for sex and/or violent crimes may pose little threat to lawful citizens. Convicted, nonviolent felons should toil for 40 hours a week on community work details, fixing roads, painting houses, picking up rubbish and sweeping streets, and performing other community work, all under the watchful eye of supervisors. Work is rehabilitating; rehabilitation is work

How You (Yes You!) Can Stop Violence in Your Town[4]

A gunman shoots up a post office in New Jersey. Another attacks a restaurant in Texas. A rash of car-jackings strikes Georgia. Any rational person would be alarmed by these horrible crimes against innocent people. And we are. National polls consistently show that violent crime is one of America's greatest concerns.

But we don't need polls to tell us this. We know it when we stop at a crowded intersection and suddenly get the urge to lock the doors. We feel it when bloody images from the nightly news fill our minds.

We are right to feel afraid. When a sniper shoots a diner sitting near a restaurant window, or when a woman is abducted outside a supermarket, we all know we could have been the victim. Schools, shopping malls, offices, and even our cars are no longer safe spaces.

But although we feel threatened, we are not paralyzed by fear. Restoring safety to public spaces has become a national cause. Smart, passionate people are standing up to the tide of violence. And in many cases women lead the crusade.

"The public is fed up with violence and is saying that enough is enough," says sociologist Amitai Etzioni, Ph.D., director of the Center for Communication Policy Studies in Washington, D.C. "There is no American who has not been touched—in some way—by violence. We are now seeing a number of concrete responses to this problem. Creative solutions are being tried all over. We have reason to be optimistic."

The experts on safety, violence, and community affairs that *Redbook* consulted suggested ten ways that America can stop violence and increase peace. Many have already met with success.

Community Policing. Already under way in many cities, community policing gets police officers out of patrol cars and onto street beats, where they can see and build relationships with the people they serve. Some community policing plans involve opening substations in neighborhoods and establishing citizen advisory committees for every precinct. Community policing has worked in many cities and towns. The Los Angeles Police Department says almost all crime figures are down, thanks in part to its citywide community policing program. Crime has also decreased in parts of Chicago, where officers hold open forums every month, where they work with citizens to set patrol priorities and find ways to prevent violence. Community policing is considered so effective that Congress has set aside $8.8 billion to

---

fund programs nationwide. For information call the Community Policing Consortium at (800) 833-3085.

Bullet control. Most Americans favor more restrictions on guns—but experts on all sides agree that strict gun control is politically unfeasible because of the lobbying power of the National Rifle Association and other anti-gun control groups. Even if we could control the sale of new guns, enough guns already exist to last us a century. Noting these roadblocks, Senator Daniel Patrick Moynihan of New York, a Democrat, suggests an ingenious alternative: heavy taxes and controls on the purchase of bullets.

Though Congress has yet to approve Moynihan's idea, some cities and towns already try to regulate ammunition. In California, specifically in Pasadena, Santa Monica, and Los Angeles, those purchasing ammunition must fill out registration cards and provide proof of their age. These programs have been in effect for less than a year, and it's too early to tell if they are helping. However, bullet regulation has already proved an effective way to bypass the stalemated debate over guns. For more information, write to Senator Daniel Patrick Moynihan at the United States Senate, Washington, D.C., 20510-3201.

> *"...bullet regulation has already proved an effective way to bypass the stalemated debate over guns."*

Rehabilitate criminals—for real. Get-tough policies for prisoners have gained political favor—as the return of chain gangs in the South shows—but society may actually be better off with a more positive approach. Wardens who have made prisons cleaner, expanded education programs, and reduced inmate stress have actually cut costs, reduced violence, and decreased recidivism. This approach has been successful at the federal Correctional Institution McKean County in Bradford, Pennsylvania, and has been adopted by the Corrections Corporation of America, which operates prisons under government contracts.

Perhaps the most unusual method for curbing inmates' violent tendencies is to teach them transcendental meditation and related stress-reduction techniques such as meditation and yoga. The argument for this approach is outlined in *Crime Vaccine* (BookCrafters; (800) 879-4214) by J. B. Marcus, an Iowa attorney, who has written extensively on crime prevention. Meditation techniques had some success in California, Michigan, Massachusetts, Minnesota, and Vermont. More information on prisons and meditation programs is available from Maharishi University of Management in Fairfield, Iowa, (515) 472-2857.

Safe corridors. In many urban neighborhoods adults take to the streets every morning and afternoon to guarantee safe passage for children walking to and from school. In North Philadelphia, for example, where churches organized one such effort, street crime has decreased substantially, and children, adults, and older persons now find the sidewalks much safer. More information about safe corridor programs can be obtained from Reverend William B. Moore, Tenth Memorial Baptist Church of Philadelphia, at (215) 787-2780.

Harlem educator Geoffrey Canada takes the concept one step further in his recent book, *Fist Stick Knife Gun*. He proposes a peace officer corps of neighborhood residents trained in conflict resolution to help avert violent confrontations.

The idea behind both this and the safe corridor plan is simple and can be applied anywhere: The watchful eyes and ears of residents are a neighborhood's best defense. A neighborhood that's alert, proactive, and works closely with local police is simply too much trouble for the bad guys.

Defensible spaces. This kind of planned community features cul-de-sacs and short streets that may end in tiny parks and play areas, and houses with expansive front porches set on quiet streets. All these design elements can make a neighborhood safer because they increase contact among neighbors and make it difficult for dangerous outsiders to get in and out.

One of the most effective uses of defensible space can be seen in Five Oaks, a neighborhood in Dayton, that has turned more than 35 streets into dead ends and cul-de-sacs. According to a study of Five Oaks, the new design scheme made the neighborhood quieter and less subject to heavy traffic, and helped cut violent crime in half. The defensible space concept, developed by architect and city planner Oscar Newman, is now being implemented or considered in cities and towns around the country. For information, call Newman's Institute for Community Design Analysis at (518) 734-4482.

Blocking out TV violence. Most experts and many in the media business acknowledge the connection between the mayhem portrayed in the media and real-life violence. Thousands of violent TV and film images can desensitize viewers, especially young ones, to the realities of violence. It's not a matter of direct cause and effect but, rather, influence. One University of Washington researcher says television violence plays a role in about half of all murders in America.

A device called the V-chip would allow parents to program a television set to lock out those programs that feature violence. Congress has already proposed ordering TV manufacturers to make the chip available in new sets, but some TV network executives have vowed to fight it as a form of censorship. For the chip to work, broadcasters would have to code their programs, a process that would lead to obvious conflicts over how programs might be rated.

Meanwhile, parents have two other choices (short of banning TV) that they can act on today. The Kid Control remote from TCI is shaped like a dinosaur or puppy and has buttons for only kid-friendly channels like PBS, the Disney Channel, and the Discovery Channel. For information call TCI at (800) 934-1111. And Primestar, a digital minidish satellite system, lets parents lock out certain channels and movies with particular ratings. Primestar can be ordered through 800-PRIMESTAR.

Training children to resolve conflicts. Called peace education, conflict resolution, or peer mediation, antiviolence training is being tried in schools across the country. Experts in crime and violence, noting that young people commit the vast majority of violent crimes, hope the peacemaking skills learned in school will calm the impulses that lead to violence on the street. In Baltimore a public school program developed by researchers at Johns Hopkins University has cut the level of violence among students in half.

"Conflict-resolution programs in schools work best when they are followed up by adults in the community getting involved in the kids' lives, " says Laura Ross Greiner, assistant director of the Center for the Study and Prevention of Violence at the University of Colorado. This kind of follow-up can be as simple as the example set by a woman in Los Angeles, Alice Harris. She noticed that teenage boys had no recreation programs and too much time on their hands. She installed a basketball hoop on her garage and invited them to play. Soon she was offering milk, cookies, and motherly advice. She has since helped several youngsters go on to college and has widened her effort to include other neighborhood parents.

"...93 percent of accidental shootings by minors occurred when children were left unsupervised."

Safer guns. Gun manufacturers are the largest producers of hazardous consumer products exempt from government regulation. The American Bar Association has suggested empowering the Consumer Product Safety Commission to help gun makers redesign weapons to make them safer to operate.

Locks, safety switches, and other devices would make it much more difficult for young people to commit either accidental or intentional shootings. Readily available guns that are too easy to use represent a very real hazard. One study in Oklahoma found that 93 percent of accidental shootings by minors occurred when children were left unsupervised. The U.S. General Accounting Office has estimated that one-third of all accidental shootings could be prevented by installing simple safety devices on guns. For more on gun safety proposals contact the American Bar Association at (202) 662-1760.

Public awareness campaigns. In Boston and Los Angeles, as well as many other cities, billboards and TV spots aim to make violence socially unacceptable. Many national organizations, including the National Crime Prevention Council, the American Academy of Pediatrics, and the American Medical Association, are conducting antiviolence publicity campaigns. The aim is to show adults and kids what they can do to make their communities safer, and spur them to action. In the Boston area a series of billboards showing children's faces implores people to end violence. Television networks use top stars to remind viewers that smart people walk away from dangerous situations. Saatchi & Saatchi advertising agency has donated its services to produce a series of highly dramatic antiviolence commercials to air as a public service.

Although the effect of public relations efforts is difficult to measure, participants in a concerted antiviolence campaign in Los Angeles believe these efforts have contributed to the recent decrease in murders in that city. For information about public awareness campaigns contact the National Crime Prevention Council at (202) 466-6272 ext. 121. The Center to Prevent Handgun Violence, at (202) 289-7319, also develops and implements antiviolence education programs.

Citizen action groups. In scores of communities, individuals and newly formed groups hold rallies, conduct vigils, march through neighborhoods, and pressure politicians, all to stop violence. These organizations, often led by concerned mothers and survivors of violence, offer support to families struck by crime and work with authorities to make neighborhoods safer. In Charleston, Massachusetts, an antiviolence campaign led by local mothers convinced government authorities to crack down on violent crime. In Los Angeles Lorna Hawkins, 43, a woman who has lost two sons to street violence, has taken her grief to the airwaves with an antiviolence program called *Drive-By Agony*.

Experts are not surprised to discover brave women leading the effort against violence. Women often take a stand where men fear to tread. "Mothers still have a symbolic power that is effective," says Deborah Prothrow-Stith, M.D., a professor of public health practice at Harvard University School of Public Health. "Mothers are often able to move police and officials to take action, and when they speak out, the media pays attention too."

Two national organizations have been formed to help survivors of violence work in their own communities. Call Save Our Sons and Daughters at (313) 361-5200, and Parents of Murdered Children at (513) 721-5683.

No one proposal or program guarantees a safe society. But taken together, these ideas and initiatives reflect a groundswell of concern and action against violence, explains Laura Ross Greiner. "We have noticed a greater awareness of the violence issue in part because people feel they are directly threatened," she says. "And when people feel threatened, they become more active, creative, and innovative."

At a recent national conference on violence prevention—the first ever—hundreds of experts and community leaders shared ideas for a broad-scale peace campaign. Susan B. Sorenson, Ph.D., an associate professor in violence prevention at UCLA, attended the conference and was impressed by the depth of public concern about this problem.

"Random, unpredictable acts may be something we have to tolerate in society," says Dr. Sorenson. "But in general people are saying they want to prevent the kinds of violence that are more common." Dr. Sorenson expects that ordinary citizens will lead the way to a safer society by creating constructive outlets for their outrage, in the way the famed Mothers Against Drunk Driving helped citizens combat another deadly scourge. "The good news is, those kinds of organizations are coming, because we are really ready for it," adds Dr. Sorenson. "I think we can be optimistic about it."

Why Can't We Control Guns?

You don't have to have a degree in criminology to conclude that gun control may be the best idea of all for stopping violence. That gun controls are strict and murder rates much lower elsewhere in the industrialized world suggests that tough gun laws work. And national polls consistently show that Americans favor more controls on guns. So why can't we pass laws that make guns harder to get?

Determined opponents of gun control, led by the National Rifle Association, have made it next to impossible for Congress to limit gun purchases or to stiffen requirements for gun ownership. The NRA's political power is legendary. The organization spends millions of dollars to defeat members of Congress who want to control guns. House Speaker Newt Gingrich, acknowledging the NRA's support, has reportedly vowed that "no gun control legislation is going to move" through Congress as long as he is speaker.

Faced with national inaction, many local communities and states have passed their own gun control laws. Meanwhile, a growing number of organizations, including the American Bar Association, continue to push for national limits on handguns. To learn what citizens can do, contact Handgun Control Inc. at (202) 898-0792.

Communities Against Crime[5]

My son David and his friend Phil Hooven were just four blocks from our suburban Philadelphia home, walking to their favorite pizza place. It was the twilight of a gentle summer day, people were out everywhere, and there was no reason to think these two deep-in-conversation 14-year-olds were in any danger.

But a young man not much older than they were raced up behind them and stuck what felt like the barrel of a gun into Phil's back. He and my son were both ordered to kneel on the sidewalk while the mugger went through their pockets. It all happened too fast for my son to feel much fear, but he came home and turned on every light in the house. And although he shows no sign of having been traumatized by the event, we certainly were. Grappling with the sad (and infuriating) reality that our young sons are not safe—even in one of the "safest" suburbs in the Philadelphia region—we quickly learned that we are far from alone.

Parents Are Accepting That
Suburban Crime Is Here to Stay

Fear of crime, in fact, is rampant. Parents raising children in cities have long been accustomed to being afraid, but what's new is that crime is now as much a part of childhood in suburbs and the countryside as it is in urban areas. In a recent Gallup poll (for CNN and *USA Today*), suburbanites ranked crime and violence as their second greatest national concern, just behind the federal deficit. And with good reason: The Council on Crime in America reports that more than 43 million crimes were committed in 1993, the most recent year for which statistics are available, and that 10.8 million of them were violent. Increasingly, children are involved: Young teens are far more likely to be both the perpetrators and victims of violent crime.

Convinced that the police and the criminal-justice system cannot stem the tide (polls show that Americans think even less of the court system than they do of Congress), millions of parents are taking matters into their own hands—not as vigilantes but as consumers and as increasingly active neighbors, banding together to fight back.

Often the battles are over quality-of-life issues, such as aggressive panhandling, public drunkenness, graffiti, and the "squeegee men" who demand money from motorists for "washing" their front window at stoplights. Sometimes the issue is garage break-ins or drug selling or the never-ending troubles coming from one out-of-control home.

---

[5]Article by Marc Kaufman, reporter for *The Philadelphia Inquirer*, from *Parents* 71:50–2 Je '96. Copyright © 1996 Gruner + Jahr USA Publishing. Reprinted with permission.

For a surprisingly large number of families, the answer has been to buy homes in a gated community. Others, fed up with what they see as the failure of the system, have joined neighborhood and town watches to become "eyes and ears" for local police. Some have embraced a more aggressive neighborhood activism.

"When people lose confidence in their police and courts, they'll inevitably look for other ways to make things safer for their families," says John P. Walters, executive director of the Council on Crime in America. "People are thinking about crime prevention, and trying to do something about it."

One Solution: Lock the Problem Out

For a fast-growing group, frustration about crime has led to simply shutting intruders out, by building or moving to gated communities. Many of these neighborhoods are private, but some are carved out from public streets, and they are especially common in California, Texas, and Florida. Housing experts estimate that as many as six million Americans live in private, gated communities today. And in a recent survey of new housing in the New York region, "virtually all of it was gated," says Oscar Newman, a renowned urban planner and architect. "It's kind of hard now for an investor to invest in anything *but* a gated community. They sell better, and the extra cost to developers is minimal," adds Newman, who has studied and promoted the idea of "defensible space" in housing since the early 1970s.

"Housing experts estimate that as many as six million Americans live in private, gated communities today."

Many such communities are built for families with young children. "You have two parents who might be away at work, and they just don't want to have to worry about how safe the kids are," says Newman. "A gated community gives them more peace of mind."

One neighborhood that essentially fenced itself in more than three years ago is the Five Oaks section of Dayton, Ohio, an area of about 1,800 older homes favored by city workers and local hospital and university personnel. Five Oaks has the misfortune of being just off a major highway, making it a convenient stop for drug transactions. Within several years in the late 1980s, the quiet family-centered neighborhood went into steep decline, says Patrick Donnelly, a father of five young children and a leader of the effort to build the gates around Five Oaks. The worried community organized, studied the idea of gating, and endorsed it in a neighborhood vote. The city volunteered to help.

"It had gotten so bad I wouldn't let the younger kids out in the front yard without someone always watching," says his wife, Brenda. "The streets are pretty narrow, but cars would zoom by all the time—people who'd just bought drugs and wanted to get out fast. Once a stray bullet flew into a friend's living room. And there was the time I pulled up in our back alley and found a prostitute and her client right there."

Since the gates—six feet high, with brick columns—went up in late 1992, all that has changed. The unlocked gates close off through streets, and Patrick Donnelly says violent crime has decreased 55 percent, while all crimes have fallen 26 percent. Housing values have also steadily increased.

Some have branded this gating of American communities as racist, calling it a destructive retreat by some affluent white people from society's problems. Kenneth T. Jackson, Ph.D., chairman of the history department at Columbia University, says the practice is divisive and sees it as part of a national trend away from "taking responsibility for our neighbors."

"Quite a few cities have sent their planners here," says Patrick Donnelly, nothing that almost half the Five Oaks residents are not white. "It may not work for everyone, but it certainly has worked for us."

Parents Police the Streets

In thousands of American communities, involved neighborhood residents have been the key to facing down crime. According to Matt Peskin, executive director of the 2,000-member National Association of Town Watch, in Wynnewood, Pennsylvania, the greatest interest now seems to be in suburban and rural areas, where crime has become a major problem. And town watches work: In 1992, when a rash of garage burglaries broke out in Richardson, Texas, residents formed the Richardson Heights Crime Watch Patrol, eventually enlisting more than 50 participants. Some patrol the streets in cars emblazoned with the town-watch logo, and some patrol on foot with radios. In the year after the town watch began, the total number of burglaries fell from 25 to 4.

"The bad guys quickly learned we were out watching," says Lynn Jeffcoat, coordinator of the watch. "Our presence scares them off, but then we also make sure residents have their garages locked and their property safely away. If someone on patrol sees a kid's bike left out on the lawn, we'll call the homeowner and remind them to lock it up."

In West Allis, Wisconsin, a suburb of Milwaukee, the town watch got involved in fighting the graffiti that was beginning to spread across town. Since many residents saw graffiti as a harbinger of crime and disorder, blockwatch captains began cleaning the scrawls themselves.

Nick Ostrander, the father of a 10-year-old and a 21-year-old, took a brush and some solvent to the spraypainted brick wall of a nearby convenience store. "Kids need to see that the adults won't be intimidated," he says. Because Ostrander and other town watchers made it clear that fighting graffiti was a high priority to them, the government of West Allis agreed to buy a power washer and the chemicals needed to clean graffiti paint. (For information on how to start your own group, call the National Association of Town Watch, (610) 649-7055.)

Neighbors Find Innovative Ways to Drive Out Problems

Town watches are less effective against persistent crime problems. Tony and Laurie Ammirato moved to their Long Beach, California, neighborhood—filled with $200,000 Cape Cod-style homes—in 1990 because it looked so peaceful and friendly. It didn't take long for them to learn how mistaken they were.

The family across the street had four boys who fought constantly, vandalized property, and lit fireworks in their house. Police were frequently summoned, by neighbors or the boys' own parents, reporting violent brawls.

"They just made life in the neighborhood horrible," says Tony Ammirato, who himself called police when one of the neighbor boys pulled what he thought was a real gun on his son, then 13, and again when the boy approached his son with a lead pipe. Now, Ammirato says, his son "seldom goes far from the house." He also worries about the effects on his daughter, who was 2 when they moved into the house.

"Many towns...are trying hard to find ways to fight crime before it starts."

As the violence and disruptions continued, Ammirato put up his house for sale, but there were no takers. (The young thugs and their friends in gang clothes didn't help.) In desperation, Ammirato and his neighbors turned to Safe Streets Now! after reading about its successes in other parts of Long Beach. Founded by Oakland, California, mother Molly Wetzel in 1989 as a way to close down a neighborhood drug house, Safe Streets Now! programs today operate around the country. (For information, call 1-800-404-9100.)

The group's tactic is simple: Enlist dozens of neighbors to complain, and if necessary haul the property owner into small-claims court. So Ammirato and his neighbors got 15 families and a total of 34 anonymous complainants—each of them suing the parents of the wild boys for $5,000 (the maximum amount awarded in small-claims court). Their suit was filed in mid-January, and within weeks a California judge ruled in favor of the community, assessing damages of $170,000.

Today, Ammirato and his neighbors are hopeful that the family will be forced to sell its home in order to pay the damages, and leave the neighborhood. "Nothing else will work," Ammirato says. "The neighborhood deserves some normalcy."

Increasingly, such new kinds of activism appeal to frustrated parents. "The criminal-justice system has essentially collapsed, and police can't resolve the kinds of drug-related and behavior problems showing up in so many places," says Betsy Bredau, a Safe Streets Now! coordinator in southern California who helped Ammirato organize the suit. "But that doesn't mean we're helpless. We can go to small-claims court against the people ruining our blocks, and our experience is that we usually win."

Catching Kids Before the Crime

Many towns—recognizing that young teenagers are often both the most violent and the most victimized—are trying hard to find ways to fight crime before it starts. By organizing mediation programs, educators hope kids will learn to solve disputes without violence. "Young people need conflict-management skills," says Erin Donovan, director of the National Teens, Crime, and the Community Program, in Washington, D.C. "We help teach them to keep small problems from becoming big deals."

Using "mock mediations," kids work together to try and find nonviolent solutions. So far, more than 500,000 youngsters have seen these mediations, Donovan says. Donovan's group recently commissioned a Louis Harris & Associates survey of school-children from urban, suburban, and rural areas. Sadly, 46 percent said they had made some change in their daily routine because of crime. But an encouraging 86 percent said they would get involved in programs to end the violence if they were offered. For more information, call (202) 466-6272, extension 161.

Working Toward
Violence-Free Schools[6]

One beautiful day in October on the Purdue University campus in Indiana, an 18-year-old freshman strolled into his dorm. Blaming his RA (resident assistant, or dorm counselor) for the trouble he had gotten into for cocaine possession, the boy pulled out a gun and shot the older student dead.

This situation shows signs of the same troubling violence that has infected high schools across the nation. Not just inner-city schools, but all kinds of schools—suburban and rural as well as urban—have been affected. Every year, there are nearly 3 million incidents of theft or violent crime in or near schools.

"Every year, there are nearly 3 million incidents of theft or violent crime in or near schools."

Have weapons become as much an accessory in a backpack as a calculator? More than 41 percent of teenagers surveyed recently by Children's Institute International said they don't feel safe at school. More than 46 percent said violence was increasing at their school. Gangs, guns, media violence—along with poverty, drugs, and disintegrating families—all contribute to the threat of violence in schools.

It's a Team Effort

Combating the complex problem of school violence must be a team effort. Students, the school, the community, parents, law enforcers, courts, and religious leaders all need to work together to make schools safe.

Many schools have effective safe-school plans. And a key to many successful schools' plans is peer mediation or mediation by outside volunteers. Working with trained mediators, both sides in a dispute hear each other out and work toward a solution that both can accept.

Safe-school plans also may include these measures:

- metal detectors to prevent weapons from being carried into school
- zero-tolerance rules for drug use, bullying, and weapons possession
- graffiti crackdown to erase gang symbols security guards to head off trouble
- locker supervision to keep drugs and weapons out of the school
- transparent backpacks to keep weapons out of the school

---

[6]Article by Marilyn Sherman, from *Current Health* F '97. Copyright © 1997 by Weekly Reader Corporation. All Rights Reserved. Reprinted with permission.

Across the country, the wave of violence is meeting with a wall of resistance. Students who violate violence-free codes are being expelled more frequently. In 16 states, students patrol and report crimes through the Youth Crime Watch program.

What You Can Do

A school action plan is only part of the answer. Each individual in the school has to be part of the solution on a personal level. Even if you're not directly involved in a confrontation, you're still involved. Responsibility rests with the majority not to allow bullying to go on at school. On a personal level, you can show your strength by helping to prevent violence in these ways:

- *Know you can be tough by backing down.* Sometimes the smartest thing to do is to walk away from a confrontation. It can take more guts-and be cooler-than to give in to anger and fight. Police say most youth homicides result from someone not backing down from a fight.

- *Understand ways of dealing with confrontation.* There are times to avoid it, times to use reason or humor, and times to assert yourself. Have an appropriate range of reactions, not an on/off switch.

- *Listen.* Use active listening skills, even repeating aloud the other person's viewpoint to make sure you understand it.

- *Know what your body language says.* Just a look can be interpreted as a staredown and may start a major fight.

- *Be assertive when it's safe and appropriate.* Effective responses can be saying "Don't do that!" or "stop it!" and walking away. Anger and combativeness only escalate conflict.

- *Get tough on yourself.* Be firm about being responsible for your own behavior. Keep your anger in check. When there're no refs to put you in the penalty box, do your own self-policing. Sit out, take deep breaths, and count to when you feel yourself becoming confrontational. Keep a lid on your own tendencies to violence. You'll thank yourself for it.

- *Avoid bad situations.* Do what it takes, whether it's sticking with a supportive group, walking away, or taking a different route home.

- *Use peer mediation.* Look to the program at your school, or request one if your school doesn't have it. Use a go between to talk out and resolve a conflict so that both sides win.

- *Go for extracurricular activities.* Make sure your school has them for all interests, and get involved. School activities, along with work experiences, are safe alternatives to gangs and can boost your self-respect.

If you have a problem with violence—either your own or someone else's—get help. See a teacher or other adult you trust. A small insult or negative look can blow up into a violent crisis. If somebody at your school gives you a bad look or hits you with a put-down, what do you do—make a joke, tell him to quit, or punch him? Depending on where you are and whom you're with, your choice could mean the difference between a falling—out and a fatality.

Schools around the country are working to be safe havens for students (see sidebar below). Safe schools put the squeeze on guns, drugs, and gangs—and squeeze out violence. But your school has to be able to count on you to come through a conflict with a cool head.

"Safe schools put the squeeze on guns, drugs, and gangs—and squeeze out violence."

Securing Safe Schools

Safety is at the top of the priority list at the Metropolitan School District of Lawrence Township in Indianapolis. "Safe schools are everyone's business. We all have to work together to resolve common issues," states Assistant Superintendent Duane Hodgin. Teachers, students, parents, and the community—all are cooperating partners working for safe schools in the district.

Four years ago, motivated by rising violence around the country, the district enacted a safe-schools plan for grades K through 12. With key elements of prevention, intervention, education, and involvement of everyone, the plan helps the district be prepared.

A district with a diverse population and economic extremes, Lawrence Township was the first in Indiana to have a board-adopted safe-schools policy. It was also first to have a crisis of incidents such as the taking of student hostages or student unrest.

An important part of the safe-school plan is having "police support officers" on the high school premises but outside the buildings. The trained, off-duty police officers are available by radio if they are needed inside. "While their role is to help, serve, and prevent, their visible presence contributes to security," says Dr. Hodgin. Since the program began, vandalism has been almost wiped out, and there have been no guns on campus, he noted.

While the school district acknowledges that there are gangs in the area, it doesn't cave in to gang behavior at school. There are little ways, such as banning hats in school, and major ways, such as working with an area gang task force.

What also counts is education for both teachers and students. Drug education and education about bullying are two prime topics. And the school trains students as peer mediators so that when disagreements arise, those involved can refer themselves to peer conflict management programs.

Other safe-school practices include having a closed campus

with visitor badges, locked doors, sign-in procedures, security cameras, mirrors, handheld radios, and an emergency communications network. The school takes surveys and conducts safety audits.

What this adds up to is a feeling of security. In a recent survey, most district high school students said they wanted law and order, and they overwhelmingly approved of the police support officers. Ninety percent reported feeling safe. Dr. Hodgin notes, "From analyzing the data, we know we're making a difference."

Bibliography

An asterisk (*) preceding a reference indicates that an excerpt from the work has been reprinted in this compilation or that the work has been cited.

Books and Pamphlets

Albuquerque, Severino Joao Medeiros. Violent acts. Wayne State Univ. '91.

*Bailie, Gil. Violence unveiled: humanity at the crossroads. Crossroad '92.

Brown, Richard Maxwell. No duty to retreat. Univ. of Oklahoma '94.

*Canada, Geoffrey. Fist, stick, knife, gun. Beacon '95.

Chevigny, Paul. Edge of the knife. New Press '95.

*Courtwright, David T. Violent land: single men and social disorder from the frontier to the inner city. Harvard Univ. '96.

Crews, Gordon A.; and Counts, M. Reid. The evolution of school disturbance in America. Praeger '97.

Crews, Gordon A.; Montgomery, Reid H.; and Garris, W. Ralph. Faces of violence in America. Simon & Schuster '96.

Derber, Charles. The wilding of America. St. Martin's '96.

Dobrin, Adam. Statistical handbook on violence in America. Oryx '96.

*Fleisher, Mark S. Beggars and thieves: lives of urban street criminals. Univ. of Wisconsin '95.

Goldstein, Arnold P. Violence in America. Davies-Black '96.

Hampton, Robert L.; Jenkins, Pamela; and Gullotta, Thomas P. eds. Preventing violence in America. Sage '96.

Harries, Keith D. Serious violence. Thomas, C. C. '97.

LaCerva, Victor. Pathways to peace. Heartsongs '96.

Leet, Duane A.; Rush, George E.; and Smith, Anthony. Gangs, graffiti, and violence. Copperhouse '97.

McKenzie, V. Michael. Domestic violence in America. Brunswick '95.

Miller, Don E. Drug wars: the final battle. Speranza Productions '94.

Monroe, William Frank. Power to hurt. Univ. of Illinois Press '97.

Parrow, Kathleen A. From defense to resistance. American Philosophical Society '93.

Parker, Tony. The violence of our lives. HarperCollins '96.

*Postman, Neil. Technopoly: the surrender of culture to technology. Vintage '92.

Sheley, Joseph F.; and Wright, James D. In the line of fire. Aldine de Gruyter '95.

Silberman, Matthew. A world of violence. Wadsworth '95.

Trexler, Richard C. Sex and conquest. Cornell Univ. Press '95.

Winter, Gibson. America in search of its soul. Morehouse '96.

Additional Periodical Articles with Abstracts

For those who wish to read more widely on the subject of Violence in American Society, this section contains abstracts of additional articles that bear on the topic. Readers who require a comprehensive list of materials are advised to consult the *Reader's Guide to Periodical Literature* and other H.W. Wilson indexes.

Domestic violence: why it's every woman's issue...and what you can do. Rosemary Black. *American Health for Women* 16:56+ Mr '97

An overview of domestic violence in the United States. According to the U.S. Department of Justice, over 1,400 American women die at the hands of an abusive partner every year, and in a 1995 poll conducted for the Family Violence Prevention Fund in San Francisco, over one-third of those surveyed said that they know someone who is a victim of domestic violence. Thanks to the Violence Against Women Act signed by President Clinton in 1994, more funds than ever before are available to help victims escape their tormentors and rebuild their lives, but money alone cannot buy safety. Guidelines on stopping the violence are presented.

Talking to kids about violence. Sandy Keenan. *Good Housekeeping* 225:76+ Ag '97

Parents must limit the amount of televised violence their children are exposed to, but it is also important to ensure that children are not so sheltered they are unable to deal with things they encounter when they are not under parental control. Dr. Alvin Poussaint, a professor of psychiatry at Harvard Medical School and the director of the Media Center of Boston's Judge Baker Children's Center, says parents have to face up to the fact that children are going to hear about violent events one way or another and that they are going to be frightened by these events. Advice is provided on helping children deal with frightening news stories by encouraging them to talk, answering their questions simply, pinning down the exact cause of their fears, reassuring them, and appealing to their logic.

The wild boys. *Men's Health* 12:62 My '97

David Courtwright is a professor of history at the University of North Florida and author of *Violent Land*, which describes how, whenever young men are left alone in a group, trouble erupts. In an interview, Courtwright discusses why he feels that single men are self-destructive and aggressive and why marrying could be the best thing a man can do for his health.

When home is not a haven. Malcolm Boyd. *Modern Maturity* 40:60 Ja/F '97

Abuse, by anyone at any time, whether physical or psychological, is dehumanizing and detrimental to an individual's dignity and self-respect. It often takes place when an imbalance in a relationship leads one partner to dominate. What is more, abuse of older women and men is a harsh reality in U.S. society that is rarely publicized in relation to its scope. Contributing factors can be addiction to drugs or alcohol or economic insecurity. Whatever the trigger, however, when abuse occurs the victim's best option is to seek outside help and refuse to accept a long-term situation of domestic violence. Individuals' experiences of abuse are recounted.

Point last seen. Hannah Nyala. *Ms.* 7:48-53 My/Je '97

In an article reprinted from *Point Last Seen: A Woman Tracker's Story*, the author discusses how she became a search-and-rescue tracker. She recounts how she escaped with her two children from an abusive seven-year marriage, only to be traced by her husband who took the children away. She explains that only the mountains could encompass the terror that subsequently consumed her and that her fierce longing for her children erupted in productive activity, which led her to become a tracker.

Behind the (bell) curve. Bruce Shapiro. *The Nation* 264:5 Ja 6 '97

Justice authorities who universally embraced the "superpredator theory" have been confounded by the latest Justice Department crime figures. Princeton professor John DiIulio's superpredator thesis asserted that "moral poverty" coupled with rising numbers of preteens necessarily means a generation of amoral thugs. The Justice Department's figures reveal, however, that arrests of juveniles for violent crimes are down by 7 percent in the past year, and murder by teens has fallen 12 percent in the past year and 23 percent since 1993.

Welfare's domestic violence. Jennifer Gonnerman. *The Nation* 264:21-3 Mr 10 '97

As the welfare "reform" is implemented and AFDC is abolished, domestic-violence victims will be among the hardest hit. The new legislation imposes strict limits on the length of time people may receive benefits. Under the bill, the time and support women need to get out of abusive relationships are missing, according to Taylor Institute director Jody Raphael. In addition, NOW Legal Defense and Education Fund legal director Martha Davis points out that tragedy could result if those stalked in the workplace feel unable to change jobs or stop going to work for fear of losing benefits. Across America, activists are now fighting to soften the blow of the welfare legislation by urging states to adopt the Family Violence Option plan, which 24 of the 40 states that have submitted welfare plans have partly or wholly adopted.

When violence strikes home. Marcia Smith. *The Nation* 264:23-4 Je 30 '97

For many African-American women, violence is an everyday affair. The violence these women experience exists against the backdrop of mainstream U.S. culture, which tolerates, and sometimes embraces, violent resolutions to problems. It is also a product of the patriarchal culture prevalent in African-American communities and elsewhere, which results in the relative powerlessness of black women and public silence about what is perceived as a private matter. The pervasiveness of violence against women presents African-American leaders with a clear imperative. The public space within the community must be opened to allow women's voices to be heard and their experiences to be validated.

Don't re-arm domestic abusers. *New York Times* A24 Mr 20 '97

Congress should reject two bills that have been introduced that would gut the law passed last year prohibiting anyone convicted of misdemeanor domestic violence offenses from purchasing or owning guns. The first bill, introduced by Michigan representative Bart Stupak, would exempt police and military personnel who have been convicted of domestic violence charges from the ban, while the other bill, introduced by Georgia representative Bob Barr and Minnesota senator Paul Wellstone, would apply the ban only to those convicted of domestic violence crimes after September 1996.

Drugs found a danger to more than users: study links substance abuse to violence. Christopher Sale Wren. *New York Times* A16 Ag 20 '97

A study that examined the effect of substance abuse on homicides and suicides in three counties that include Seattle, Memphis, and Cleveland found that people who do not use illegal drugs but live in households where such drugs are used are 11 times as likely to be killed as those living in drug-free homes. The study by researchers at the University of Washington, the University of Tennessee, Case Western Reserve University, and Emory University, as reported today in the Journal of the American Medical Association, also found that killings were 70 percent more likely among non-drinkers in households where alcoholism exists.

Gangs at school. Bob Herbert. *New York Times* 15 (Sec 4) O 12 '97

Ruth Messinger has tried to make the school system the one main area in which she could show her credibility while putting incumbent New York City mayor Rudolph Giuliani on the defensive, but the most important issue in the schools now is the growing influence of violent Los Angeles–type gangs, and these play to the strengths of a law-and-order mayor. The threat of gang violence in the schools and on the streets seems to be more serious than many New Yorkers believed, and the issue has become a point of contention in the mayoral race. Voters may feel that Messinger has the edge in most school issues, but not when it comes to crime in the schools.

Gun association is trying to lure children, its foes say. Katharine Q. Seelye. *New York Times* A24 N 19 '97

A new study by the Violence Policy Center says that the National Rifle Association is trying to cultivate a new generation of gun owners by using the same strategies to hook children on guns that the tobacco industry has used to hook them on cigarettes. Faced with a slump in gun sales and a raft of negative publicity, the NRA uses characters like Eddie Eagle to teach gun safety.

Judge upholds law making gender-motivated crime a civil-rights violation. Nina Bernstein. *New York Times* A16 Jl 10 '97

Federal judge James H. Jarvis, of the Eastern District of Tennessee, has "quite reluctantly" upheld the constitutionality of the Violence Against Women Act of 1994 in the case of *Laurel Knuckles Seaton v. Kenneth Marshall Seaton*. Two earlier decisions have also upheld the constitutionality of the law, which makes crimes motivated by gender a violation of civil rights, while another found the law to be an unconstitutional federal intrusion into state matters. The issue is expected to make its way to the Supreme Court, where the reach of federal authority has become a deeply divisive issue.

Security failures in the schools. *New York Times* 10 (Sec 4) My 25 '97

Sexual violence has swept through New York City schools, pointing up the significant lapses in school management and security. The recent cases strengthen Mayor Rudolph Giuliani's call for police control of school security. School Chancellor Rudy Crew opposes a police presence, but the Board of Education should accept any help it can get, as its record on safety is abysmal.

Spate of skinhead violence catches Denver by surprise. James Brooke. *New York Times* A18 N 21 '97

A series of attacks by racist skinheads belies Denver's modern image of tolerance and affluence. The unexpected outbreak of violence, most of it by young, white skinheads, is part of a national trend in which skinhead groups are expanding as Ku Klux Klan and neo-Nazi groups decline, according to the Southern Poverty Law Center.

TV rating system may actually lure youths to violent shows, study finds. Lawrie Mifflin. *New York Times* A22 Mr 27 '97

Joanne Cantor, a professor of communications arts at the University of Wisconsin, compared the reactions of 374 children to eight types of ratings systems and found that the Motion Picture Association of America's age-based ratings and labels that said "parental discretion advised" more often attracted children to a program than did labels identifying a program as having "mild violence" or "graphic violence." Cantor's comparisons were part of a three-year study commissioned by the National Cable Television Association to study different aspects of televised violence.

The wisdom of children who have known too much. Fox Butterfield. *New York Times* 1+ (Sec 4) Je 8 '97

Life has changed for young people in Harlem and in other inner cities across much of the United States as record levels of murder and other violence have begun to fall. Young people, backed by social workers, probation officers, and psychiatrists who work with young people from troubled families in poor neighborhoods, say that the crime rate is falling because there has been a change in attitudes among the young. Many who have seen someone shot or have a close relative or friend who has been incarcerated do not want to repeat the mistakes of older siblings, and, in general, guns and violence are much less socially acceptable than they were a few years ago.

Damaged. Malcolm Gladwell. *The New Yorker* 73:132-8+ F 24–Mr 3 '97

Part of a special issue on crime and punishment. Dorothy Otnow Lewis, a psychiatrist at New York's Bellevue Hospital and a professor at New York University School of Medicine, and Jonathan Pincus, a neurologist at Georgetown University Medical Center, Washington, D.C., have published a series of groundbreaking studies on murderers and delinquents, painstakingly outlining the medical and psychiatric histories of the very violent. They both believe that the most degenerate criminals are, overwhelmingly, people with some combination of abusive childhoods, brain injuries, and psychotic symptoms. They also believe that, although each of these problems in isolation has no connection to criminality, these factors together create such terrifying synergy as to hinder these individuals' ability to play by the rules of society. Lewis and Pincus's work is described in detail.

A chip of fools? Hara Estroff Marano. *Psychology Today* 30:10 My/Je '97

Norway is the first country in the world to enact an education campaign against visual violence. Rather than imposing censorship, Norway is seeking to breed individual responsibility through an innovative campaign that teaches school children skills for interpreting visual imagery. Students examine who makes a film, who it is intended for, and what gets omitted. In addition, by creating their own videos, they learn how media messages are fashioned. In contrast, by relying on the so-called V-chip to block violent programs in the home, the United States is, in effect, placing the blame on broadcasters for children's viewing habits.

Listen to your fear. Gavin De Becker. *Reader's Digest* 151:128-33 S '97

An article condensed from *The Gift of Fear*. The writer, a security consultant who has predicted the behavior of murderers, stalkers, irate former employees, rejected boyfriends, and mass murderers, discusses the benefit of fear, an excellent internal guardian that warns of danger. He offers advice for trusting this survival instinct and acting on it, and he discusses an incident in which a woman missed crucial signals from her attacker before she was raped but later listened to her fear and saved her own life in the process.

Danger decrees get confidence boost. Bruce Bower. *Science News* 152:157 S 6 '97

A new study reveals that the confidence that clinicians place in their own judgments concerning the potential danger posed by psychiatric patients can be quite insightful. If a clinician feels almost or entirely certain about a violence estimate, this estimate typically proves to be accurate, says Dale E. McNiel of Langley Porter Psychiatric Institute in San Francisco and his collaborators. The researchers maintain that modest or low certainty frequently accompanies inaccurate predictions of violence, however.

Emerging from the shadows. John Q. Kelly. *Vital Speeches of the Day* 63:748-52 O 1 '97

In an address delivered to the Ob/Gyn Informational Update Conference, Long Branch, New Jersey, the lead attorney for the family of Nicole Brown Simpson during the O. J. Simpson civil trial discusses domestic violence as a medical issue. The medical community is the first line of defense many women have against domestic abuse and is the single most effective means of identifying and rescuing victims. Although more than 1 million women seek medical assistance for injuries caused by domestic violence, only 4 percent of the injuries are correctly identified. Complexity is one reason battering can be missed, but there are other reasons: Many doctors are unaware of how pervasive a crime domestic violence has become, most medical schools and training programs have been slow to include domestic abuse on the curriculum, and victims are usually unforthcoming. The speaker suggests that all doctors who have contact with female patients should receive continuing education on how to handle cases of domestic abuse.

Appendix

Organizations and Help Hotlines

National Resource Center on Domestic Violence (800)537-2238

Domestic violence toll free hotlines:

Arkansas: 1-800-332-4443

Florida: 1-800-500-1119

Indiana : 1-800-334-7233

Indiana (Central Indiana Serves 12 counties): 1-800-221-6311

Illinois: 1-800-603-HELP or 1-800-603-4357

Michigan: 1-800-99-NO ABUSE or 1-800-996-6228

Montana: 1-800-655-7867 (24 hours)

Nevada: 1-800-992-5757

New Hampshire: 1-800-852-3311

New Jersey: 1-800-572-7233

New York: 1-800-942-6906 (English)

New York: 1-800-942-6908 (Spanish)

North Dakota: 1-800-472-2911

Oklahoma: 1-800-522-7233

Pennsylvania (eastern): 1-800-642-3150

Texarkana area: 1-800-876-4808 or local calls 903-793-help.

Vermont: 1-800-ABUSE-95. (1-800-228-7395)

Virginia: 1-800-838-8238

West Virginia: 1-800-352-6513

Washington: 1-800-562-6025

Wisconsin: 1-800-333-7233

Wyoming (SAFV Task Force of Uinta County): (307)789-7315 or (800)445-7233

Abused, missing, runaway or exploited children:

800-I-AM-LOST (800-426-5678) Child Find Hotline (parents reporting lost children)

800-4-A-CHILD (800-422-4453) Child Help USA (for victims, offenders and parents)

800-999-9999 Covenant House Hotline (for problem teens and runaways)

800-A-WAY-OUT (800-292-9688) Hotline for parents considering abducting their children

800-843-5678 National Center for Missing and Exploited Children

800-231-6946 National Runaway Hotline

800-442-HOPE (800-442-4673) National Youth Crisis Hotline

800-782- SEEK (800-782-7335) Operation Lookout, National Center for Missing Youth (for missing child emergencies and sightings)

800-HIT-HOME (800-448-4663) Youth Crisis Hotline (reporting child abuse and help for runaways)

Index